Connecting
with **Reluctant**
Teen Readers

TIPS, TITLES, AND TOOLS

Patrick Jones

Maureen L. Hartman

Patricia Taylor

Neal-Schuman Publishers, Inc.
New York   London

Published by Neal-Schuman Publishers, Inc.
100 William St., Suite 2004
New York, NY 10038

Printed and bound in the United States of America.

The paper used in this publication meets the minimum requirements of the American National Standard for Information Sciences—Permanence of Paper for Printed Library Materials, ANSI Z39.48–1992.

Library of Congress Cataloging-in-Publication Data

Jones, Patrick, 1961–
     Connecting with reluctant teen readers : tips, titles, and tools / Patrick Jones, Maureen L. Hartman, Patricia Taylor.
          p.   cm.
     Includes bibliographical references and index.
     ISBN 1–55570–571–5 (alk. paper)
   1. Young adults—Books and reading—Handbooks, manuals, etc.   2. Teenagers—Books and reading—Handbooks, manuals, etc.   3. Young adults' libraries—Book lists.   4. Children's libraries—Book lists.   5. Young adults' libraries—Administration—Handbooks, manuals, etc.   6. Young adult literature—Bibliography.   I. Hartman, Maureen L.   II. Taylor, Patricia, 1952—   III. Title.
     Z1037. J65 2006
     028.5—dc22   2006012355

Contents

Stating the Problem with Sound Bites!

"Reading ability is positively correlated with the extent to which students read recreationally."

—National Center for
Education Statistics

"Young people who cannot read at all are far outnumbered by young people who can read (poorly or well) but won't. The latter, who chose not to read, for whatever reason, have little advantage over those who are illiterate."

—H. Holbrook, "Motivating
Reluctant Readers: A Gentle Push

"I just don't like to read because I can never find a book that has enough suspense to keep me from falling asleep as I read. Every now and then, I will find a good book, but it's not often. I only like to read my magazines because they are the only thing I enjoy reading. Reading is just boring unless it's something that I care about."

—Fifteen-year-old boy

"I think the bottom line is respecting the reluctant readers' reading choices while letting them know about the huge variety available to them."

—Di Herald, *Teen Genreflecting*

"Prepared by the YALSA Quick Picks for Reluctant Young Adult Readers Committee, the Quick Picks list comprises books that will attract teens who, for whatever reason, choose not to read."

—Young Adult Library Services
Association (YALSA) Web site

"I try to leave out the parts that most people skip."

—Elmore Leonard

Preface

We all have that one thing—cooking or balancing a checkbook—that we absolutely avoid doing. More than likely, that something is avoided because the person (a) doesn't do it well, (b) doesn't enjoy doing it, or (c) doesn't do it regularly enough to either enjoy doing it or do it well. For those of us who are lucky, it is something that only comes up once a year or that can easily be handed off to someone else—income taxes come to mind. For others, it's something that should be done every day—exercise or flossing.

As most of us are librarians, the one activity that likely isn't coming to mind is reading. Most—though admittedly not all—of us would classify ourselves as readers. We know how to read, choose to read, and would describe reading as something we do for pleasure. But we also serve a large population for whom reading is that one thing they avoid doing. These reluctant readers—especially the reluctant teen readers—hold that they do not enjoy reading, aren't good at it, or simply find other activities (dating, studying, playing games, e-mailing, chatting) more appealing.

And yet they still come to the library. The Internet seems to have brought a whole new group of teens into school and public libraries. They come for the Net, but they stay for, well, the Net. The fact that they are surrounded by books that might interest them is usually lost. Even if they did take stock of all the titles, they might still doubt that a book fits into their jam-packed schedules.

So is it avoidance? Poor performance? Better things to do? There's a lot going on. Classroom teacher Laura Gajdostik provides us with a great summary of the problem at hand:

> I believe that students lack the skills, practice and confidence in reading by the time I meet them (high school). Somewhere in their school histories, they have been "turned-off" by an assigned reading, reading beyond their levels or interests, lost confidence by receiving poor grades with reading and/or boring assignments to accompany reading. I also believe they may have associated all reading with school (which has also become laborious and unappealing). In my classes, I think reluctant

readers (the majority of my students) are intimidated by reading a "whole" book and lack the confidence and desire to even start a "whole" book. I don't think they are willing to "commit" the time, desire or even perhaps the struggle in reading a "whole" book.

So, what to do? Librarians, teachers, and those in the publishing industry all have their reasons for wanting teens to read, but are these reasons being adequately conveyed to teens? And do these reasons even matter? Sometimes talking to teens about reading is like talking vegetables with a fussy eater. You can tell them it's good for them, but that won't get them to open their mouths—or, in this case, the covers of a book.

But there are things we can do to get reluctant readers reading—and we've divided them here into the best tips, titles, and tools available. Let's be very clear up front: we are talking about reluctant teen readers, a kind of catch-all phrase to describe persons ages 12–18 who have the ability to read but choose not to, often because they lack confidence, access to reading materials, or a positive view of reading. While many of these teens may have some reading challenges, we are not talking about illiterate teens but aliterate teens. More than just a compendium of our own research, experience, and intuitions, *Connecting with Reluctant Teen Readers* shares the thoughts of authors, publishers, editors, librarians, and teachers to get "talking points" on the topic about what works, what doesn't, and why we should push teens to read.

Part I, "Tips That Work," provides solutions for some of the most challenging issues. First, it explains who reluctant readers are and why they feel the way they do about reading. Next, it offers techniques for librarians, educators, and concerned parents to use, through exploration of the formats and genres that are most likely to convert nonreaders. Along the way, you'll find that many of your most frequently asked questions will be answered; in addition, you'll benefit from the advice of many experienced professionals, including librarians who've served on the Young Adult Library Services Association Recommended Books for Reluctant Young Adult Readers Committee—hereinafter known as Quick Picks—as well as other librarians, classroom teachers, and experts.

Part II, "Titles That Work," brings together many lists of books that will grab teens' attention. This isn't one straight A–Z list but specific, carefully crafted lists—with annotations where appropriate—that will meet your readers' needs. You'll find our list of fifty-seven turnaround titles as well as fiction, nonfiction, graphic novels and comics, and specialty lists. If you need to make a book/movie connection, you'll find it here, along with literary titles, magazines, books for boys, and more. There's even a section for read-alikes that can help fan the fire once one title has ignited a spark.

Finally, Part III, "Tools That Work," presents book talks, sample reading interest surveys, and an extensive bibliography. To augment the printed bibliography, visit our Web page: www.connectingya.com/reluctant.htm to gather links to Web-based resources. While most of the items in the bibliography are from the years 2001–2005, there are a few older items that are necessary for understanding these issues. The bibliography has both tools for using (other bibliographies) and for understanding (articles on boys and reading). While the majority of items are from the library professional press, we've included many resources aimed at teachers.

While we've collaborated on the project throughout, each of us has focused on specific areas based on our expertise. Patricia, a former classroom teacher and current tutor and author, focused on understanding the obstacles, partnering with teachers and parents, and creating reading ladders to help aliterate readers succeed in school. Patrick, a former young-adult librarian and current young-adult (YA) author, conducted the author interviews that produced many of the insightful sidebar quotes; developed the booktalks; and contributed to the tips section. Maureen, a public librarian who chaired the Young Adult Library Services Association's Quick Picks committee, focused on lists of titles that empower teachers and librarians to connect with reluctant teen readers. We've adopted a FAQ format to help you get the most out of this resource, so you can focus on the areas in which you're most interested or read straight through.

We think you'll find here not just titles but also ideas, activities, and inspiration to connect reluctant readers with the library collection as well as classroom reading. We hope to give you both skills and confidence to help your reluctant readers discover what we know: the power, the glory, and the joy of reading.

Acknowledgments

Patrick: Of course, thanks to all the people listed on the next page who took time out of their busy schedules to share their ideas/expertise with us. In particular, I want to thank Dr. Kylene Beers, whose breakthrough work about aliteracy inspired and guided my thinking on this issue. Thanks to the staff/members of the Young Adult Library Services Association for supporting the work of the Quick Picks committee, creating Teen Read Week, and providing leadership in this area. Thanks to Cathi MacRae and Linda Benson at *VOYA* magazine for rounding up and letting me use the Perfect Tens lists. Finally, thanks to Dr. Erica Klein for her continued support.

Maureen: Thanks to all those who have given great advice, conspired on brilliant ideas, and continue to guide me in my professional journey, especially Carey Conkey, Linda Braun, Terry Turner, Ginger Bush, Tonya DePriest, and Emily Watts. And a final thanks to my family and especially Yen Nguyen, who paid the rent while I was in library school, cooked dinner while I was "just finishing up a few things at work," changed plans when I had my nose buried in a book, and has always believed in me and supported me in everything I've attempted.

Patricia: Gratitude to every librarian and teacher who helped a reluctant reader, love to all my students who shrugged off the mantle of "reluctant reader" because we trusted each other (especially Lori Redd Huffman), and lots of thanks to those who understood why my face is always blocked by a book, most importantly Mary Earle Popham, Travis Alexei Taylor, the late LaVelle Wittmer, the late Nell Whitman Gurley, Zandrah K. Ralphs, and Sandra Felix Shroyer.

Special Thanks

To the following authors, editors, librarians, teacher librarians, and teachers who provided us with talking points. For authors, we've listed only their most recent Quick Picks book (as of 2005).

Alessio	Amy	Librarian/Author	*Teen Read Week: A Manual for Participation*
Apollo		Author	*Concrete Candy*
Arnold	Mary	Librarian	Former YALSA president
Atkins	Catherine	Author	*When Jeff Comes Homes* (Quick Picks 2001)
Beers	Kylene	Author	*When Kids Can't Read: What Teachers Can Do: A Guide for Teachers 6–12*
Bennett	Cherrie	Author	*Love Him Forever* (Quick Picks 2001) with Jeff Gottesfeld
Brookover	Sophie	Librarian	Camden County (NJ) Public Library
Bruggeman	Lora	Librarian	Former Quick Picks chair
Cansano	Jean	Librarian	Springfield (MA) City Library
Cart	Michael	Author/Editor	*Love & Sex* (Quick Picks 2002)
Cheney	Amy	Librarian	Alameda County (CA) Juvenile Hall Library
Claudio-Perez	Marina	Librarian	San Diego (CA) Public Library
Cohn	Rachel	Author	*Gingerbread* (Quick Picks 2003)
Coons	Martha	Librarian	Springfield (MA) City Library
Coy	John	Author	*Crackback* (Quick Pick nominee 2006)
Crowe	Chris	Professor	Brigham Young University (UT)
Digiacomo	Delores	Teacher	Carmon-Ainsworth High School (Flint, MI)
Doyle	Miranda	Librarian	Teenlibrarian.com
Enslow	Mark	Publisher	Enslow Publishers
Evarts	Lynn	Librarian	Former Quick Picks chair

Flinn	Alex	Author	*Breaking Point* (Quick Picks 2003)
Gajdostik	Laura	Classroom Teacher	Hudson (WI) High School
Gallaway	Beth	Consultant	Rogue Librarian Inc.
Gantos	Jack	Author	*Hole in My Life* (Printz Honor 2003)
Giles	Gail	Author	*Playing in Traffic* (Quick Picks 2005)
Glenn	Mel	Author	*Foreign Exchange* (Quick Picks 2000)
Goldsmith	Francisca	Librarian/Author	*Graphic Novels Now: Building, Managing, and Marketing a Dynamic Collection*
Gorman	Michele	Librarian/Author	*Connecting Young Adults and Libraries* (3rd edition)
Gottesfeld	Jeff	Author	*Love Him Forever* (Quick Picks 2001) with Cherie Bennett
Griffith	Jessy	Librarian	Mt. Vernon (IN) Public library
Hardacre	Mari	Librarian	Fort Wayne (IN) Public Library
Harlan	Mary Ann	Librarian	Quick Picks Committee
Hartinger	Brent	Author	*Last Chance Texaco* (Quick Picks 2005)
Helmrich	Erin	Librarian	Ann Arbor (MI) Public Library
Herald	Diana Tixier	Librarian/Author	*Teen Genreflecting*
Hrdlitschka	Shelley	Author	*Dancing Naked* (Quick Picks 2003)
Jenkins	A. M.	Author	*Breaking Boxes* (Quick Picks 1997)
Jensen	Tori	Librarian	John Glenn Middle School (MN) and member Minnesota Youth Reading Awards
Johnson	George	Librarian	Houston (TX) Independent School District
Kan	Kat	Librarian/Author	"Graphically Speaking" columnist for *Voice of Youth Advocates*
Keane	Nancy	Author	*Booktalking across the Curriculum: Middle Years*
King	Cory	Librarian	Carson City (NV) Public Library

Koja	Kathe	Author	*Blue Mirror* (Best Books 2005)
Korman	Gordon	Author	*Son of the Mob* (Quick Picks 2003)
Kropp	Paul	Author	*Raising a Reader: Make Your Child a Reader for Life*
L'Allier	Darla	Librarian	Tulsa (OK) City County Library
Lerner	Alan	Publisher	Lerner Books
Lesesne	Teri S.	Author	*The Right Book for the Right Reader at the Right Time*
Levin	Nancy	Librarian	Cleveland Heights (OH) Public Library
Lubar	David	Author	*Hidden Talents* (Quick Picks 2000)
McBride	Jenny	Teacher	Formerly at Arcata (CA) High School
McDonald	Janet	Author	*Spellbound* (Best Books 2002)
Mikaelsen	Ben	Author	*Touching Spirit Bear* (Best Books 2002)
Mowry	Jess	Author	*Ghost Train* (Quick Picks 1997)
Myracle	Lauren	Author	*TTYL* (Quick Picks 2005)
Odean	Kathleen	Author	*Great Books for Boys*
Paone	Kimberly	Librarian	Elizabeth (NJ) Public Library
Peters	Julie Ann	Author	*Define Normal* (Quick Picks 2001)
Plumb	Dania	Teacher	Dundee (MI) Alternative School
Reynolds	Marilyn	Author	*Telling* (Quick Picks 1997) and *I Won't Read and You Can't Make Me: Reaching Reluctant Teen Readers*
Scieszka	Jon	Author	*Math Curse* (BBYA 1996)
Shusterman	Neal	Author	*Downsiders* (Quick Picks 1999)
Sleator	William	Author	*Rewind* (Quick Picks 2000)
Stewart	Kathy	Librarian	Richland (SC) County Public Library
Stine	R. L.	Author	*It Came from Ohio: My Life as a Writer* (Quick Picks 1998)
Stoehr	Shelley	Author	*Crosses* (Quick Picks 1992)
Suellentrop	Patricia	Librarian/Author	*Connecting Young Adults and Libraries* (3rd edition)
Sullivan	Michael	Librarian/Author	*Connecting Boys with Books: What Libraries Can Do*

Sweeney	Joyce	Author	*Players* (Quick Picks 2001)
Taylor	Deborah	Librarian	Enoch Pratt Public Library and former YALSA president
Watson	Jamie	Librarian	Chair, Quick Picks (2005)
Weatherfeld	Scott	Author	*So Yesterday* (Quick Picks 2005)
Weaver	Will	Author	*Farm Team* (Best Books 1996)
Welch	Rollie	Librarian	Cleveland (OH) Public Library
Werlin	Nancy	Author	*Killer's Cousin* (Quick Picks 1999)
Woodbridge	Andrews	Publisher	Orca Books
Woodson	Jacqueline	Author	*Behind You* (Quick Picks 2005)

From the Authors

PATRICK JONES

"I'm thirty years old and I have these dreams." That's the beginning of *Ball Four*, the book that turned me from a magazine/newspaper reader (not that there's anything wrong with that) into a book reader. Published in 1970 as a controversial best-seller, this diary by baseball player Jim Bouton was the first book I remember reading outside of school. It was the summer before my sophomore year, and by fall, lines from the book ("consider the source") had worked themselves into my conversations. While I liked baseball, I don't recall reading much about it other than box scores and newspaper stories in the *Flint Journal*. I opened the book because of an interest, but left it inspired to read. I don't know if it was the humor, the language, the sexual content (I was an adolescent boy after all) or the "worldview" of Bouton, but something clicked. I reread the book several times while in high school, and still read it once or twice a year. It was *the book* that taught me everything about reading: that words on a page could make you think, make you laugh, make you angry, and thus bring you pleasure. I was hooked.

I wasn't much of a reader as a kid and didn't visit libraries (most people know that story, but if not, see my essay "Wrestling with Reading" in *Guys Read*, edited by Jon Scieszka), so I was lucky that for some reason my mom had a copy of the book. And while I don't read baseball biographies anymore, I still read about the game—in particular, writers like Bill James. Mostly I read about professional wrestling. The highlight of my week is the arrival of my *Wrestling Observer* newsletter on Saturdays. I don't read fiction, except YA stuff, and I can't imagine ever wanting to read one word of a Harry Potter novel. But for me, Jim Bouton was my J. K. Rowling, just as Sister Souljah, R. L. Stine, Gail Giles, Alex Flinn, or any of the authors included in this book serve to inspire today's reluctant teen reader. I wasn't reluctant to read; I just didn't understand why I should until Bouton threw me a pitch I could hit out of the park.

PATRICIA TAYLOR

I believe that the world can be divided into two groups: readers and nonreaders. The readers have all the advantages; just ask any nonreader. I used to tell my students that language was what got us out of the caves and kept us out. My reluctant readers usually made a crack concerning cavemen not having to deal with book reports and reading quizzes, and that if they had, we'd still be in the hollow hills.

They had a point. Every year I was met with high school students who hated reading and—by extension—school because their reading skills were below level and had been that way for most of their memories. To respond to the situation, we instituted a class for reluctant readers, which I taught for fifteen years and whose components I still use in consulting and private teaching. Most of the material in this handbook comes from the experiences of those years, and every suggestion and activity has been "road tested" and proven viable.

One thing they don't tell you in teacher or library school: how much intuition can play into success with reluctant readers. Listening to them—and to their histories—can reveal a great deal, and a sympathetic ear is something many of them are not accustomed to having. Sometimes a large part of bringing reluctant readers into the fold is nothing more than cheerleading. They have to believe they can learn to read with joy as well as competence. And they can, most of them, if they are relieved of the pressures they've come to expect about their performance in the book arena.

As a child, the book I read until I wore the pages out was *Gone With the Wind*. I was ten years old my first time through it, and I had an older, well-meaning cousin who told me I was much too young and shouldn't be reading it. Thank the gods of books and little girls that my mother paid no attention to such spurious advice. In the intervening years, an avalanche of books have come into my life, but it is still Margaret Mitchell's masterpiece that I look on most fondly. I was always a reader, but Ms. Mitchell taught me I could read anything I liked, even if it was supposed to be for "grown-ups." Now when teens ask me what they should read, my answer is always, "Anything you like." Reluctant readers are generally flabbergasted by such direction.

There is no greater pleasure than opening a book to someone who once could not see the pages. In doing so, you have given another human being the ability of a lifetime, and it can be a life-changing experience. The adage "Give a man a fish and he eats for a day, teach him to fish and he eats for a lifetime" applies to the world of literacy. "Give a child a book and she'll read if she must, teach her to read and she'll have books all her life." And what is life without books? Just another day in the caves.

MAUREEN L. HARTMAN

My first job out of library school was as a children's and young-adult librarian in a small branch library outside of Boston. It was five blocks and six and a half minutes from the middle school and one of the elementary schools. The branch was only open three days each week, but on each of those days, at 2:25 P.M., students—primarily middle school—would arrive to spend anywhere from ten minutes to three hours at our branch. Evidence of their presence was everywhere—giant backpacks thrown on the ground near computers, candy wrappers hidden between books on the shelves, and a near-constant pleading of "Maureen, I am sooo bored; don't you have anything to do?" Like many of us who chose to be librarians and educators, I found the concept of being in a library and having nothing to do almost inconceivable. The building was full of "things to do"; all they needed to do was walk up to a shelf and select a book. But without anyone to connect them with the titles on the shelf or anyone to understand the kinds of books they might enjoy, they wandered around disconnected from the great titles painstakingly selected from the ever-decreasing materials budget. From that day on, I've recognized the significance of reluctant readers and the power we have to engage them in reading.

In my continued work with teenagers, I still love talking with avid readers, but I get much more personal enjoyment from spending time with those who are just like the teenagers I encountered on my very first day as a librarian: reading is the last thing they would choose to do with their free time. But just as in the case of those students in Watertown, who I—and others— connected with books like *Walk Two Moons, The Wreckers, Party Girl* and *Speak*, we hold the power to connect our would-be readers with books that will speak to them personally, and to use strategies that will engage them in the habit of reading. We have the great responsibility to create lifelong readers out of teenagers. We can do it; we just need the right tools.

Part I.   Tips That Work

FOREWORD TO PART I BY GAIL GILES

Gail Giles is the author of *Shattering Glass, Dead Girls Don't Write Letters,* and *Playing in Traffic*. All three books appeared on Young Adult Library Service's Association "Quick Picks" for Reluctant Young Adult Readers list. Portions of these remarks were first delivered at the American Library Association 2005 Annual Conference during a session sponsored by the Young Adult Library Service Association's Quick Picks Committee entitled "Reaching the Reluctant Reader."

First of all I'll start with Grand Theft Syntax. I was one of the gazillion people listening to Laurie Halse Anderson speak at the Texas Library Association conference in Austin and I'll paraphrase her thoughts. "These teens are not 'reluctant' they are 'discriminating' readers. For these kids to read a novel it has to be goooooooood. Face it, all of us in the room are promiscuous readers, book sluts, as it were. We'll read anything, anytime, anywhere. The 'discriminating' readers are much more picky."

I have felt this way for many long years and have tried to explain it, but Ms. Anderson articulated it elegantly enough that I shoplifted it.

I had the honor, and I mean that sincerely, of teaching high school remedial readers. Remedial. Let's just say I have a problem with that term too. Some of the students were in my classroom because their reading skills were below grade level. Some were there because they just didn't want to read. Some were there because they had pissed some other teacher off and they ended up with me because I had pissed someone in the administration off.

But we were together and not too many people came near us so I was able to plan and write my own program. Believe me, I ditched those skill sheets and other reading programs in a big hurry and bought classroom sets of novels. I wrote my own units that fit the pattern of these "discriminating" readers and off we went. I was able to find out what novels worked and what didn't for the kids and for me. And I had empirical evidence. The books that worked were in short supply at the end of the day. The kids stole them to read ahead.

What makes a book good? Here are some of their common traits. It has to start fast from the giddy-up. These kids won't give you more than a sentence to snag their attention. You have to have a great first sentence. And a really good second sentence. And third, and ninth, and twenty seventh, and maybe if you're lucky they will cut you some slack and let you have just an okay two thousand and third sentence, but you better pick it back up on the two thousand and fourth. These kids don't have time to mess with a sloppy writer. They only read the good stuff so everything in the book has to be good.

The book has to have a really great main character. Maybe one a little outside the margins. These readers are more broadminded than the promiscuous reader. The main character can be flawed and even unsympathetic, but the character must be understandable. This reader demands the all-important why. Why does this character behave the way he or she does?

Now, it's not enough just to have good characters. Lots of books have good characters that spend their time just "characterling" around. But the "discriminating" reader wants more. This reader wants his fully developed character to DO something. Something has to happen. The character has to make it happen and it has to happen quickly.

Fast paced. Remember the old adage, immediate gratification takes too long? Good plot. For the discriminating reader, plot is not a four letter word, so throw in a few unexpected turns please, and a breakneck pace, leading to a walloping ending. We like an ending that takes the breath away. Something that makes us say "Wow!" Something that makes us discuss. Or just cuss. Maybe even argue. Maybe offends our sense of justice. Maybe something that makes us wonder. And please do this in under 200 pages. There are books the "discriminating" reader will love that are big and heavy and long. But they are the exception rather than the rule. I love that they love them.

But for the most part, teens like books that reflect the teen years. So much is packed into the few years between twelve and eighteen. Physical changes are huge, intellectual changes are, hopefully, just as big. A kid goes from being babysat to being a babysitter. From riding in the backseat to driving. From carrying a lunchbox to applying for college. It is amazing to me how much change, how many emotions, how much angst, how much stuff is jammed into so few years.

I think YA books usually reflect that. They are lean, mean, fighting machines. They don't give themselves up to long descriptive passages about the color of the sky or waxing poetic about what someone is thinking. YA novels don't tell much at all. They show. They are stripped of author self indulgence.

Well, the good ones are and those are the ones that reach our discriminating readers.

Now for the most important thing of all. The discriminating reader demands that the YA book be honest. The discriminating reader won't let you get away with pulling the punch at the last minute. You can't throw the fight. If the character is flawed, you can't get away with a quick redemption and a promise of happily-ever-after at the end. The discriminating reader does not want to be insulted. He might be reluctant, but he got that way for a reason. Deal with him or her honestly. Play the story out as the character would, not as the author wants it.

So, how did learning all this from my students affect my writing? I got the germ of the idea for *Shattering Glass* by eavesdropping on a group of kids when I was substitute teaching so long ago that I refer to that period as "when I was still alive." The idea nestled in my head for a long time.

I had an idea. How did I start? I spent an entire year writing short stories and learning that craft. Not with any intention of writing and selling short stories, but with the idea that most novels start too slowly, but short stories, by necessity, shoot right out of the gate. A year. When I got comfortable with what worked and what didn't, I started writing novels with a short story-type opening. You're never going to read a lot of them. But when I dredged up the memory of that eavesdropping incident and the ideas it had engendered, I began. And began. And began again. I think I began seventeen times. Until I had it right.

> Simon Glass was easy to hate, I never knew exactly why, there was too much to pick from. I guess, really, we each hated him for a different reason, but we didn't realize it until the day we killed him. (*Shattering Glass*, p. 1)

I think every teen in the world, marginal or not, has had a person they hated. And maybe they didn't even know exactly why. And hated so much they'd liked to kill. They don't, of course. But this opening sets off a series of questions that lets the reader know that he or she isn't the only person ever who harbored such internal rage. And they want to find out what happens if that secret rage is fulfilled.

> Things had been getting a little better until I got a letter from my dead sister.
>
> That more or less ruined my day. (*Dead Girls Don't Write Letters*, p. 1)

That is the opening of *Dead Girls Don't Write Letters*. I get a lot of e-mail from teens. Some that like my books and some that don't. And some that say, "Ms. Giles, you are the greatest writer ever. I was assigned your book for my class. It was the greatest book I ever read. Could you write me back today and tell me the plot, the theme, and some thumbnail sketches of the main characters? It is very important I have these today." But other than these desperate attempts for me to be the greatest writer ever of their book reports, I have gotten more e-mail about Sunny than any other character I have written.

Look at what we know about Sunny from her opening remarks. Wow, she gets a letter for her dead sister and it ruins her day. Worse, it MORE OR LESS ruins her day. She's not only hard hearted, she's sarcastic to boot. Flawed? Check. Unsympathetic? Double-check.

But our discriminating readers want to find out why Sunny might be this way. Believe me, they may have wanted a sibling to disappear a time or two themselves. Maybe not for real, but . . . enough to keep reading and see if Sunny has reason not to want to hear from her dead sister. And how does one get a letter from a dead sister anyway?

And they find out. Sunny wasn't an only child but her older sister Jazz certainly was. How many letters have I gotten from the "forgotten" siblings? Those unfavored children in the family, the ones that don't quite live up, the ones that stand in the shadow of another sibling's glow? This was THEIR book. The one that said, I can love my parents and my sibling and be rightfully angry at the same time. And while they were finding that out—it didn't let them laze around. Things happened fast and in remarkably few pages. Remember the rules my students gave me—the characters have to do stuff, do it fast, and in under 200 pages. This story essentially takes place in under nine hours.

Next thing those students wanted was an ending that made them wonder and argue. Let me talk about e-mail again here. *Shattering Glass*. Lots of e-mail about "how can you break up Young and Ronna? How can you let Rob get away?" My biggest surprise was that no one questioned the killing of Simon or of Young's guilt. The kids found these things inevitable and thanked me for the honesty, for not backing away, but I wounded their sense of justice about Rob's run from the law and their romantic sensibilities about Young and Ronna. Good for them. Losing is hard and not just the overt bad guys lose when you get caught up in bad things.

The end of *Dead Girls Don't Write Letters* has produced a lot of e-mail too. I love this. Provoke the reader to wonder. I have been called upon to settle arguments between readers. Did Jazz exist or not? Ah, I say, that's up to you. There's evidence there to support either conviction. A puzzle within a puzzle. Yes, endings are good things.

> "Make your choice. Me, you, my parents, your sister. Who do you want dead the most?" She put the barrel once more to her temple.
> Back to me.
> Back to her.
> Now I knew there were levels of rage. And I had just reached critical mass.
> She had moved the gun back to me. I stared into the barrel. I stared into those dark eyes.
> And I hated.
> She moved the barrel back to her own temple.
> Who did I want dead the most?
> I didn't look away when I spoke.
> "You," I said.
> I think the shine in her eyes was tears.
> And her lips moved.
> But I'm not certain what she said.
> I couldn't hear over the roar of the gun. (last section of *Playing in Traffic*)

This is the conclusion of *Playing in Traffic*. A conclusion that validates Matt's opening lines that he was doomed from the moment he met Skye. This is the book about the colorless kid. The kid that flies under the radar and hopes he gets out of high school unscathed. In high school he doesn't have anyone to hate or anyone he especially feels close to—he just goes along to get along and get out.

And then it all changes. How can he refuse that impulse to be the bad boy, or if he can't do that—to hang out with the bad girl? To play in traffic for just a little while? So many of my e-mailers liked Matt, many of them actually liked Skye, but the readers knew their collision would inevitably lead to damage. It hurt the reader to see that damage, but there was no honesty if it didn't occur. I couldn't flinch. Those "discriminating" readers wouldn't have allowed it. So as much as the readers hated it—Skye ends up dead and Matt ends up ruined.

I don't write books to change the world. I don't write books to change the world one kid at a time. I don't want to change anyone. When I was fourteen, a librarian handed me a bookmark. I have always been powerfully affected by the quote on it from C. S. Lewis: "We read to know that we are not alone."

That's why I write. That's why I hope teens pick up my books and read. I think that's what the reluctant reader is searching for. The book that tells him or her "What, you too? I thought I was the only one." And for that day and for that book they are not alone. And maybe the next time they feel alone it will be easier to reach for and read a book, knowing there might be a friend waiting for them within the pages.

Chapter 1

Who Are Reluctant Readers?

1.1 WHO ARE RELUCTANT TEEN READERS?

By reluctant teen readers, we mean persons ages 12–18 who choose, for whatever reason, not to read. They can read, maybe not always at grade level, but it is not so much a matter of skill as a matter of choice. A person who can read but chooses not to is aliterate (although we've also seen the spelling *alliterate*). Aliterate readers face significant obstacles to becoming teens who are self-defined avid readers, then later lifelong readers. The key to this work is understanding the obstacles, then seeking tips, titles, and tools to overcome those obstacles. The understanding starts with knowing that nonreaders are not lacking in intelligence but lacking in the desire to make reading a priority in their lives. Dr. Kylene Beers first defined these first four types of aliterate readers:

1. **Dormant readers:** Teens who like to read, may even identify themselves as readers, but rarely do because they do not take the time. Their time is spent in other pursuits, such as schoolwork, sports, and socializing.
2. **Uncommitted readers:** Teens who, if presented with the right book, will read it and most likely enjoy it. They won't search for books on their own and may not define themselves as readers; it is just something they do.
3. **Unmotivated readers:** These teens have very negative attitudes toward reading and toward those who choose to read. They are our most difficult to connect to reading because reading has no value in their lives. This is normally the group most people think of as reluctant readers.
4. **Unskilled readers:** These readers won't read because it is too hard. Not only do they not find joy in reading, but they find negative emotions, mainly frustration.

Another type of reader who might be found within all of these groups but no doubt overlaps mostly with unmotivated readers is the "anti-literate reader." These readers actively hate reading, and will express that sentiment to teachers, librarians, and parents. This isn't so much based on reading skills and attitudes as on developmental tasks of adolescence. They are anti-reading because reading is seen as something that pleases adults, not peers. They are often secret readers as well—they will read on their own for pleasure but will not admit it.

Rather than reinventing or reshaping the wheel, we present the following chart by Dr. Beers, which gives us a framework about what works with each type of reader. This chart—which you should hang on your wall—is a start to understanding, and certainly does not provide the only strategies available to teachers and librarians. Although we may still refer generically to the term "reluctant reader" within the text, as that is the term most people are more familiar with, generally speaking, it is unmotivated and uncommitted readers that we are looking at: kids who would read if we got them connected to the right reading materials. Notice that all four groups have one thing in common: they want to choose their own books. We added the term "avid readers" but dropped "unskilled readers" from this chart as those nonreaders are not the primary focus of this book.

Avid and Dormant Readers	Uncommitted and Unmotivated Read
They do want to:	*They do want to:*
1. Choose their own books	1. Choose their own books from a narrowed choice
2. Have teacher read aloud a few pages	2. Have teacher read aloud an entire book
3. Meet the author	3. Compare movie to book
4. Buy books at a book fair	4. Read illustrated books
5. Keep a reading journal	5. Do art activities based on books
6. Go to the library	6. Read nonfiction material and comics (handbooks, drawing, car, fashion, makeup magazines)
7. Participate in panel debates and small-group discussions or share books with friends	
They do NOT want to:	*They do NOT want to:*
1. Write book reports	1. Meet the author
2. Do many art activities	2. Buy books at a book fair
3. Have teacher read aloud an entire book	3. Go to the library
	4. Read for a charity
	5. Keep a reading journal
	6. Participate in panel debates and small-group discussions or share books with friends

Our second assumption is basic, yet the basis of most controversies in this area. We assume a value in all reading; that is, the goal of any person working with a reluctant teen reader is to overcome that reluctance and get that person reading. Whatever the format, quality, or genre, reading is an end. One librarian interviewed for this book mentioned that she felt "ashamed" that her son was not a reader since he "only" read magazines and nonfiction. This negation of any reading other than fiction, in particular school-assigned classic reading, must be overcome. This second assumption goes a long way toward knocking down the obstacles for aliterate readers, allowing for reading materials that attract all types of these readers. Reading magazines, nonfiction, graphic novels, and just about anything but "required" reading is noted over and over again by every person interviewed for this book. Yes, books offer a fuller and often more engaging reading experience, but they are not better—just different.

But many books don't engage readers, which leads to our third assumption—also mentioned by just about everybody as a primary obstacle. This was best proposed by Don Gallo in his groundbreaking essay for *English Journal* called "How Classics Create an Alliterate Society." While Gallo argues strongly and convincingly for more use of YA literature in classrooms, he puts forth—as the title of his throwing himself to the lions piece suggests—that, generally speaking, English teachers and the curriculums they follow are a significant obstacle to teens reading for pleasure. Gallo argues that the literature teens are required to read sets them up to fail and almost guarantees that reading will become an unpleasant experience. Yet we all know that reading is required to succeed in high school and move on to college. We all know the figures about the incomes of those with college degrees and of those without. So, how do we get teens ready in high school for college reading if they hate the classics and have moved beyond adolescent or children's literature? Our assumption is that by working with teachers, we can build for students reading ladders that will move them from frustration with assigned reading to appreciation, for as former Quick Picks chair Lynn Evarts noted, "I think many reluctant readers become that way because no one has ever really shown them that there are interesting things to read beyond *Great Expectations*."

Finally, our last assumption is that teachers, librarians, and even authors and editors are in some ways the worst positioned to assist aliterate readers because, quite simply, we don't "get" it. As one author noted, "Most books for children are written by middle-aged women and edited by middle-aged women. The critics that review them are all middle-aged women. Now I happen to like middle-aged women a lot, but their sensibility is not necessarily that of a teenage boy, or even a teenage girl." Thus, almost all of us closely involved lack a simple understanding of how a teen could *not* read for pleasure. We lack not only understanding but also perhaps empathy for teens who choose not to read. Is a group of people who find reading pleasurable the best choice to motivate others to read? Yes and no. Yes, because we are passionate on the subject. No, because we are passionate on the subject. We have to help aliterate readers find their own way for their own reasons in their own time to become lifelong readers, not because it validates us or our experiences.

> "I once heard someone describe reluctant readers as not so much reluctant as not motivated. And I think that is the heart of the matter. We can motivate kids with more choice in reading, less lecturing and testing, and more laughing until you fall down and pass out a little."
>
> Jon Scieszka

1.2 WHAT ARE THE CHARACTERISTICS OF DEPENDENT READERS?

Dependent readers rely on sources outside of themselves to tell them what to do, and, in many cases, to do it for them. They have strategies for moving through a difficult text—strategies that look very different from the ones an independent reader would use.

- Dependent readers might lack the cognitive abilities to read independently. Without the cognitive confidence, they might struggle with comprehension, vocabulary, word recognition, or fluency and automaticity.
- These readers might have negative attitudes toward reading. They might claim that reading is boring or a do-nothing activity. They have had so many moments of failure with reading that they do not dislike it but have come to believe that they cannot do it. They are disengaged from the reading process so that whether or not they have cognitive abilities to read independently does not matter. Their attitudes toward reading keep them distanced from reading. These students lack social and emotional reading confidence.
- Dependent readers don't know what types of books they might enjoy, which authors might excite them, or what range of genres exist for them to read. To them, all books are the same. They read a textbook like a YA novel they read in their language arts class. Additionally, these readers

lack the ability to stick with a difficult text and lack the stamina to even find a text.

- Dependent readers only see reading as a means; it is too hard for any other purpose than to complete the assignment.
- Dependent readers often fail because they have nothing but the text itself. They lack the ability or interest to connect the words to events in their personal experience.
- Dependent readers give up easily. Like any person engaged in an unenjoyable task, they look for the first excuse to stop it, the first hurdle they cannot clear. Then, stepping away, they see the fault not in themselves but in the activity. They are not stupid—reading is stupid. Dependent readers are defensive readers.

Independent readers, on the other hand, do the opposite: they won't give up after a few pages, they'll connect the text to their lives, and they will read just to read. We know these teen readers very well—they are in our libraries. But because they are independent readers, they don't need us as much—even if they *are* easier to work with when all of us have too much work to do. As Chris Crowe noted, "[I]t's easy for schools and libraries to focus on the students who are already institutionalized and to neglect kids who don't know how—or who don't want to—play the game the way schools want to play." Another reason they are easy to work with is because we know them: we were them.

1.3 SOME PEOPLE EQUATE RELUCTANT READERS WITH MALE READERS. WHY IS THAT, AND IS IT TRUE?

Almost any school or public librarian who has visited a secondary school classroom to booktalk could tell the tale about the student, always a male, who will defiantly and proudly announce to the librarian that he doesn't read. Chances are much of that is for show, to mark turf and to challenge. Chances are that boy *does* read—but not the stack of novels the booktalking librarian no doubt has in front of her; instead, that male is probably reading newspapers (especially the comics, sports, and entertainment sections), magazines (the same list of subjects, but throw in video-game magazines for younger teens), and maybe even heavily illustrated nonfiction.

After years of neglect, there is now a growing body of research to explain the reading and nonreading habits of boys. In the first chapter of Michael Smith's indispensable *Book Reading Don't Fix No Chevys* is a quick review of a dozen major findings of that research related to boys (not just teens) and reading:

- Boys don't comprehend narrative (fiction) as well as girls
- Boys have much less interest in leisure reading than girls
- Boys are more inclined to read informational texts
- Boys are more inclined to read magazine and newspaper articles
- Boys are more inclined to read comic books and graphic novels than girls
- Boys like to read about hobbies, sports, and things they do or want to do
- Boys tend to enjoy escapism and humor
- Some groups of boys are passionate about science fiction or fantasy
- The appearance of a book and cover is important to boys
- Few boys entering school call themselves "nonreaders" but by high school, over half do
- Boys tend to think they are bad readers
- If reading is perceived as feminized, then boys will go to great lengths to avoid it

Thus, the boy at the booktalking session who says he doesn't read might simply be saying that he doesn't read what the library offers.

Most young-adult sections in public libraries are filled with fiction; there is little recreational nonfiction. If there is recreational nonfiction, it is likely to be self-help, health-related, about teen issues, or pop-star biographies. There might be magazines, but chances are they are aimed more at girls than boys. Comic books will more than likely not be there, and graphic novels, if collected, are not featured. There probably isn't a newspaper lying around. Boys who venture into the YA area will find shelves so jammed that there will not be the opportunity for a catchy cover to grab their interest, and it is doubtful if anything but new fiction will be on display. Given these choices, a teen boy, especially a younger one, will opt for something safe like a series (boys like brands), only to get the message from a teacher, parent, or maybe even a librarian that the book is okay because "at least they are reading something."

The tools and titles are here in this book, as well as in other professional books; the research is there; and the need is staring us right in the face. According to the Justice Department, one in thirty-two people in the United States is currently in jail, in prison, on probation, or on parole, or has been one of these things. The majority of these people are male. Most of the male prison population has limited education; many are high school dropouts. The limits of education are almost always related to reading problems. If we want young men to have their hands clutching a graduation diploma rather than the bars of a cell, then it is time to start overcoming the obstacles we've set up in schools and public libraries so that young males will read.

"From what I've heard from my Guys Read fans, they see most all reading as some kind of school assignment. They feel like they are going to have to answer ten questions or write an essay for anything they read. The limited definition of reading material is another factor. I've heard from a lot of teens who say they are not readers. But it turns out that they read magazines about cars, music, wrestling, fishing, computers, style. They read information books. They read graphic novels. They read and write online. They just don't read the relatively narrow collection of literary fiction that is defined as 'real reading' in schools."

Jon Scieszka

1.4 ARE THERE SPECIFIC REASONS THAT GIRLS IN PARTICULAR DON'T CHOOSE TO READ?

We used to joke that the Recommended Books for Reluctant Young Adult Readers Committee could instead by called Books for Boys. And while research does suggest that boys are more often reluctant readers than girls, that doesn't mean there are no female reluctant readers. While most of the techniques we've outlined here work for both genders, here are some specific things to keep in mind when working with female reluctant readers.

1. "I don't want to look like a dopey bookworm in front of my friends. They'll think I'm being a snob."
2. "I don't want to look like a dopey bookworm in front of boys. They'll think I'm being a snob."
3. "I don't want to look like a dopey bookworm in front of my boyfriend. He'll think I'm saying I'm smarter than he is."
4. "I'm a swimmer/volleyball player/basketball player/track star/softball pitcher, and I don't have time."
5. "Reading is for girls who can't play sports."
6. "Reading is for girls who don't have lives."

This is hardly a complete list, but it is a good sampling of the beliefs we have heard over the years. Once these beliefs have been assimilated, trying to root them out is very difficult and very slow. So, how can we do it?

1. Don't read in front of your friends. And would they *all* think you're a snob? If so, pick a book and tell them you're reading it for extra credit or that your teacher assigned it.
2. Don't read in front of boys. God forbid they should think you're a snob. You might, say at lunch, see if there are any cute boys actually reading themselves. If so, you could use a book as bait!

3. Well, we certainly don't want your boyfriend to think you're smarter than he is. (You must keep a straight face when uttering these words. If your reluctant reader [RR] takes her fear seriously, then so must you.) Have you ever thought of reading a book together? Some very romantic couples do this, you know. They take turns reading to each other and talking about it. Really. No kidding.

4. Say something like, "I understand. I wish I had your athletic ability, and I know it takes a lot out of you. But even if you took ten or fifteen minutes when you're waiting for your ride after practice, it might be a pleasant change in concentration. I know a couple of titles about girls who play baseball/basketball/volleyball/track events/swimming you might enjoy. Perhaps you'd be interested in this title about _____." Fill in the blank of whatever subject could intrigue this particular RR.

5. Did you know that both Venus and Serena Williams reads? Again, it's useful to do some research into the reading lives of contemporary women athletes, but they all have Web sites, and you can even e-mail some of them with questions about their reading. Tell them you're using them as examples for the young women athletes you know who need encouragement in reading, and you're very likely to get answers straight from the horse's mouth, so to speak.

6. What do you mean by that? Do you mean some girls have nothing else to do so they read? Do you actually know anyone like that? You do? That's the saddest thing I've ever heard. Of course, you have so much going on, you could never be accused of "having no life." But I bet you'd find your very busy life might even be more fun if you sometimes read a book like, _____. Once, more fill in the blank to suit the RR.

1.5 CAN AN HONOR STUDENT BE A RELUCTANT READER?

These are the readers who can be the most difficult to reach with the notion of pleasure reading. What to do? Honor students will offer you one advantage: they know reading is important. But for the honor student who doesn't read well, the humiliation can be almost unbearable. Teens who are predominately left-brained, who excel at mathematics and science, are often confused and self-critical when they have to work three times harder than their peers for good grades in English. Other honor students may honestly believe they cannot take the time from their studies to "waste time" reading when no grade is involved. Their question, even if unasked, is "Pleasure reading? What's in it for me?"

What's in it for them is something they may never have considered: time for exploration and reflection, time to examine the world beyond themselves and their own responses to that world. Honor students often drive themselves so hard, they lose sight of the importance of quiet time for themselves. They have to be told again and again that it is not a sin, or even irresponsible, to choose a noncurricular book, sit down, and let themselves be lost in it.

For the honor students who have overcompensated in English—or other classes requiring extensive reading—the idea of pleasure reading may not compute. Help them understand that reading without pressure will help them improve their skills; the more they read without anxiety, the easier all reading becomes for them. "Honor" student does not mean "easy reading" student; depending on their schedules, their curricular interests, and how much reading at home is emphasized, the opposite may be true.

"A good reluctant-reader book will have many levels to challenge the reader—because a 'reluctant reader' doesn't mean a kid who isn't smart. Many readers are reluctant because they don't have patience for a book that doesn't engage them. An engaging book will make readers think and feel, and allow them to delve deeper, if they choose to."

Neal Shusterman

"I don't pull back from vocabulary because I think a potential nonreader will be reading the book. That's not being honest with my reader. He or she can get the meaning from the sentence usage, look it up, ask, or just skip it, but just because he or she is a nonreader doesn't mean he or she is a nonlistener. I don't ever take a 'discriminating reader's' intelligence for granted."

Gail Giles

Chapter 2

Why Are They Reluctant to Read?

2.1 WHY SHOULD TEENS READ FOR PLEASURE?

> "I think teens have a lot of things competing for their time and attention. If they haven't gotten intrigued by reading as a pleasurable activity 'before' they're teens, they're rarely going to have the time and patience to pick it up 'as' a teen."
>
> Nancy Werlin

Our answer to students who ask us this question is often "Why shouldn't teens read for pleasure? As Scout said in *To Kill a Mockingbird* about reading from an early age, "Until I feared I would lose it, I never loved to read. One does not love breathing." The curricula of many secondary schools is so demanding in the age of ever-increasing competition for college admission that students often say they have no time for pleasure reading. Ask them: Have you time for breathing? Eating? Instant Messaging your friends? Take fifteen minutes a day, if nothing more. Carry a paperback in your bag or back pocket. Everyone has times during the day when they must wait for a ride, wait in line, wait for their next class. Don't sit and be bored. Read! And why should they? Because those who never read for pleasure accustom themselves to thinking of reading only as a chore or, worse, tedium. Opening a book should never be a reinforcement of unpleasant work or mere duty; it should be an opening to many doors, behind which are joys, sorrows, escape, pleasure, and—okay—work. The point is, there are a variety of experiences available to active readers, and they should not expect the worst every time they look at the printed page.

Many reluctant readers suffer from slow reading speed, and barring severe learning differences, there is one certain method to increase it: more reading. Teens reading for pleasure will find their speed increasing, sometimes quite rapidly, if they take on books that they enjoy. There is no pressure, no test coming, no time limit. "Just read as you will" is a concept many students have never considered, or if they have, it seems as alien as an episode of *The X-Files*. What they need is encouragement and, perhaps more important, permission. And you can give them that.

One of the dirtiest words in the teen lexicon is "vocabulary." This conjures up SATs, workbooks with endless exercises, flash cards to be memorized, and such classroom admonitions as, "We'll have a vocabulary test every Friday!" If language were presented to you like that, you would dread it, too. How can you make the learning of language more palatable? Suggest reading for pleasure. Books capturing the imagination also offer a no-anxiety method to learn words in context. If you get it, great; if the word "reconnaissance" passes you by, there's always another time. Most people with an extensive command of the language gained it in two ways: by being reared in a household where words were used often and well, and through reading widely. If you dangle the pleasure-reading word carrot at teen readers, many will bite.

We've often told teens, "If you read for your own pleasure, you'll never be bored, and you'll never be lonely." Feedback sometimes came years later, but invariably it was the same. The former reluctant readers had stories to tell about how reading had saved them from the great horror of all teens: ennui. Picking up friends at the airport? Take a book! Waiting for your carpool? Take a book! School canceled for bad weather? Yea! You can read! Often teen readers don't consider how much time is lost to forced inactivity until they try regaining the loss with a few chapters of Chris Crutcher or Walter Dean Myers.

How often have you heard "I don't need to read the book; I saw the movie"? Certainly movies can be useful in bringing the written word to animate image, but after the reading, please—not before. *To Kill a Mockingbird* is a case in point. The film's reputation is that of a classic and deservedly so; however, what readers discover is that several important subplots were severed from the story, necessitated by the time limits of film. Teen readers who read the book first can love the movie but still appreciate how much richer the book is. Or, more recently, there was the teen who said, after seeing the movie of *The Sisterhood of the Traveling Pants,* "It was a pretty good movie, but they left so much out, and they actually changed things. I was so mad!" This from a young woman who had lived as a reluctant reader most of her life, until Ann Brashares's series opened the gates of pleasure reading for her.

To read for pleasure is to follow a cultural map. One book may point to another, and that to yet another, until teens can find themselves in a journey we might call the Sister- and Brotherhood of the Traveling Books. Some years ago, in an assignment requiring oral presentations to her class, a teen reader had taken on *Roots;* in the book was the admonition to stop, go and read *The Autobiography of Malcolm X,* and then return to Alex Haley's autobiographical/history/memoir. She did, and discovered a book that she cherishes even now. She didn't have to read it; no one would have known if she hadn't. But she did and thereby discovered the pleasure of reading for her own occupation.

"Young people should get into the habit of reading for pleasure because as they get older, reading comprehension and the ability to think analytically—skills that other mediums often fail to provide—become increasingly important in the business world and in the realms of career choices. For instance, so much of our communication is done through e-mail today that it is key to be able to think and communicate by way of the written word."

Apollo

2.2 WHY DON'T TEENS LIKE TO READ?

"I asked my almost-sixteen-year-old son (a nonreader) why he didn't like to read. He said, 'Reading sucks.' I told him that wasn't a reason. He said, 'It takes up too much time.' I said that still wasn't a reason. He said, 'Well, I do like to read stuff that "I'm" interested in. Not like *A Tale of Two Cities*.' 'Tale of Two Cities' was said in a tone of great disgust. He's having to read it for Honors English."

A. M. Jenkins

2.2a Survey

As part of the celebration of Teen Read Week, which took place from October 12 through October 20, 2001, SmartGirl and the American Library Association (ALA) put out a survey asking all about reading. Just over 2,800 teens responded. The average age was fourteen, but the gender makeup (as one might suspect from a Web site called SmartGirl.com) was not equal; 61 percent of the respondents were girls, and more than 37 percent were boys. While the entire survey is of interest, let's focus on two charts:

Answers to "How often do you read?" (percentages rounded)

Statement	Girls	Boys	Total
I read constantly for my own personal satisfaction, and I love it.	35%	17%	28%
I don't have much time to read for pleasure, but I like to when I get the chance.	41%	40%	41%
I only read what I'm supposed to for school.	13%	24%	17%
I basically don't read books much at all.	5%	9%	5%
No answer.	6%	10%	7%

Answers to "If you don't read much or don't like reading, why not?" (percentages rounded)

Response	Girls	Boys	Total
No time/too busy	41.4%	29.8%	36.1%
Boring/not fun	29.3%	39.3%	33.7%
Can't get into the stories	6.3%	7.7%	6.9%
Boys are more interesting	.2%	N/A	.1%
Like other activities better	7.8%	11.1%	9.2%
Too much schoolwork	5.5%	1.4%	3.7%
Makes me tired/causes headaches	1.9%	2.5%	2.2%
I'm not good at it (dyslexia, poor comprehension)	2.6%	4.3%	3.4%
Video games/television more interesting	1.8%	2.3%	2.0%
Books are too long	1.2%	.9%	1.1%
Friends make fun of me	.4%	0%	.2%
Other	1.9%	.9%	1.5%

This data speaks for itself, in particular about the gender differences: almost 40 percent of boys say reading is boring. This was the third year of the Teen Read Week survey, and the results all three years were very similar. Our own reading surveys (equally unscientific) are very similar. Almost every expert interview views teens finding reading "boring" as the most important reason teens don't read more. And in a peer-dominated world, how many teens want to openly and actively engage in an activity deemed boring?

> "There may be as many reasons as there are stars in the sky. Do we blame disabilities, language skills, parents, teachers, the curriculum, community, society, publishers—access to books? I don't know who is to blame; what I do know is that if the experience of reading a book is good, then chances are the reader will want to repeat the experience."
>
> Jack Gantos

2.2b Teens Speak Out

The "why don't you read" question from this survey produced some interesting answers. You can see full results of all the surveys at http://www.smart girl.org/speakout/archives.html, but here are some of the highlights—and lowlights, as it were:

> "I think that reading is EXTREMELY boring and that it gives me stress!! The only thing I will willingly read is a magazine!!!"
>
> —girl, 17

> "The reason I don't read is because I basically don't have enough time. I go to work right after school and go to school right away at 5:30 in the morning. But when I do read, I love it and wish I could do it more often."
>
> —boy, 17

> "I have a pretty busy schedule, and I like getting school reading done before pleasure reading. So I don't get confused, I don't normally read any other books besides assigned ones during the school year."
>
> —girl, 17

> "Because most books can't keep me interested, so I guess I have a short attention span."
>
> —boy, 17

> "I don't really read for pleasure. If I do, then it is from a beauty magazine like *Teen* or *Seventeen*. No books really interest me anymore. I used to read *Babysitters Club* when I was little. I also read other little kids books all the time, but not anymore. At my age, no books really interest me."
>
> —girl, 17

> "I think that reading takes up a lot of time that I don't have, and I enjoy reading when it's a good book that I'm interested in, but I don't have the time for books like that since the reading that I have to do is for school, and I don't like the books they choose for me."
>
> —girl, 17

> "I don't read because I am a visual learner so I find it hard to learn with pages and pages of words. I like to see what I'm being taught."
>
> —boy, age 17

"I don't mind reading for myself but when school starts I don't like reading anymore. School seems to have boring books to read. Most of the books that I'm assigned to read have nothing to do with my profession. And I feel that it's a waste of time. If I have to read something I feel that it should at least offer me some type of helpful knowledge."

—girl, age 16

"I don't find many books I like."

—boy, 16

"I don't read because it is boring."

—boy, 15

"I don't really have time to read during school days and I don't really know which books are worth reading."

—girl, age 15

"I usually don't read because it gives me headaches trying to focus my eyes on the words."

—boy, age 14

"I think the reason I don't read is because I never run into a book good enough to keep my attention."

—boy, age 14

"I like to read, but it's having the patience to make time for it that gets in the way! Plus, a lot of the books seem to be sci-fi these days, which I hate, so it's also availability."

—girl, age 14

"I'm more of an outdoors person and don't like to stay cooped up inside with a book."

—boy, age 13

Reasons teens don't read based on what I see as an alt ed teacher are:
- Student does not understand the book due to unfamiliar vocabulary.
- Student cannot relate to the plot so doesn't find a reason to pick up the book.

- Student sees reading as a forced "school" activity and doesn't want to do it on their free time.
- Student has ADD/ADHD; it's hard for them to sit and concentrate for long periods of time.
- Student is dyslexic; reading is a struggle and *not* enjoyable for them in any way.

Catherine Atkins

2.2c Interview

Daniel Sandoval is a teen in the Chicago suburbs. In the summer of 2005, he spoke on a Young Adult Library Services Association panel on reluctant readers. While one reader can't represent all, his comments led us to ask for an interview to learn more about him and, thus, reluctant readers.

Q: How would you describe your view of reading? Would you say that you are currently an avid reader, a reluctant reader, or a nonreader?

A: Reading I would describe as something that cannot and should not be forced on someone. Personally, if I am forced to do some reading whether it is required or assigned, I will not want to do it. Reading should be a choosing. It should be something only you like and something only you can enjoy. An example would be when a school does a "one book, one school" type of thing. That doesn't compel people to read. They'll think, "Urgh, I *have* to read that damn school book," and then they won't feel like doing it at all. I would describe myself as a reluctant reader. I used to love reading anything that sparked my interest. Once my high school started to assign books, however, it all changed. Now I find myself SparkNoting most of my assignments.

Q: Outside of school, how many books do you normally read a month? What's the last best book you read, and why?

A: Outside of school, the only reading I do is on the Internet. I simply search up what interests me and spend hours reading. Books? Hardly. Last thing I read was *Stargirl* for the school and that was because there were no SparkNotes for it. I got halfway through *Interview with the Vampire,* then school started.

Q: Do you read other than books? Magazines, newspapers, Web sites, etc? Do you get a sense that teachers/adults don't count that as real reading, and all that matters is reading literature?

A: Besides Web sites, I also read *Nintendo Power*. It's a magazine all about Nintendo. . . . I do believe that people don't think it is "real" literature simply because it involves entertainment, but I do think it is a good form of literature. Overall, *Nintendo Power* is a good read, which has both lengthy and short articles of interest.

Q: Have your reading tastes changed over the years? Do you read mainly books written for teens or more adult books? If you stopped reading outside of school, when did that happen? In other words, what is your reading autobiography?

A: As you can probably make out, my reading habits have changed. I have become more reluctant and prefer not to read things forced on me. In the past, I read fantastic book series that people my age would normally read. Now, I'm all about *Nintendo Power* and comic books. Every Wednesday I head down to my local comic book shop and pick up an average of five books a week. I've read a mixture of adult and teen books, but I'm more focused on teen reading right now, if comic books are considered to be for teenagers.

Q: What should—or maybe just as important, shouldn't—school libraries be doing to promote reading?

A: To promote reading, there's a great section of my high school library that tells the "Top 10" books read by teens and stuff like that. Whenever I walk past that area, I always try to stop and check out what they have to offer. Nothing too much can be done about making teens read more besides simply promoting some suggested books. Nothing else seems to really work like clubs or anything like that. Honestly, with today's media, it's really difficult to pull away from the convenience and entertainment of a computer.

2.2d Findings

In early fall 2005, we surveyed—with the assistance of various classroom teachers—those students who often fall into the category of reluctant readers: secondary students in juvenile detention centers, juvenile correctional facilities, and alternative classrooms. Note that this is hardly a scientific survey or random sample; instead, we went where we knew we'd find nonreaders. The majority of the population was, of course, male. Here's the raw data as well as some connections we made.

Reading Survey 2005

1. How would you describe your view of reading?

11% Love reading—I enjoy reading for pleasure and for school

25% Really enjoy reading—I enjoy reading for pleasure when I have the time

46% Tolerate reading—I will read for school, but not for pleasure

18% Hate reading—I will read only if I had to

2. How would you rate your own reading skills?

5% Advanced—I like to read books meant for people in higher grade levels

16% Above Average—I read some at my grade level and some above it

49% Average—I am comfortable reading books for people at my grade level

21% Below Average—I can read books at my grade level, but sometimes have trouble

9% Poor—I have trouble reading most books at my grade level

3. Outside of school, how many books did you read a month?

zero	1–2	3–5	6–10	11–15	16–20	More than 20
55%	**23%**	**10%**	**6%**	**4%**	**2%**	**0%**

4. When do you read, what do you read most? PLEASE CHECK ONE

books	magazines	comic books	newspapers	web sites
22%	**48%**	**9%**	**1%**	**20%**

5. If you read books, what type of books? PLEASE CHECK ONE

fiction / stories	nonfiction / stories	graphic novels
33%	**51%**	**16%**

6. In fiction, what THREE types of books do you like best?

5% Adventure

9% Fantasy

2% Historical

17% Horror

8% Humor

19% Mystery/Suspense

16% Realistic

1% Romance

7% Science Fiction

15% Urban Fiction

1% Other

7. In nonfiction, what THREE types of books do you like best?

6% Biography
5% History
15% Sports
1% Health
4% Self-help
12% Humor
31% Music/TV/Movies
9% Poetry
14% True Crime
1% Science
2% Other

8. In magazines, what type of magazine do you like best? Choose only ONE

Music	Sports	Fashion	Video games	TV / Movies	Other
44%	**11%**	**5%**	**28%**	**10%**	**2%**

9. If you said you tolerated or hated reading, why? Check all that apply

26% I like reading, just not reading books
12% In books, I just can't get into the stories or relate to the characters
39% Reading is boring compared to other things I could be doing with my time
5% Reading makes me tired/causes headaches
4% I'm not good at it
11% Books take too much time
2% Friends make fun of me
1% Other

10. If you said you tolerated or hated reading now, when you were younger did you:

[ ]love to read	[ ]enjoy reading	[ ]tolerate reading	[ ]hate reading
25%	**55%**	**12%**	**8%**

11. What grade are you in?

10% 7th
11% 8th
18% 9th
29% 10th
21% 11th
11% 12th

12. Are you?

78% Male

22% Female

Ten quick observations and connections from three nonresearchers about the teens who reported they hated or tolerated reading:

1. Much more likely to be male (few of the girls reported hated or tolerated) and older.
2. More likely to report they were below average or poor readers.
3. More likely to report they read two or fewer books outside of school.
4. More likely to report that when they did read, they read magazines.
5. When asked about books, most preferred fiction.
6. When asked about fiction, they preferred the genres of horror, mystery/suspense, and urban. Few reported science fiction, fantasy, or historical.
7. When asked about nonfiction, they mostly preferred only music/TV/movies, with some interest in biography, sports, and poetry.
8. Among magazines, they overwhelmingly preferred music magazines.
9. They were most likely to report reading problems such as headaches than other groups, but "reading is boring compared to other things I could be doing with my time" was the primary response.
10. More likely to report they hated or tolerated when younger, although there was a significant percentage who went from love or liked reading to hated or tolerated reading.

2.2e Research Reports

There are many reasons advanced from these surveys and short takes on what makes a reluctant reader reluctant, but if we're going to remove the obstacles, we need to understand them first. Perhaps the most concise list—based on research as opposed to observation or informal nonscientific surveys—may be old, but we believe it still applies. In their 1977 article "Why Won't Teenagers Read?" Lance Gentile and Merma McMillan outlined the following common factors:

- By the time many students reach high school, they equate reading with ridicule, failure, or exclusively school-related tasks.
- Students are not excited by ideas. They prefer to experience life directly rather than through reading.
- Many active adolescents are unable to sit still long enough to read for any prolonged period of time.

- Teenagers are too self-absorbed and preoccupied with themselves, their problems, families, sexual roles, etc., to make connections between their world and books.
- Books are inadequate entertainment compared to other competing media, such as television, video games, and the Internet.
- Persistent stress from home and school to read constantly is counterproductive for some adolescents.
- Adolescents may grow up in nonreading homes void of reading material with no reading role models. There is no one to pass down the value of reading.
- Some adolescents may consider reading solitary and antisocial.
- Reading is considered "uncool" and something adults do. For boys, it is seen as something girls do and not a masculine activity.
- Some adolescents view reading as part of the adult world and reject it outright, which is cool.

While it does not appear on this list, another factor is the reader's level of independence in reading. As with any task, if we can do it independently, it is more enjoyable and satisfying than if we require help. If we enjoy reading, we do it more; because we do it more, we get better and require less assistance. Thus, a reluctant reader is also often what Kylene Beers would call a dependent reader.

2.3 WHAT ARE THE OTHER FACTORS THAT EXPLAIN WHY MANY TEENS CHOOSE NOT TO READ FOR PLEASURE?

"At the risk of sounding simplistic, I think readers are most often reluctant because they've not yet stumbled across a book they like. And I think schools in general, and many English teachers in particular, do potentially avid readers a terrible injustice by attempting to shove 'good literature' down the throats of kids who aren't ready for it. And if that's all they know of reading, why would they seek it out? The other side of that, since I'm already feeling guilty for criticizing English teachers, is that when teachers offer a wide variety of books for their reluctant readers, and provide ample time for independent reading, the resistance to reading falls by the wayside."

Marilyn Reynolds

We've talked about research, but the fact is, most teachers and librarians are not in the position to do that research—or, in many cases, to even read that research. Therefore, we've asked librarians with a history of working with reluctant readers to give their take on the primary reasons that teens choose not to read for pleasure, based on observation, experience, and instinct. We've eliminated those reasons that validate the research, and instead offer ideas that will make us think about the issue in new ways.

1. **READING "SUCKS ASS"** (to quote *South Park*). "If teens saw more celebrities reading in movies and on television, that might have some influence. Why don't YA publishers advertise on MTV? Increased YA novel ads in teen magazines influenced requests for purchase in my last job."—**Beth Gallaway**

2. **CLASSROOM TEACHERS.** "They may have had negative experiences with fiction titles in the classroom in the past. It seems to me that very few classroom teachers use current, relevant YA literature. Many of these reluctant readers are guys. I don't think classroom teachers get what guys will like in literature."—**Tori Jensen**

    Let's also add here that even teachers who try to bring in YA lit don't always succeed, especially if they don't understand the types of books that will appeal to reluctant readers, in particular male reluctant readers. "When my son was in eighth grade, everyone had to read *Izzy Willy Nilly*—he was so disgusted he read nothing but *Sports Illustrated* until he graduated from high school."—**Mary Arnold**

3. **JUST DON'T KNOW HOW TO READ FOR PLEASURE.** "They have no idea *how* to read for pleasure. They're shocked when I tell them they can skim through the boring parts, or choose books by their covers, or quit reading a book if it's boring. It is the opposite of how you're supposed to read in school. The reading that they do in school is often not geared toward their interests, so they think that all reading is *The Scarlet Letter* or *Oliver Twist*. Just last week a new student was complaining about not liking to read and was being very verbal and resistant to the idea of reading in class. One of the girls that was here last year (and who was also very resistant to reading at first) looked at him and said, 'You just haven't found the right book yet.' That's the same thing I always tell them. By the end of the hour, he had a book that he seemed to like, but it took some doing."—**Dania Plumb**

4. **CAN'T FIND THE GOOD STUFF.** "They're not finding things to interest them *where they are*. There is a lapse between what is offered and what they want in their area bookstores, libraries, schools. Or they are not finding out about the offerings at those places. Lots of reluctant reader teens, like reluctant reader adults, are narrow-minded about what they like to read. If the perception is that the library will not have

their video game magazines, they will not bother to see what else we have to offer."—**Amy Alessio**

5. **INHERENT NATURE OF TEENAGERS.** "They're a jumpy crew, and a social crew. Reading is a sitting-still-by-yourself kind of activity, and if you aren't prone to that, and if your parents haven't instilled the love of reading in you, it can be hard to go against that and get kids to read. Plus, even I was turned off by the gung-ho cheesiness of some of reading's strongest advocates—both as a teen, and more recently."—**Jessy Griffith**

6. **LACK OF AWARENESS.** "Sometimes I think the primary factor is about lack of awareness and marketing. Teens are bombarded with music, movie trailers, and the ready access of friends through personal interaction, computers, and today's ever-present cell phone. Because books aren't successfully marketed like movies, and they take more time, I think reading becomes low priority, also because it is seen as a solitary activity, not a social one. But books that are hot—that get word of mouth and media attention—become a social activity and teens read them and talk about them even if they are reluctant readers. I think the number-one problem is how to market reading as a cool social activity and not a solitary nerdsville thing to do."—**Mary Ann Harlan**

7. **OVEREXPOSURE TO THE CLASSICS.** "Forcing kids to read and digest titles they may not be ready for (especially over the summer, when there is no one to help them get through it) is another factor. Shakespeare was meant to be viewed, not read. There is a dichotomy between what teachers think kids should read and what librarians think kids should read. I understand the importance of knowing the canon, but if all teens are ever exposed to are books that are classics, which can only be understood with the help of a teacher, I'd never read again either! More balance between literary tomes and fun books might go a long way in easing anxiety and reluctance to read."—**Beth Gallaway**

8. **PERSONAL HISTORY.** "I think I see a kind of parallel with math: some people develop the abstracting ability to do math easily later than others and are frustrated earlier with years of 'not getting it.' Some reluctant but capable readers have the life experience of remembering *not* being capable, not getting why anyone would find the activity pleasurable, and thus have to be coached into trying it again. I think audiobooks help with this, as well as with those who really need to be physically active to feel engaged—very possible to do while listening."—**Francisca Goldsmith**

9. **PRESSURE.** "There's so much pressure from parents and teachers and peers to be able to read by grade 1; however, everyone develops and

learns differently and this is unrealistic! Every child starts school excited about learning and reading, and then they start to get lost when it doesn't come as easily to them. Reading becomes not a source of joy but one of fear and frustration."—**Beth Gallaway**

10. **TIME AND TRADITION.** "Time is the number-one factor. I think teens read for pleasure more than they think they do—they are just not reading 'traditional' literature. They read Web sites, blogs, e-mail, chat transcripts, video-game strategy guides, song lyrics, magazines, subtitles on anime, the back of the cereal box, the Sunday comics. They don't have time to sit down and read a whole novel, so they read in bits and pieces."—**Beth Gallaway**

So we've covered a lot of reasons teens don't like to read. Now that we've identified all the roadblocks, let's start taking them apart brick by brick, starting with understanding something very basic. What is reading anyway?

2.4 WHAT ARE THE FOUR LEVELS OF READING?

To understand this work, we need to break it down into its parts. We started with four assumptions and outlined four types of readers, but let's look at the four levels of reading. Like characters in a video game, many reluctant readers get stuck on a level because they don't have the resources to advance to the next. If given a passage to read, such as a chapter in a novel, readers who want to get fully connected to the text need to succeed on all four levels.

Level One

Read ON the line. The key questions for the reader are:

- What is the LITERAL meaning of the passage?
- Can you describe WHAT is happening.
- WHO is the writing talking about, and WHERE are they?

Teens with reading difficulties get stuck. They can't figure out what is going on, so how can they possible enjoy it? It's like watching a foreign film without subtitles.

Level Two

Read BETWEEN the lines. The key questions for the reader are:

- What is the IMPLICATION or suggestion of the passage?
- WHY is the writer presenting the passage or scene?
- HOW is it important to understanding?

This is where unmotivated readers get stuck: they read the passage, but now what? They can't—or won't—tell you what it means because they are stuck on the concrete level of the story itself. Many a reluctant reader can tell you what happens in a book, and that's where it ends. They can recite the plot to extreme detail but can't go beyond that. Because they can't go further, they stay on the surface of reading, without roots to understanding. Thus, when the next thing comes along—a video game or another distraction—the roots are not strong enough to hold.

Level Three

Read BEYOND the line. There's only one key question for the reader here:

- What OPINION or IDEA do the lines reveal about the writer's world-view both inside and outside the book itself?

You're asking readers here for introspection: You read the book and you may even understand it, but what does it mean in the big picture? Given the narrow worldview of teens, the big picture is probably more what it means to them. What truth does it tell about yourself? This is the issue of relevance, which is the strongest case for using teen fiction with teens. If nothing else, they might be able to relate the truth of the book's world to their own. A connection is made.

Level Four

Read for WHOLE MEANING. The key question for the reader is:

- What is the RELATION of the lines to the meaning of the entire book? Connect the passage in question with another passage with the same explicit meaning.

And the last connection: they can connect the dots to form letters, words, and sentences, and to even understand the plot. They can understand what the author is saying and why he or she is saying it, but can they assume what comes next? This is reading with imagination; this is reading as a creative act and often where many reluctant readers get lost, not because they're being asked to do the work but because they are often inexperienced readers and therefore can't see the patterns or make the connections. Like trying to put together a jigsaw puzzle without being able to see the patterns, the end result is frustration. To be lifelong readers, teens will need to succeed on all levels. To move beyond being nonreaders, they need to succeed on at least one.

But let them understand the puzzle. Explain that a book, long or short, is like a jigsaw puzzle in which the pieces do fit together, even if at first the whole thing looks like a jumble of disconnected parts. No one would expect to complete a thousand-piece puzzle at one sitting, or without trial and error to see how the various parts lock together to make a whole. Reading a book is a similar experience. Don't look at the size of the puzzle; that invites discouragement. Examine a few pieces first to see what part of the picture they are. A little at a time adds up. As much as you can, offer your reluctant readers a choice of evaluation methods.

Chapter 3

How Can We Help?

3.1 WHAT'S THE SINGLE MOST IMPORTANT THING ABOUT WORKING WITH RELUCTANT TEEN READERS?

The most important aspect of teaching the reluctant reader is to remove his fear. Your readers need to know that they control their reading, not the other way around. Stress that reading is active, not passive, that it is *inter*action as well as action. A high school student once observed, "I wish I could just open up a slot in my head and shove the book through. Then I'd know everything." How many of us projected a similar wish at one time or another! In understanding the frustration inherent with reading difficulties, we can point out that, short of a scalpel to the forehead, there are other ways to "shove the book through."

While these techniques are certainly most applicable to the classroom setting, they present the school librarian with a remarkable opportunity for collaboration, which is the foundation of a successful school media program. Librarians working in public libraries could easily use these techniques with groups of readers they meet outside their four walls—such as during outreach to correctional facilities, group homes, residential treatment centers, homeless shelters, and home-school groups—as well as with book discussion groups inside the library. All of these could be key components to turning passive summer-reading programs into active summer-reading experiences.

3.2 WHAT ARE THE TOP TECHNIQUES FOR TEACHERS WORKING WITH RELUCTANT TEEN READERS?

> "Reading is associated with school and is, thus, thought of as 'required,' which is the kiss of death. If we could give students more opportunities to self-select from among books they regard as being relevant to their lives, we'd have more willing readers, I think. Another reason they choose not to read is ... that there are simply too many demands made on their time. Creating more opportunities during the school day for pleasure reading might help."
>
> Michael Cart

1. Make Your Own Reading Guide

Answering questions of who, what, when, where, and why is the time-honored activity for sorting out what happened, who did it, where the doing took place, and what the heck all that doing was for. Reluctant readers gain a valuable sense of control when they chart the course themselves, rather than writing out answers to a series of preselected questions. You are in a better position to judge their progress by the choices they make in their reading guides. The format is simple, and you can either prepare it for them or have them create their own from your direction. They should fill in the columns chapter by chapter, leaving space for later additional notes. You can check individual guides quickly to see that the initial objective has been met, then discuss the generic questions and individual answers as a group. As a result of this class discussion, readers can fill in anything they previously missed. Columns should be noted with chapter and/or page numbers for everyone's easy reference.

Reading Guide for Any Book				
Who?	What?	When?	Where?	Why?

2. Book Marking

Okay, librarians, just relax for a second. Substitute "Post-it notes" for "pens," then take a deep breath. If students are fortunate enough to own their own texts, you may have some difficulty convincing them that they are not only permitted but encouraged to break the first commandment of reading and mark in their books: Generations of great writers—Hemingway, Dickens, Woolf—wrote notes to themselves in their own reading, and what better examples could there be to lead the way to interactive, dialogue-rich reading? Readers often make the mistake of thinking that if they highlight important passages, they've done all they need to do. In reality, such a technique leaves us with nothing more than a book yellow (or green or pink) with highlights: a colorful display of pages, perhaps, but nothing to help decode the puzzle.

3. Storyboards

Steven Spielberg (*E.T., Indiana Jones, Schindler's List, Minority Report, War of the Worlds*) seems to never fail. Every movie he makes turns out to be a favorite, if not a classic, and he credits part of his success to storyboarding. Every scene in every script is drawn out on a series of panels before he begins shooting, thus removing the guesswork from his moviemaking. Your students can use the same technique to remove the guesswork from their reading; often the reluctant reader is left-brained, and can draw or paint quite well. Even if students are not proficient artistically, they can manage a few stick figures or create a collage. One former student with serious difficulties in reading was both athletically and artistically gifted; she managed to master every book in the senior English curriculum by including storyboards in her compensation activities. She was eventually able to visualize scenes as she read without drawing them first.

4. Create Your Own Reading Quiz

While the reading quiz is a staple of evaluating progress in reading assignments, for reluctant readers, it can serve as a trigger for anxiety. To avoid setting up such readers for failure, allow them to create their own quizzes. Guidelines for quiz creation are as follows:

• Decide how many questions there needs to be. The number could be anywhere from five to twenty, depending on the length of the assignment. (Questions must span the length of the assignment. If the reading covered ten pages and the quiz is five questions, then each question must roughly cover two pages.)

- At least one vocabulary question should be included. Quiz makers must choose one word in the assignment, look it up, and use it in a question-and-answer format.
- Answers, which must be included, cannot be yes or no. Quiz makers must be prepared to defend each question as to its relevance to the text and its importance to the story. Often, such defenses reveal to the readers that they knew much more about inferences than they thought.
- Readers should be given the choice of making their own quiz or taking one prepared by the instructor.

5. Make Your Own Book Cover

As associate professor of Slavic literature at Cornell University College in 1948, Vladimir Nabokov was delivering a lecture on Robert Louis Stevenson's *The Strange Case of Dr. Jekyll and Mr. Hyde*; deploring the garish cover on the paperback edition his students were using, his first assignment to them was "you will veil the monstrous, abominable, atrocious, criminal, foul, vile, youth-depraving jacket—or better say straitjacket." (Nabokov was nothing if not agile with adjectives.) While he made his point about the vagaries of publishing house art directors, he also served as the inspiration for another path of discovery for reluctant readers. Following the reading of the text, you can instruct your students to create book covers that reflect their understanding of the story. One class of reluctant readers who had completed *Phantom* by Susan Kaye re-covered their books with their own interpretation of the various themes in the story, photographed them, and sent them to the publisher to suggest better artwork than the unfortunate, vile (see Nabokov) stuff gracing the latest paperback version.

6. Creating a Timeline

For reluctant readers, books that do not follow a chronological timeline can be frustrating, confusing, and—in the worst cases—a deal breaker in terms of completing the reading. Timelines may serve as a guide to alleviate such difficulties. For less-demanding novels, readers should try to make their own, either individually or in groups. Group work is very effective, as it can give rise to vigorous discussion, allowing readers to feel as if they are truly mastering the reading on their own. For more difficult literature, you can provide the timeline before the reading begins as sort of a security blanket.

7. Devise a Family Tree

Works of literature with many characters or with a potentially confusing cast can put off even non-reluctant readers. As with a timeline, devising a family tree of characters can be individual or group work, or it can be provided by you.

8. Student Writing for Publication

Independent exploration often assures reader enthusiasm; writing a book report just as often demolishes it. How, then, can you convince young-adult readers to write about what they have read? Through two methods: (1) the student-generated Read This Book! list, and (2) book reviews online.

READ THIS BOOK!

Generally, the term "book reports" is met with groans and eye rolling. Students often see them as dead-end assignments, something they must grind out to prove that they have completed an assignment. However, if their written assessments generate purpose beyond the grade book, they can enjoy the writing practice, work on locating their own writing "voices," and often inspire their peers to do some non-assignment reading.

Rather than writing a simple synopsis of the plot, reviewers write an actual review: synopsis, character analysis, examination of writing style, appropriate audience, and—most importantly—the reviewer's honest emotional opinion. ("I couldn't stop reading it even when my favorite TV show was on." "I had to read it with a dictionary, so don't pick this one unless you have a lot of time.")

The reviewers should employ language reflecting their own way with words. I tell my students that after seeing two or three writing samples, I should be able to know who wrote what without seeing any names. Writing should be as individual as speaking; everyone's style is different. The reviews should be brief—every sentence has to count! Once collected, this valuable information can be typed, assembled into a booklet, and shared with the rest of the school (one copy to the library, and copies to other teachers giving reading assignments). Word of mouth usually spreads to interested students, and reviewers will gain a small measure of fame with their "published" work. Artistic students (usually the ones who are good with storyboards) may illustrate selected reviews. It should be noted that negative reviews can be included as long as the writer's disapproval or disappointment is valid and well-defended.

BOOK REVIEWS ONLINE

Amazon.com! Besides being a swell place to buy books and research information about them, it's a gold mine of publishing opportunities. Reviewers also receive feedback from their readers ("did you find this review helpful?"), so writers can gain a taste of the "real" world—their work matters beyond a grade. The reluctant reader should choose a book he or she is enthusiastic about—positively or negatively. Before submitting a review to Amazon.com, your students should read a range of comments already published there to get a sense of what is helpful to other readers and what is not. It is much more difficult, for example, to write a helpful negative review than a positive one, although negative feedback on a book is certainly sometimes necessary. After reading their books, reading others' reviews, and considering what direction they wish their critiques to take, students should write their own and submit them according to Amazon's directions. It usually take a few days for a review to appear, but when it does, the reluctant reader feels a part of an internationally published group. As a good modeling exercise, you should submit a review, too. Your participation makes the playing field level for reluctant readers. Following are a few samples of reluctant readers eager to express an opinion about an assigned classic. Giving readers a chance to react improves their chances of enjoying any book. When we write about something, we grow to understand it. When we understand, we appreciate. When we appreciate, we seek to replicate.

Samples:

Reviewer: A reader

Rebecca *is an enchanting story that captures your attention and won't let go until the last page is read. The second Mrs. DeWinter arrives at Manderley to a house filled with memories of the first Mrs. DeWinter, Rebecca. Rebecca, it seems, was the perfect woman; beautiful, sociable, intelligent. Manderley and the people who knew Rebecca were shattered and shocked by her death. As the second Mrs. DeWinter discovers all of the things that made everyone love Rebecca she begins to feel like she doesn't belong. Will she ever find her place at Manderley? A mystery encased in a love story,* Rebecca *is filled with descriptions that make the story come alive and keeps you turning the page to find out what happens from the enticing beginning to the surprising end.*

A classic tale of romantic suspense. A wonderful read!

Reviewer: A reader

Rebecca *is the underlying novel for the Academy Award winning Hitchcock classic movie and a recent* Masterpiece Theater *entry.* Rebecca *is a story seen through the eyes of a young girl who we only know by name as the second Mrs. DeWinter. She meets the charming, dashing and much older Maxim DeWinter in the South of France while she is employed as a paid companion. After a whirlwind romance they marry and he whisks her off to his home in Cornwall: Manderley. Manderley really is the main character of this gothic romance. The girl projects all of the insecurities brought on by youth and inexperience onto Manderley and the title character Rebecca. The most enjoyable part for me of reading* Rebecca *is the description of the house and grounds, the dishes, and the bushes. Maybe Martha Stewart read* Rebecca *in her formative years. Daphne Du Maurier departs from the classic "whodunit" and is more concerned with the character of the place and the people involved. She shows us magnificently how perception and reality can be almost diametrically opposed at times and the consequences of our often wrongheaded but very natural assumptions about other people and their motives. A wonderful read.*

9. Running Wild in the Bookstore/Library

Reluctant readers do not go to bookstores. In their view, it's a foreign country where they do not speak the language. By the same token, a library is a place where the password is "shh!" Reluctant readers are often extroverted personalities, and when we force them to be silent, we quash their enthusiasm and creativity.

Reluctant readers need to make friends with books, and a good beginning is to become comfortable with places that house books. The school library is an excellent beginning.

Most schools allow you to reserve the entire library for one period. During your allotted time, take your reluctant readers in and tell them that for the first five minutes, they can make all the noise they want. Let them run in the aisles, laugh out loud, yell across the stacks to each other. Allow them to literally run around and behave as irreverently as you and the librarian can stand. After the "breaking in" period, explain that you want each one of them to choose a book to read for a class presentation or online publication. They should take the whole period if they wish, pulling books out, reading a few pages, putting them back, consulting with each other if they find stories they think their fellow students might like. Circulate among them to answer questions or make suggestions, but the students should know they are directing themselves. Libraries that subscribe to NoveList can offer reluctant readers further opportunity to research reading possibilities as well as hone their reading skills.

Once your reluctant readers have completed their library safari, a wonderful field trip is to repeat the experience in a good local bookstore (sans the yelling and running). The plan works well if you contact the manager of the bookstore in advance, tell him or her that you'd like to bring your class in to become comfortable and spend a couple of hours. Managers are almost always ready to welcome a whole group of future customers! A store with a coffee shop is an added plus, as the students can meet there after they've made their purchases, have a snack and a drink, and compare notes. Let them know they can take a book off the shelf and sit on the floor or reading chairs and really look through it to decide if they want to buy and read it. When they perceive that bookstores can be warm, welcoming, and non-elitist places, your students will realize that they can return on their own to explore reading possibilities. Becoming comfortable in buildings filled with books is a necessary step toward enticing the reluctant reader from his or her fear.

10. Alternative Forms of Evaluation

A critical step in bringing reluctant readers into the literary fold is to destroy their fear of "the test" and their accustomed practice of "reading for the test." Worry over the evaluation stage of reading is almost a guarantee of ruining the pleasure of reading. There are several ways to evaluate your students' grasp on literature without multiple-choice and fill-in-the-blanks guessing.

Essay tests do not have to be tedious to take or to grade. To measure a reader's understanding over a series of several books, pose the question: If characters X, Y, Z, and D were either stuck in a stalled elevator together or locked in a closet, what would they talk about? Whatever the subject, they must remain true to their personalities and experiences.

Students often find creating dialogue much less threatening than other forms of writing, and they can usually reveal a great deal of understanding of the literature while flexing their own creativity. Furthermore, every answer is going to be different, which brings a freshness to your reading and grading.

In lieu of an actual test, completing an audiovisual representation project can bring your reluctant readers to a level of enthusiasm they might not ordinarily enjoy, particularly for the left-brained readers for whom three-dimensional work is often more clearly expressed than two-dimensional testing. To get started, meet with your reluctant readers individually and ask them to create an audiovisual project to represent the idea about the book that they found most important. They can do artwork, write poetry, create music, film videos—anything through which their natural talents and interests can be translated into literary comprehension. Once their projects have been approved and completed—the hardest part is convincing them that they can do anything and it will really count for a grade—each reader should present his or her creation to the class, explaining its thematic importance. You may be surprised how much you learn about your students beyond their grasp of the literature. Such evaluation can be graded upon presentation, which will make your life somewhat easier in the crush of constant evaluating and grading. In some cases, students' work can also be displayed, which adds to their pride of workmanship and constantly reinforces the literary information you want them to retain.

Teacher for a Day provides them with the opportunity to demonstrate their progress in comprehension techniques. Each student can take a chapter of a book, a short book, a poem, or a scene of a play and present it to the class as if he or she were the teacher. Students must conduct the class in such a way as to indicate their understanding of the work in question and elicit answers from the class. When students must bear individual responsibility for a particular work or a portion of a work, they tend to take it very seriously. The extroverted "hams" can often conduct a very lively and informative class. This form of evaluation also gives reluctant readers a sense of ownership of their reading, and your confidence in allowing them to "take over" the class temporarily generally inspires a great deal of self-confidence in them.

3.3 HOW DO WE GUIDE RELUCTANT TEEN READERS THROUGH REQUIRED READING?

Reluctant readers often suffer under the misconception that reading anything is an exercise operating in a vacuum. They don't see that all ideas are related, and that, thematically (as Shakespeare said), "there is nothing new under the sun." Some of the most fascinating modern literature has been inspired by the so-called classics, and giving your readers a chance to read the same basic material in several different formats reinforces what they read while giving them a new understanding of the connections between the many forms of the written word.

Building a Stairway to Reading Heaven

If reluctant readers are at the bottom of the reading ladder, there must be a way to help them ascend, rung by rung. On the ground, there is no reading. Young-adult novels are the first steps in the climb, and they are invaluable. For readers who must survive the curricula of high school and college, however, there must be a place between YA and the Western canon. The middle steps on the stairway are contemporary books that are more challenging than YA, and that connect more emotionally or intellectually than Shakespeare, Dickens, Hawthorne, or Twain. Comparative literature studies—which will be discussed in more detail later—is a hefty name for a simple plan. Take one contemporary work, mix well in the reluctant reader's mind, then add a similarly themed classic piece and mix well. When the reluctant reader knows the inside story (read: "theme") in advance, Shakespeare and Dickens are not nearly so daunting.

A SIMPLE PLAN TO MACBETH

There is no greater horror for the reluctant reader than a meeting with that monster of all monsters, William Shakespeare. For generations, lovers of the Bard have been trying to find ways to make his Elizabethan English relevant to modern readers who feel they may as well try reading Japanese as read one of the world's greatest plays. Of course, Shakespeare was meant to be seen rather than read, and there are countless productions, as well as some splendid films, available. But what about the reading?

In 1994, Scott Smith published his remarkable first novel, *A Simple Plan,* in which three men discover a cache of money, and evil ensues. (The novel has also been made into a film with Bill Paxton, Billy Bob Thornton, and Bridget Fonda.) While *A Simple Plan* has garnered excellent reviews and enthusiastic reader response, what is rarely or ever mentioned is that the construction of the plot is based on *Macbeth,* with all of Shakespeare's moral ambiguities intact. The tale of a good man gone wrong when presented with an unexpected windfall translates almost seamlessly to the modern Midwest.

Shakespeare:	Smith:
Macbeth	Hank Mitchell
Lady Macbeth	Sarah Mitchell
Banquo	Jacob
The unexpected: 3 Witches	The unexpected: plane crash
The bait: "All hail, Macbeth, thou shalt be king hereafter!"	The bait: Four million dollars in cash

At first, Macbeth is faithful to his own sense of decency by insisting, "If chance will have me king, why chance may crown me / Without my stir." Similarly, Hank Mitchell tells his brother, Jacob, and Jacob's sleazy friend, Lou, that they should turn the money over to the authorities. Had moral superiority won the day, both stories would have died aborning. Fortunately for readers, Macbeth loses his grip and descends into the longest murdering spree by a single man in Scottish history, and Hank follows suit. As Macbeth is bullied into more and more horrific acts by his wife, so Hank is tutored in correspondingly evil schemes by Sarah. All's not well that ends not well in both works.

Filmography

> *Macbeth*, directed by Roman Polanski (rated R), Tri-Star Columbia. Lots of gore and some brief nudity; Polanski releases Macbeth from the chains of literature and lends it plenty of blood, but this is the way Shakespeare would have wanted it if he had ever dreamed of movies in 1604. There are many tamer versions of the story, but if you want the shock value that accompanies the true loss of soul, this is the film to see.
>
> *A Simple Plan*, directed by Sam Raimi (rated R), Paramount. Violence is the key to the rating here, but again, it follows Shakespeare's and Scott's original intent that horrible violence is the result of vaulting ambition or insane greed.

HERE ON EARTH TO WUTHERING HEIGHTS

Arguably the greatest novel of the nineteenth century, *Wuthering Heights* has been made into so many movies that countless people know the story without ever having read the book. Cinematography aside, Emily Bronte's masterpiece is as difficult for the reluctant reader as any novel in the high school or college curricula; therefore, a good way to introduce the RR to this story of passion, betrayal, and love that transcends death is to begin with Alice Hoffman's *Here on Earth*, which made it into Oprah's Book Club.

Bronte:	Hoffman:
Catherine Earnshaw	March Murray
Heathcliff	Hollis
Nellie Dean	Judith Dale

Catherine Earnshaw is soulmate to the antisocial Heathcliff, and when she deserts him, he exacts a terrible revenge on everyone around him. She returns to him, after a fashion, her spirit wandering the earth to haunt him until his own death many pages later. Nellie Dean, the housekeeper at Wuthering Heights, has a good deal to do with how the story plays out. The moors— spooky, beautiful, and wild—are both setting and character. Meanwhile, in the spooky, beautiful, and wild Northeast of the United States one hundred years later, March Murray returns to bury the housekeeper who reared her, Judith Dale. There, she reconnects with Hollis, an antisocial man who was her first love and, as the story reveals, her last. Hollis, furious with March for her desertion twenty years earlier, rekindles their passion, which may consume everything and everyone around them. The supernatural makes more than one appearance here, as it does in *Wuthering Heights,* but Hoffman's tone is restrained enough that the unusual, as in Bronte's novel, fits right in with the landscape. Anita's Shreve's novel *The Last Time They Met* is a wonderful follow-up on the *Wuthering Heights* ladder.

Filmography

Wuthering Heights, directed by Peter Kosminsky (rated PG), Paramount. Starring Juliette Binoche and Ralph Fiennes. Of the four existing English-language versions, this one is the most recommended. It covers the entire book, unlike the famous Merle Oberson–Laurence Olivier film; it is a very recent production; and it depicts the bleakness of the setting of the house and the beauty of the moors. Ralph Fiennes may not be as smoldering as Timothy Dalton is in the 1971 version, but he certainly captures the character of Heathcliff's amoral gothic anti-hero.

REBECCA TO JANE EYRE TO THE EYRE AFFAIR

Jane Eyre continues to grace the high school English curricula, although girls are more likely to appreciate the romantic mystery more than boys. Daphne Du Maurier's fine, and underappreciated, novel *Rebecca* has a framework so nearly identical to Charlotte Bronte's masterwork that you can make a matrix puzzle and have readers fill in the blanks. If the RR finds joy in these two novels, an excellent follow-up is Jasper Fford's witty *The Eyre Affair,* a parallel universe in which thieves can break into the texts of novels and kidnap characters, thus changing the books forever. Detective Thursday Next has her hands full when Jane goes missing and Rochester leaves the book to find her. Fford can teach the RR that it is possible to do what English teachers have been saying for years: "Have fun with the book!"

Filmography

Jane Eyre, directed by Julian Amyes (not rated), Twentieth Century Fox (originally a BBC production). Starring Timothy Dalton (yes, he gets around in Gothic cinema) and Zelah Clarke. *Jane Eyre,* directed by Robert Stevenson (not rated), Twentieth Century Fox. Starring Orson Welles and Joan Fontaine. Of course, Orson Welles is the quintessential Rochester, and this film has never been improved on, but it does omit the last third of Jane's adventures in Moor House; Amyes's version is an excellent supplement.

Rebecca, directed by Alfred Hitchcock (not rated), Anchor Bay Entertainment (originally Selznick Studios). Starring Laurence Olivier and Joan Fontaine. 1940 was a great year for Fontaine, starring in both *Rebecca* and *Jane Eyre.* There have been other movie versions of *Rebecca,* but none as powerful or as emotionally compelling as this one. Hitchcock was forced to change some of Du Maurier's plot to fit the censorship of the times (Max doesn't murder Rebecca for one thing—it was an accident), but that's almost a quibble considering that sixty-five years later this movie has lost none of its original mystique.

Reluctant Readers and William Shakespeare

The greatest challenge to the classroom teacher is to find an intersection where the paths of the reluctant reader and Shakespeare can cross. The key is to treat the greatest of all English-speaking writers with a little less reverence than your students expect while revealing his matchless genius. But how?

Keeping them out of Cliffs Notes (which are often riddled with errors) is not difficult if you make them your own guide to the Bard. It is time consuming, granted, but once it is done, as Lady Macbeth would put it, 'tis done. A guide to *Macbeth* that keeps reluctant readers on task with the language while easing them into understanding of the Elizabethan dialect is worth your time in constructing it. For many RRs, secondary school is the last time they will ever read Shakespeare, so here's your chance to make the experience a good one for them. You can use whatever format you like, including maps, articles, timelines, literary allusions (there are thousands for every play), illustrations—whatever works for you. Your guide to Shakespeare can inspire your reluctant readers to create their own guides to other works later on.

Reading Aloud: It's Not Just for Kindergarten Anymore

Most people who read well and quickly do not read individual words; in fact, they generally see pictures of what they're reading, as if opening the covers of a book were exactly like taking a seat in the nearest cineplex. Unfortunately, most reluctant readers are not blessed with such wiring and must read every word, and sometimes every part of a word. They see no pictures at all. Some can be trained to pick up speed, but some are simply aural learners who do not capture information completely by reading about it. Hence, reading *to* them can often ignite their interest and give them a jumping-off point from which to dive into a book themselves.

Experience has revealed that whether your readers are reluctant or accelerated, elementary level or high school, they all love to be read to. For those twelve and up, an excellent read is "My Name Is Margaret," from Maya Angelou's *I Know Why the Caged Bird Sings* if you're serious, and Louise Fitzhugh's *Harriet the Spy* if you're not. In the end, it doesn't really matter; you know your audience and the best choices with which to engage them. At the conclusion of your reading, open things up for discussion; you will immediately be able to tell who best responds to aural teaching.

Students should read aloud. The rule is as self-evident as knowing the wind blows and the river runs. However, with reluctant readers—particularly older ones who are not reading "at level" with their peers—this can be an exercise in humiliation for them and impatience for the rest of the group. So rather than have them read to the group, it's a good idea to schedule individual time for each of them to read to you privately. It is startling what you can discover by watching your students closely as they read aloud. Some reluctant readers are undiagnosed dyslectics; some read as if every line were endstopped; and some, surprisingly enough, simply need glasses. Lots of problems can be solved fairly quickly with private readings, and you can get a good handle on who needs a trip to the optometrist and who needs serious professional dyslexia counseling. A phone call to the parents generally takes care of the former; the latter can be referred to the school counselor.

Reading Fridays

If your schedule permits it, Reading Fridays can encourage all readers, reluctant or otherwise, to explore beyond the requirements of the curriculum. Many students are so overloaded with activities, homework, family and community obligations, and their social lives that they never have time to read for pleasure. Fridays are often a day when everyone, including you, is pretty parched mentally. Suggest to your students that they may read anything they want—no censorship—and bring it in on Fridays. Check what they're reading and make suggestions. While *Flowers in the Attic* is a perennial favorite, it isn't particularly brilliant. If a reluctant reader loves it, more power to him, but when that book is finished, suggest an alternative. There are plenty of novels about gruesome parents and their heroic children, and lots of "trash" novels with a decent level of literacy. In the end, they must make their own decisions; some of them, however, will listen to you. A critical component of Reading Fridays is that you must read, too. Do not grade papers, do not prepare lessons, do not organize your calendar; read! And the same rules apply to you: your choice cannot be something from the curriculum, and it shouldn't be something you "ought" to read. When you model reading behavior, it is surprising how much attention is paid. Often libraries and classrooms have reading corners with comfortable cushions or chairs. Allow your readers to assume whatever position makes reading easy for them. Sitting upright in a wooden student desk is the choice for about 2 percent of readers in my experience. If you need to push all the desks to the perimeter of the room and let the students all lounge on the floor, do so. If it takes the reluctant reader five months to finish one book, so be it. The point is to give them a safe, quiet, no-hassle zone for regular reading that they can anticipate and plan for. Some of them are going to fall asleep, especially if it's right after lunch or last period. Here's the deal you can make: "You slept through my Reading Friday, you owe me forty minutes of reading this weekend." Usually they'll try to live up to their end of the bargain. If sleep overcomes any reader week after week, then that's a problem having nothing to do with literacy, and you should address it appropriately. Sometimes you may want to spend the first five minutes reading from your own book; younger people are always interested in what interests us, even if they pretend otherwise. I once read a few pages of Karen Hall's *Dark Debts* to an AP class that was curious about this book I was so interested in. After class, they all got together (including the few bona fide RRs in the group) and agreed they'd all get the book themselves and read it over spring break. They returned from vacation insisting I give them a class period for discussion. Did I? What would you do if your class volutarily read a book they didn't have to—and over spring break, no less? You never know where your own interest in a book may lead your students or patrons.

About every fifth Friday, take fifteen minutes for a volunteer only book report; readers can express their satisfaction or dismay with what they've read and make recommendations to the rest of the class.

Reluctant Readers believe the eleventh commandment is "Thou Shalt Finish the Book or Fail," and are thus accustomed to failing. A radical departure for them is to hear, "You don't have to finish a book if you don't like it. Read five chapters or thirty pages, and if you're bored, try something else. Life is too short to force yourself through something you hate." It is amazing how many reluctant readers hear this exhortation as "Free at last!" Of course, it can't apply to required reading, but on Fridays, the word "required" is not part of the language.

I've often heard readers of all levels comment that Reading Fridays are the only time they have to pursue reading for pleasure and they look forward to it all week. You should, too!

Writing from Another Dimension

It's a dimension of sight, of sound, of mind. It's limits are the limits of imagination—watch out for the signpost up ahead! You are now entering *The Twilight Zone*.

One of the most famous episodes of the classic television series is called "Time Enough at Last," in which Burgess Meredith plays a bibliophile who, while reading in a bank vault on his lunch hour, manages to be the sole survivor of a nuclear holocaust. When he emerges, he contemplates killing himself to avoid the unspeakable loneliness with which he's faced until he notices the fallen sign, "PUBLIC LIBRARY," and it comes to him that he now has enough time—all the time in the world, as a matter of fact—to read anything he wants. He stacks books up and down the library steps, counting the piles off as months, and then sits down to dip into Dickens. As he reaches for another volume, his glasses slip off and shatter. He's blind as the proverbial bat without them. Well, this is *The Twilight Zone,* that great trader in irony. An interesting writing assignment for reluctant readers would be to show them the episode and then ask them to write about how they would look on the prospect of reading if there were all the time in the world and no one else in it. What books would they stack up for January, February, March? Which writers might keep them company for the rest of their lives? This program was numbered 25 in TV Guide's "100 Most Memorable Moments in Television." Keith Olbermann wrote: "It is as fine a piece of theatrical bitter irony as has been constructed. Greek playwrights would look at that and go, 'Pretty Good!'" This episode is so famous it has been spoofed on *Family Guy, Futurama,* and *The Simpsons.*

But Serling and Meredith weren't done. "The Obsolete Man" is an episode from the second season. In a future totalitarian society, Romney Wordsworth (Meredith) is a man put on trial for the crime of being obsolete. Note the character's name; the reluctant reader may be introduced to William Wordsworth here, and be asked to consider the significance of the nomenclature aside from the great poet. In this future society, written words are worth nothing, so a man named after the worth of words must be useless if not dangerous. Secretly, he is a librarian (punishable by death) and a religious man (also punishable by death). He is prosecuted by the chancellor, who passes judgment from the bench that Wordsworth is not needed by society. Eventually, Wordsworth is sentenced to die and is given his choice of execution method. He secretly chooses his punishment, known only to him and his assassin, to be administered at midnight. In his room is a video camera broadcasting live to the nation, so they can see the condemned in his final hours. He summons the chancellor, who shows up at 11:15 P.M. Wordsworth reveals that he has locked the door and that his chosen method of death is by bomb. He intends to show the nation how a spiritual man faces death. As the last few moments before the bomb explodes elapse, the chancellor begs the old man to let him go ("In the name of God, let me out!"), and Wordsworth releases him. Of course, since religion is obsolete, the chancellor has just condemned himself. He races from the room and down the stairs just as the bomb explodes, killing Wordsworth. In the final scene, the chancellor, now stripped of his rank, is on trial for obsolescence. A challenge to reluctant readers is to examine the possibilities of a world in which a love of books is a capital offense, and to research current totalitarian societies in which certain books are forbidden. There is no shortage of examples. Thirty minutes of video can lead not only to a new perspective on books but to an awareness of the history and current status of societies in which books are forbidden. *Fahrenheit 451* would be an excellent tie-in to this activity.

In "Printer's Devil," a special hourlong episode written by Charles Beaumont (after his own story, "The Devil, You Say?"), a failing newspaper editor hires "Mr. Smith," actually the Devil in disguise. The protagonist is approached by Mr. Smith, who proposes a trade of success and fame in exchange for his immortal soul, although the editor is unaware of the particulars of the deal at the time it is made. Meredith's Satan (sans horns) smokes cigars and runs the printing machine like, well, a devil. Such machines no longer being part of the newspaper business, the reluctant reader can learn the meaning of "printer's devil" and thus appreciate the pun. The catch in the deal, and there's always a catch, isn't there? Is that whatever Mr. Smith prints comes true. The editor now lives in a small town beset with murder, mayhem, and (un)natural disasters. The denouement comes when the editor's fiancée becomes Mr. Smith's target, and the editor must find a way to negate the deal and save his love. This episode can serve as a springboard for the consideration of the power of words, both used and misused.

The Twilight Zone field trip can take place in a classroom or a library—I used my classroom and provided refreshments. Following the viewing, we talked about why books and their availability seemed so common a theme, and reluctant readers came up with their own writing ideas on the three programs, focusing on irony and the old warning about being careful what you wish for. "You have just crossed over . . ."

3.4 WHAT ARE THE TOP TECHNIQUES FOR LIBRARIANS WORKING WITH RELUCTANT TEEN READERS?

1. **Library cards:** Getting teens their own library cards is the first step; whether it means hosting library-card drives in schools or an amnesty program to get back lost users. These programs could tie-in with school curricula, such as September back-to-school drives, October's Teen Read Week, and whenever term-paper time rolls around. With more and more libraries requiring library cards for in-house use of computers, putting these cards into students hands is nothing but essential. There are numerous examples of library-card campaigns, big and small, and the Public Library Association's "smart card campaign" provides libraries with all the tools to make it happen. One great example, albeit a few years old, is from the Multnomah County Public Library in Portland, Oregon. The "Get Carded!" campaign aimed at middle and high school students. The key aspect of the program was the creation of the KewlCard, which was issued to every student (as well as faculty and staff) who either applied for or already had a library card. The KewlCard

added value to the library card by offering students discounts at a wide variety of merchants, such as Barnes & Noble, Bike Gallery, Tower Records, and Powell's Books. There were a total of fourteen participating vendors, who all had their logos printed on the Get Carded! promotional materials. The KewlCard could be used at any one of the merchants during the month of April. Secondary schools were sent letters, which contained a postcard to request kits. Kits were sent; applications were returned, with a tally sheet noting the number of students with cards and the number applying; and then cards were issued by the teachers. A great number of library cards were handed out in the process, with five schools—two suburban schools and three private schools—all reporting 100 percent registration. Before the program, only 15 percent of students, faculty, and staff at area middle and high schools had cards; after the program, the number stood at 50 percent.

2. **Book lists:** Although we tend to depend too much on these, they still have some purpose if aimed at the reluctant reader. Take a piece of legal-size paper and cut it vertically in thirds. Taking one of the vertical strips, fill it with the author, title, and one-word description of books under 150 pages. Now you have a list of skinny books on skinny paper. Or, you could do "read-alikes" for popular titles (*Child Called It*) or for those with movie tie-ins ("If you liked *Soul Food,* then try . . .").

3. **Booktalking:** Be patient, that section is coming.

"I don't believe a lot of teens are even aware of the wonderful material available to them for reading. . . . If every student could have a selection of books 'book-talked' to them each semester, I believe there would be a lot more interest in reading. YA lit. needs to be made more available, more 'in the face' of teens."

Shelley Hrdlitschka

---

4. **Build relationships:** While this is the key to working with all teens in libraries, it is even more so with reluctant readers. Either they don't know anything about libraries, or what they do know about them isn't good. Nancy Levin told us you have to "hand-sell to kids you know by name, and knowing what their interests are will succeed far more often than wholesaling a book." As Jamie Watson noted, "You can't just take a Quick Picks list and say 'All these books are good for reluctant readers.' All of the books are good for someone, but no one will like all of them. Teens are individuals with their own tastes, and must be treated as such." And for all these tools, talking points, and titles, this work

always comes back to a relationship. Nancy Keane reminded us of this when she wrote, "I think the most important factor in turning kids on to reading is a teacher or librarian who can connect with the students and help them find that magical book. It may take time, but when it works, it is worth everything!"

5. **Celebrate Teen Read Week:** Simply go to www.ala.org/yalsa to learn all about how easy this is to do, what other people have done, and how you can get involved. Teen Read Week gives us a concentrated time to get everyone—readers and nonreaders, teachers, and parents—thinking about teens and reading. If nothing else, Teen Read Week should get everyone in a school or community thinking about teens, reading, and the roles that libraries play in connecting the two. Teen Read Week is a great time to catch teens reading. As Beth Gallaway noted, "This is a great townwide promotion that a community can do together. Create your own 'READ' posters. Have a book-review column in the school paper. Bring back SSR and read aloud to the classrooms. Start a reading buddies program." One similar example is getting teens involved in video/art or other media projects that promote reading.

6. **Contests:** Run trivia contests about authors or subjects that connect YAs with your collection. Many boys respond to any sort of challenge, although we're aware of the issue that if you reward reading, then reading becomes just a way to get something, not something in and of itself. This brings us back to the discussion of means and ends. One could argue that regardless of why kids read—whether it's to earn a chance to win something or simply because they want to—it's a good thing. Often the problem is not the contest idea but the design. As Di Herald noted, "Goal-oriented reading will never turn a reluctant reader around and in my opinion is counter-productive because it turns reading into work. Sometimes prizes can be an incentive but they can also detract from the pleasure of reading if they are awarded for volume of reading. I've always liked to give a drawing entry for each book comment form turned in, which gives even a kid who only reads one book during the summer a chance at the prizes as well as multiple opportunities for those who read more but no guarantees that the one who reads the most books will even win a prize."

7. **Displays:** This goes without saying, but nonreading teens who come to the library are not going to find books the way that avid readers find them: they're not going to use the catalog, ask for help, or even browse the shelves. We need to use displays throughout the library to show nonreaders what they are missing. Just as important, as Martha Coons noted, "Make sure your collection is thoroughly multicultural. Seek out

entertaining series books with characters of different cultural backgrounds, not just *Gossip Girls* upscale series books. Display books with multicultural characters on the cover."

"The greatest thing a librarian or teacher can do for reluctant readers is booktalk books. Offer choice and possibility. Keep collections current. Display new books (we love the look and feel of new books), and set up a table or shelf of books that are recommended by peers, with their comments. Model reading behavior. Discuss good books you've read. Reading is a learned behavior and the more we do it and enjoy the experience, the more addicted we become to reading. No one ever OD'd on literature—but hey, what a way to go."

Julie Ann Peters

8. **Follow-up and free-up:** Finish up by asking teens to come back and tell you how they liked the materials they picked out. As Chris Crowe noted, what many teens need and want is "authentic discussion of a text with someone else." The key is conversation with teens about what they like in story, which may lead to conversations about books. As Michele Gorman noted, "The best thing for librarians to do is talk to your teen patrons. Talk about movies. Talk about video games. Talk about the latest superhero graphic novels, mange, and anime. In other words, take the time to get to know the teens *and* be aware of pop culture. Armed with both a knowledge of the teens' likes and dislikes and a familiarity with pop culture, it is very possible to make ties to books you have on your shelves *and* to make recommendations the teen might actually take."

9. **Freedom and choice:** However, as Chris Crowe also noted, such concepts are "unfortunately . . . antithetical to the institution of school. Just as writers write best when they choose their own topics, topics they care about, readers who are free to select their own reading material are more likely to read for pleasure. Any sort of authentic reading experience is superior to a forced one." In addition, not letting teens choose isn't only anti-reading but anti-developmental. As teacher Dania Plumb noted, "I mean, come on, at sixteen we'll allow them to operate a motor vehicle and at eighteen we expect them to decide what they want to do for the rest of their lives, but we won't let them decide what they want to read? That's crazy!"

10. **Get input:** Use it, tell them you've used it, and then ask again. Though this can happen in the library, it mainly has to happen outside

of the library. You can't ask people eating in a McDonald's why they don't eat at McDonald's. We've included sample surveys in part 3, but you can't use them unless you . . .

11. **Get out of the library** and into the teen community. Not just schools but comic-book stores, boys clubs, girls clubs, etc.

12. **Get over yourself:** It is not about you, your reading interests, or even values. Quick Picks chair Jamie Watson perhaps put it best, noting that librarians and teachers should put their own values aside. "If they want to read *Fantasy Football* magazines, or horoscope books, or only *Gossip Girls,* then remember this. And tell them when the next *Fantasy Football* magazine, or horoscope book, or *Gossip Girls* book comes in. Respect their opinions, and find things that fit with their opinions. Once they know they can trust you, you can sneak in some other stuff. It *works.*"

13. **Get them in the building** somehow, someway. As Tori Jensen noted, "you have to make the library a place that reluctant readers want to hang out. You do this by not pushing reading but other cool stuff. I always have a 500–1,000 piece jigsaw puzzle going in our library. Kids love to sit and talk and try to put the puzzle together. You have to have comfortable places to sit and hang out and you have to not be too picky about how the kids choose to use these spaces. I have a cheapo coffee table in my library. . . . Students put their feet up on it and I put out magazines and other picture-intensive materials on it. To me, the key is to get them into the library; then they might just start to read."

14. **Go to the shelves:** As Sophie Brookover reminds us, "If I send a reluctant reader into the stacks with a slip of paper that has some call numbers and titles on it, I will find that slip of paper and a stack of those books on a table at the end of the day, completely abandoned. If I go to the shelves with him, and help him find the books on the list, we can have a conversation about them—are they what he was looking for? Are they not quite right? Can we refine the search a bit more? Let's find what 'is' right together—and send him on his way with something that he thinks will suit his reading needs for today."

15. **High-visibility merchandising:** Pull out the Quick Pick books and others with high appeal and get them in people's faces by setting them up by the computers. Put the books where the kids are: they're on the computers, not near the shelves. Reluctant readers are often not reluctant library users, so you can find them and help them find you. It's different than doing displays; merchandising is a philosophy, not a practice.

16. **Honesty:** If you don't know about a subject, admit it. If you don't know about an author, fess up. If you haven't read the book, don't fake it. And be honest with kids about reading: no, you haven't read every book in the library, and yes, you know mostly about books from reviewers and word of mouth. And just as important, even for the books you *have* read, you probably didn't read every word and some you didn't even finish. Di Herald noted that something as simple as "giving permission for the teen to stop reading something that isn't working for him and switching to a different book or magazine" can be very effective. Lynn Evarts echoes that advice, noting, "It's also very important to let a reluctant reader know that it's okay if he or she doesn't want to take the book you're offering—there are many more available. Also, they don't have to finish the book if they find they don't like it. I have found that this pressure to finish a leisure reading book puts a lot of kids off reading. I always tell them that I didn't write it so I won't be the least bit offended if they don't like it. Just bring it back and we'll try again. There's a lid for every pot, as my grandma used to say."

17. **Listen:** Make sure you give teens a chance to tell you about what they've read, not just because it empowers them to tell but because it builds your capacity to recommend titles by listening. And then once they've told you about a book, find a way for them to share that with other (non)readers. Most reading surveys indicate that teens find out about books not from teachers, lists, or librarians but from other teens; use this. As Miranda Doyle noted, "Use peer pressure— reluctant readers are much more likely to read something if it's recommended by a peer, so have teens review and recommend books to each other.

18. **Nonjudgmental attitude:** Just as we would not tell an adult patron at the desk: "Hey, you're reading Danielle Steel; too bad, you should be reading James Joyce or John Fowles," we should never place any value on the reading materials selected by a teen. Teens will never trust us to help them if they sense we'll first condemn, then recommend. That's one reason teacher Dania Plumb stresses funny books and even picture books. She noted, "I often let kids read stuff that they loved as children. They went crazy over *Where the Sidewalk Ends, A Light in the Attic,* and *Falling Up.* Some kids even chose to read these during sustained silent reading time. I think all kids respond well to humor and comedic stories. I try to 'reel them in' and gain their trust at the beginning of the year by reading funny stories aloud (*How Angel Peterson Got His Name* and *King of the Mild Frontier*).

Once they know that I'm not going to choose boring stuff for them, they're a lot more willing to trust me when it comes time to help them choose their own books."

19. **Reader's advisory:** Lots of research has told us the bad news: librarians are often not where YAs turn to get advice on what to read. Because they don't ask us enough, we don't offer advice enough. Because we don't offer advice enough, we can't or don't keep up with the literature. Because we're not caught up, when we *do* give advice, it's often bad. In addition, because there are so few designated YA librarians, most library staff are probably not reading YA books. Because we don't read it, we don't feel comfortable recommending titles. Finally, given lack of training and lack of information, too many librarians fall back on prejudices about what YAs should read as opposed to what they want to read. What we need to do in every reader's advisory relationship is determine what a reader will respond to in a book. We do that by learning what that reader has responded to in the past. For all the rules below, one trumps all. The most important question to ask teens is not why they liked a book. Perhaps this is because teens don't often analyze that deeply what they have read. Instead, ask them to tell you about the book. In doing so, they will tell you what they liked, what they responded to. Once you understand the nature of the response, the work can begin to connect readers to another book that will provide a similar positive experience. For nonreaders, or teens whose only reading is composed of the books assigned and despised in school, asking about reading response isn't going to work. Instead, ask about movies or TV shows—anything that will give you an idea about what interests this YA. As Beth Gallaway reminds us, "Instead of asking about what a teen likes to read or what his last three books read were, ask more personal questions: What kind of music do you like? What movies do you like? What video games do you play? From those responses, direct the student to read-alikes." If you can't find out what a nonreader might like in reading, then find out what they don't. A lot of nonreading teens might be inarticulate in telling you the books they like but real quick to list all the things they don't like about a book, with "fat" and "boring" being chart toppers. There's nothing wrong with them wanting a "thin one," but just make sure you and the teen understand that thin doesn't always mean easy. Often in the library, the person we talk to isn't the teen but the parent.

20. **Weed the collection:** Reluctant readers want to choose their own books, but only from among the "good" books. Moreover, having old

stuff on the shelf reinforces every negative stereotype about librarians/ libraries not being cool. Finally, the more you weed, the more room there is on the shelves for face-out displays. Show them the covers.

21. **R-E-S-P-E-C-T:** Relationships are built on mutual respect. If you want teens to respect "our world," then we've got to respect theirs as well; otherwise, how shall the two ever meet? As librarian Martha Coons noted, "Talk to teens, including boys, respectfully and engage them in conversation about their interests. Don't bad-mouth video games and other aspects of teen culture in a way that makes them feel the library is not for them." What we're really talking about is influence: we want to influence other people to do something we want them to do which they don't want to do. Even all the gimmicks of marketing and promotion can only go so far because so often this work comes back to finding the right book for the right teen at the right time, which can only happen if we know the teen at the center of this equation.

3.5 IS THE ACCELERATED READER PROGRAM A GOOD OR BAD THING IN PROMOTING RELUCTANT READERS?

A hot-button issue with librarians and teachers, this could be a "Point/Counterpoint" from *60 Minutes* in the 1970s. We've seen articles demonstrating the success of the Accelerated Reader (AR) program and heard testimonials from parents about their effectiveness. We've also seen articles pointing out the failings of the program in theory and practice. Librarians seem more frustrated with not getting the lists from schools or getting them and discovering that half of the books are not in the library's collection. Some believe, as noted by Kathy Stewart, that an AR program can be counterproductive, for while the program is "well-intentioned, it has an adverse effect because the list, by definition, automatically limits the pool from which they might select. When I'm taking a look at any given list, to try and help a teen select something good to read, I almost always have the feeling, 'There's nothing good on this list.'" But perhaps the biggest issue isn't the practice of the program but the theory. Librarian/information goddess Beth Gallaway makes one of the best cases against AR, stating:

> Reading should never be used to punish or reward. Kids should read for pleasure and to improve their minds, not to answer test questions or win stuff. The only appropriate incentive for reading is more reading materials. . . . Any program that teaches by memorization of facts alone does not help children become critical thinkers or help them evaluate

information. According to an SAT book I read recently, the best way to improve your reading comprehension is to read the editorial and OpEd pages in your local newspaper. I thought AR pigeonholes kids into reading from small groups of books—if it's not on the list, it doesn't count. That doesn't seem fair! It deprives readers of all kinds of books. Reading and contributing to a classroom book discussion on a blog about *Tuck Everlasting* would be ten times better than taking a ten-question multiple-choice quiz on the book. Publishing book reviews on a classroom Web site may also reward and motivate. A reader's advisory database like NoveList may help identify titles of interest to a reluctant reader (again, I'm convinced a reluctant reader only needs to find the right title). Getting reluctant readers to see that reading is cool by creating "READ" posters with ALA software and Photoshop could also be a motivational tool via technology and more effective than AR, IMO.

AR doesn't encourage reading for pleasure; it requires reading for a test, as Jessy Griffith notes, "AR doesn't work because it enforces reading as something one has to do, with empirical results. I see plenty of kids going through the motions of reading just to answer questions to get AR points."

But it's not an easy question. For librarians working with an AR list, in part the answer is that it doesn't matter what we think because our jobs are to support teachers, schools, and academic success. That's the practical approach, but this is about the philosophical, which often boils down to reading as a means, not an end, as is often the case with summer reading programs. As Chris Crowe noted in discussing the complexity of this issue:

> I have some problems with AR, but I know for scorekeeping kinds of reluctant readers, the program offers an appealing, concrete incentive for reading. For other kids, though, AR only reinforces what they already believe: "I don't know how to read" or "I'm stupid." Incentives work for some reluctant readers, but I worry that we sometimes rely too much on incentives and then turn kids into readers who only read when Pavlov's bell rings. If we want to turn students into independent readers, we need to find ways to get them reading without external incentives.

Thus, the issue with AR is both philosophical as well as practical. From a practical standpoint, one of the drawbacks of most AR lists we've seen is that they are loaded down with exactly the kinds of books that won't appeal to male reluctant teen readers: historical fiction, female coming-of-age stories, and award-winning slices of mostly rural life stories. The books teen boys in particular might read for rewards isn't in the test bank; thus, teen boys might see AR as just another reading "thing" that dismisses and discourages them.

Although AR is often promoted as a reading motivation program, perhaps it is actually more of a reading management tool for teachers. AR makes assigning outside reading easy: read a book, do a test, get some points, repeat process. By making the assignment of outside reading easier for teachers, it might lead to more of it, which is a good thing—that is, if the assigned reading isn't more of the same but something teens might actually read. When working with students who are motivated to read a particular book they've heard about or that attracts them because of the cover/blurb/title, librarians are often discouraged to find that if the book's not on the list, the teen reader won't check it out. The list becomes not an access provider but something that limits access. For avid readers, AR is thus counterproductive in many cases.

So who is pushing for AR or similar programs, other than the companies that develop them? While in some school districts it comes from the top down, in others, classroom teachers think AR is the Holy Grail, since it allows them to assign outside reading but have someone else do the grading.

That said, not all classroom teachers feel the same. As sixth grade teacher Jenny McBride noted:

> Incentive programs for reading defy the purposes of reading. We read to connect to the lives of others, to learn, to enjoy language, to laugh, or just to kill time. The reasons for reading are infinite and variable. Reading for prizes does not make this infinite and variable list. And, let me add, this is coming from a twice chosen "Royal Reader"—5th and 8th grade—and the person who, as a kid, charted "pages read" the way Galileo must have charted stars. The kids who excel in reading incentive programs are the kids who already love to read. Reading incentive programs may motivate reluctant readers. They may want to succeed but do not have the tools to do so, just as the failing student may not be able to bring up his grades no matter what dollar amount his parents offer. We must cultivate a reading ethic within our students, just as we strive to cultivate work ethic. Both must come from within. At some point in life, we want our kids to read when there are no more gold star stickers or pats on the back. How many of us have thankless jobs but still work hard? Apparently we think reading is important. We read to our babies; we provide books for our children in and out of the classroom; we set good examples. Why do we do all of it? Is it just one big competition? I hope not. Reading can change and even save lives. Let us not cheapen our message with cash or junk "prizes."

Yet many public libraries are loaded down, especially in the summer, with incentive-based programs.

> "I think one of the main factors is the way reading and writing are taught in school. If you go into a first grade classroom, you will see students of all abilities excited about learning how these marks on the page are connected to words. The joy of discovery of this magic code is visible and the enthusiasm is contagious. If you visit these same students a few years later, it is shocking to hear how many of them don't like to read. What happens in such a short time to turn off so many kids from reading? One factor I think is the way we teach reading, emphasizing a sense of hierarchy. We have good readers and struggling readers. . . . I don't think we focus enough on the individual needs and challenges of students, and I think the intense focus on testing is making this even more pronounced."
>
> John Coy

3.6 SHOULD LIBRARIES PLAN PROGRAMS, SUCH AS SUMMER READING CLUBS, THAT OFFER INCENTIVES FOR READING?

Like AR, there's plenty of passion on both sides of this argument. The main consensus, in particular with reluctant readers, is that summer reading programs conducted inside the library merely reward regular readers, not motivate reluctant readers. For a summer reading program to be successful with reluctant readers, it must adopt three strategies:

1. The program is promoted and conducted outside of the library's four walls—at free lunch sites, summer schools, and any other place you might find reluctant teen readers in the summer.
2. The program must not be just about reading but also about the library. Since many reluctant teen readers believe that anything having to do with reading is marked for failure, they won't listen to the rest of the message. A better chance of success is if the program is a teen summer activity that rewards/encourages not just reading but such things as volunteering, attending programs, paying off fines, writing reviews, and helping select materials.
3. The program must define reading very broadly, so that the goal is never the number of books read. Number of pages, time spent, or some other measure must determine how incentives are going to rewarded. If not, then both reluctant readers (who may struggle through even a thin

book) and avid readers (who decide to knock off *The Once and Future King* just for kicks) don't get a fair shake. Perhaps the best idea would be to work with readers as they sign up to set their own goals, rather than using an arbitrary and thus usually unfair objective determined by the library. Referring to the summer reading program at her library, librarian Mari Hardacre noted, "Our summer reading program allows teens to read whatever they want, including magazines and internet sites. I don't know if it motivates them to read, or to read more than they usually do, but maybe it helps them see themselves as successful readers."

3.6a Summer Reading Success Stories

The staff and I determined that we had several things working against higher involvement—kids with huge fines on their cards from videos so they could not check out books, and reluctant readers. So, we devised a couple of solutions to these two problems. First, for those kids who wanted to use their library cards—tasks around the library could be completed for fine disappearance. Then, a couple of times a day, every day I read aloud. I'd read fast-paced fiction, intriguing nonfiction, picture books, whatever I liked and thought made a good read aloud. And, if you showed up for the reading, you got prizes for participating in SRP (oh—I did not make those coming fill out all the details for SRP registration . . . just asked their name and age). I started out thinking I'd get mostly younger kids, but ended up with mostly middle school kids. Everyone lying around in the air-conditioned library for an hour or so just listening to me read. I was amazed at the numbers that would come and the age ranges that would come. I even had an up-and-coming gang leader that would come with his admiration group. Of course, flexibility is required. I'd start reading aloud to the staff at the same time everyday and before long, I'd have some kids/teens. I'd try to have extra copies of the books in case someone wanted to stick around and read some more for themselves. If there were books, I'd move on to another book on my pile. And I learned that sometimes it may be the simplest thing that proves effective.—**Crystal Faris**

My big success story is one boy I knew since he was a high school freshman. Every summer I tried to get him to join the summer reading program, and he turned me down. Until the summer before his senior year—we had switched to counting time and not books, and he was so jazzed that we would count the time he spent on the computer in chat rooms and reading pro wrestling magazines. He was a total pro wrestling fan, and when I showed him that we had some books, including autobios by Mick Foley, the Rock, and Chyna, He was determined to get every single one we had. He completed the program, got his books, and he read them. The book by Foley, this teen came around almost every day asking about it. He even let me put a hold on it for him. The day the library copy came in, he danced into the YA section to show me he got it.—**Kat Kan**

3.7 WHAT ROLE CAN/SHOULD PARENTS PLAY IN MOTIVATING RELUCTANT READERS?

> "Reading and study often become a family tradition. When kids sees Mom and Dad reading—it can be Nora Roberts and Tom Clancy—they're more apt to be readers, too. Once the pattern is shattered, though, it's damn hard to reestablish it."
>
> Cherrie Bennett

1. Read yourself! Modeling behavior is how children, even teenagers, learn to be adults. If they see you reading, especially for pleasure, they may reconsider their own avoidance issues. Read frivolously in front of your teens. If they see that's it all right for their parents to "waste time" reading something nonessential, they may gradually allow themselves the same "luxury."

2. Try not to censor what your children read. It's natural for parents to want to protect their teens from "inappropriate" material, but there is very little in today's world they haven't encountered on television, movies, and CDs. If they read something disturbing to them, that's your chance to discuss it with them and answer questions; in turn, they will appreciate your respect for their ability to handle "adult" themes. Many young-adult novels these days deal with everything from sexual abuse to alcoholism to homosexuality to teen pregnancy to drug dependence. Believe me, your teenagers are probably more well-versed in these subjects than you are. So-called "adult" novels, from Steinbeck to Atwood, are mild in comparison.

3. Provide your reluctant readers with time and space for reading. If you see them without a textbook but reading nonetheless, don't ask, "Have you finished your homework yet?" That only reinforces the idea that pleasure reading is like dessert and must wait until all the main courses of academia are finished. If you apply that rule, dessert will never come. The amount of homework many teens are given today would stagger students of a generation ago. Plus, you can't gauge how much of their pleasure reading will roll over into their history, English, or even science classes.

4. Have your own reading circle at home. When Patricia was in the class-room, every Friday was Reading Day. There were no rules, just reading. Nothing was required, either. Whatever the students wanted to read was fine. She later discovered that many of them had only that forty-five minutes in the entire week to read for themselves. "I can't wait for Fridays in your class," she was told over and over. To say that Patricia was surprised would be putting it mildly. She had supposed that there would be time to read on the weekends, not realizing that their calendars were bulging with sports, church, community activities, family outings, work, and—of course—the mountain of homework to be completed by Monday. Designating a couple of evenings a week for a half-hour reading circle could be just the thing. Simply enjoin everyone in the family to flop in the family room after dinner and read anything they like. There's a coziness inherent in a family reading circle that you won't find anywhere else. Let the dishes stack in the sink, take out the garbage later, put off your committee work or that stack of papers in your briefcase for only a half-hour. It won't be much in the scheme of a whole week, but will repay you and your reluctant readers over and over.

5. Take your reluctant readers to the library—not for them; for you. Browse for a book you might like to read, and while you're grazing among the shelves, your children might do the same. If you get in the library habit, eventually it might wear off on your children. Ditto with bookstores.

6. Give your reluctant reader a book you've read and say, "I'm wondering what you would think of this. I'd like someone to talk to about it, and I'm really interested in your opinion. Would you do me the favor of reading this over, so later you could help me understand some things in it?" If your child wants to know when the book is "due," you know the answer must be, "whenever you're ready." A gentle nudge from time to time is encouraged!

7. Read the books required for your child's English class and ask if you can talk about them together. If your reluctant readers see you taking an interest in the novels, plays, or short stories, their own interest may be sparked.

8. You can lead a horse to water, and you can lead a reluctant reader to a bookshelf, but the drinking and the reading are up to them. Don't apply pressure; believe me, it never works. Reading is a joy, and you can't force joy on anyone. You can only allow them to see it in action and take their own wary steps toward it. After all, teenagers generally don't

want to do what they are supposed to do; don't make reading a duty; make it irresistible.

3.8 ARE THERE ANY COUNTERPRODUCTIVE STRATEGIES THAT LIBRARIANS OR TEACHERS ENGAGE IN WHEN TRYING TO REACH RELUCTANT READERS? IN OTHER WORDS, WHAT DOESN'T WORK?

We've done too many workshops after which a participant will come up and say something like "I enjoyed your workshop, but don't you think—" and then advance a contrary position to what has just been described. Maybe it's because people don't like to change or because they're not aware of the current research/best practices, but a big part of the issue isn't doing lots of new stuff but moving away from what doesn't work. According to librarians in the field, the most counterproductive strategies include:

1. **Audiobooks.** While audiobooks work for some, they're not for everyone. As Francisca Goldsmith noted, "Audiobooks are great, except that when we force older kids to use print text with audiobooks, it is clunky and discouraging. By their teens, people seem to be set in their learning style (visual, auditory, kinesthetic), and making the demand that one engage two styles at once can be frustrating or even overwhelming."

2. **Blinders.** This is a nice way of saying we don't see or understand what reluctant readers want and need because we're too tied to the visions of what we think they should want to read. As Jessy Griffith noted, "I think there's a danger in trying to blindly apply profession-side lists and ideas to your specific kids. Examples: Award-winning graphic novels aren't necessarily what your kids will read. I've got a copy of *Goodbye Chunky Rice* with a layer of dust." This was echoed by Martha Coons, who noted, "There does seem to be a gap between the world of review sources and awards committees on one hand, and the world of teen nonreaders on the other. Too many well-reviewed books are those that succeed as quality literature but fail on the popularity side, to use *Voice of Youth Advocates (VOYA)* concepts. As I select from the reviews, I find my shelves filling with very long fantasy books or very abstract works of fiction with odd-looking covers." Perhaps worse than wearing blinders is thinking the rose-colored reading sunglasses many of us wear fit all: not only will teens want to read what we think they should read, but they'll want to read what we read and they'll love it, too! But as Sophie Brookover noted, few things are as counterproductive as

"saying, 'well, I loved this book when I was your age!' I am at least twice as old as teen reluctant readers. I am old enough to be their parent, and they know it. 'When I was your age' means 'before the Internet,' which means that the book in question has to be at least fifteen years old, which is just not going to fly. Please, don't say it. Ever. (The one exception I can think of is if you have already established a good relationship with the reader, and he or she knows that your opinion is worth entertaining, if sometimes dead wrong.) This is not to say that you can't recommend a book you loved when you were a teen. Just don't use that aspect of it as a selling point."

3. **Denigrating reading tastes.** This is perhaps the most dangerous and self-defeating attitude we can possess. It is counterproductive, as noted by Di Herald, to "ban magazines and repair/technical/game manuals as legitimate reading materials." The effect is that rather than encouraging reading and readers, we engage in a judgmental process that Herald noted "denigrates reading tastes" other than our own. Sophie Brookover noted, "I often find myself in the position of working double-time to undo years of negative conditioning about what constitutes 'real reading.' This is another situation in which I find myself often giving permission to a teen to read what he or she wants to read. As much as I relish the opportunity to encourage a reluctant reader, it feels very strange to realize that someone might 'need' permission to do what he or she ought to feel is his or her right to do. It's positively heartrending in the case of giving that permission to parents of reluctant teen readers, who are often vexed and frustrated after enduring years of criticism over their kid's reading habits. Often, these are people who know in their hearts what's right for their kids, and would rather see their teens happily reading anything of interest, but who've been led to think that those interests are wrong or unworthy in some way."

4. **Graphic novels.** Too often graphic novels are seen as the answer, but they are no more for every reluctant reader than James Joyce is for avid readers. Graphic novels are not easy to read; they are, instead, different to read. Francisca Goldsmith, who has written extensively on graphic novels, noted, "a big mistake is assuming that graphic novels are all easy to read and interesting; this is an over-inclusive generalization that can give many kids just another kind of book to not like on principle." Michele Gorman states that while she loves graphic novels, "to assume that a reluctant reader will automatically love this format is wrong. This happens so often, and the truth is that reluctant readers may or may not like the graphic format. They may like action stories or nonfiction or stories about war and conflict, and you will never know unless you

don't make an automatic assumption that because they are reluctant to read they will most likely be engaged by a book with illustrations."

5. **Ignoring what we don't know.** Chances are that many of the things that might interest a reluctant reader are not the same things that would interest us as readers, nor are they things we might have read as teen readers. Thus, a teen who might know about books like *Coldest Winter Ever* or graphic novels like *Blade of the Immortal* might find us ignorant of reading materials they are smart to. As Sophie Brookover noted, because these materials are "outside of our own personal areas of interest, we cannot recommend works in these areas and genres. This generally sends a subtle message of disapproval, and in the worst cases, a teacher or librarian unaware of and uncomfortable with these subject areas will say directly, 'I don't know anything about [Lurlene McDaniel/*Gossip Girls*/monster trucks/heavy metal/building soap-box cars/insert interest area here]. Why don't you read this instead?' No teen reader, reluctant or otherwise, will return to that teacher or librarian for assistance. Worse yet, many teen readers will assume that this type of ignorance and blasé disengagement with their interests extends to all teachers and librarians."

6. **Overanalyzing.** We looked very early on at the four stages of reading, noting that reluctant readers often get hung up at an early stage. They're about plot—books where stuff happens—but that's not how books are discussed in the classroom or even in library book discussion groups. Its not about what happens, but why. While that's a good thing for many readers, Rollie Welch noted how this works against reluctant readers who "will stop in the reading of an assigned passage and have a quiz or try to start a discussion with the question, 'What do you think this means?' If the reader is into the book, they don't really care what it means, but they want to know what happens next! The halting of reading to analyze is like letting a boy sit in a Corvette and start the engine and then reaching over and turning off the key."

7. **Page requirements.** There's not a single librarian who hasn't faced the "I have a book report due and the book has to be x number of pages" assignment. The intention of teachers making this assignment is obvious but again counterproductive to helping a reluctant reader succeed. Rather than being able to read a book they might be interested in, they are often forced to read something else because it meets a page requirement rather than their personal requirement of what makes a good book. This strategy, as noted by Sophie Brookover, then "focuses the teen's attention improperly on reading the shortest book possible, whether it's of interest or not, instead of finding the best book for them

that also meets the page requirement. To me, this is a double-whammy: the teen often picks up a book of no interest whatsoever just to get the assignment done, which in turn reinforces the idea that reading equals work, period."

8. **Reading assignments.** Nancy Levin put it best: "Reluctant readers need to buy in to the process by making their own choices, even if they can choose from a pool selected by the teacher or librarian." Reading assignments don't narrow choices; they close them off completely. Chris Crutcher often tells the story of turning in his brother's book reports rather than completing a reading assignment. The Cliffs Notes corporation has made a bundle off reading assignments, perhaps the only real winner. Teachers get kids who show off their intelligence in avoiding reading the book, and reluctant readers are once again set up to fail. Tori Jensen noted that "assigning a book doesn't work as well as allowing readers to choose. Reading assessments such as Reading Counts are the kiss of death—*the kiss of death*—for reluctant readers, as is not allowing reluctant readers to choose a book report product themselves. The typical book report form teachers give the kids in some schools is the most boring thing in the world."

9. **Reading lists.** While we talked earlier about how reading lists can work with some readers, too often librarians depend on lists rather than listening to readers. After all, most of the lists are put together by adults for other adults, although there are the occasional "readers' choice" lists, but even those feature many titles they seem more likely to appeal to teachers than to reluctant teen readers. As Amy Alessio told us, "My reluctant teen readers hate suggested lists. They want only lists suggested by teens—if they see that teens have direct input, they will keep coming back. Or they want things particularly targeted to them, like e-reviews of the latest game code books or writing guides sent to them in a newsletter. Books from lists suggested by others, such as summer reading lists or award titles, may be particularly shunned, and should be marketed in proactive ways, where it is easy to see what would be good in those titles."

10. **Summer reading lists.** Yet another horror story told by most librarians is about the world's worst summer reading list. The worst offenders are those featuring not just titles that no teen would ever want to read, let alone in the summer, or be able to read, without some sort of guidance, but titles that can't even be gotten because they are out of print or otherwise unavailable. Beth Gallaway has some interesting ideas on these lists: "When I finally got asked for my input about creating a list, I told the school administration, here is

the perfect summer reading list: Send a letter home to parents instructing them to give their child $20 and set them loose in Barnes and Noble. Let the student pick out and read whatever he or she wants. And, encourage them to register for the library summer reading program, which rewards their reading with . . . more free books, magazines, and comics!"

11. **Time constraints.** As we've noted, the reluctance of some readers is a coping strategy for dependent readers. The more pressure to read, the more defensive—and creative—these readers become. Such is the case with time constraints on reading. Mary Ann Harlan noted, "It takes some kids forever to read a book, and having due dates, fines, etc., really discourages them. I let two kids last year have the same book all year long, and went out and purchased a copy of the book for one kid so he could finish it over the summer. Plus, it's possible it is the first book he has ever owned; for sure it is the first book that was his in like ten years."

12. **Treating fiction as the only reading that matters.** You knew this one was coming: almost everyone we interviewed talked about this issue. Sophie Brookover noted that the emphasis on fiction "from pre-K to grade 12 is more damaging than any other reading-discouraging behavior I can think of. It also makes no sense, since once teens enter college, skills developed by reading nonfiction—critical thinking and analysis of the text—are the ones most highly prized by professors. These skills can be developed by reading fiction, too, of course, but in my experience, this is almost exclusively accomplished in the classroom and, of course, requires that the reluctant reader actually 'read' the book in question." A similar argument was advanced by Mari Hardacre, who noted that "putting too much emphasis on fiction (i.e., novels) can deter some readers. I have met some teens who read quite a lot, but don't consider themselves readers because they have the idea that readers are those people who like to read long novels or classics. So they might say they don't like to read. And some readers just prefer nonfiction—true stories or informational works."

13. **Treating reluctant readers like avid readers.** We started off this section discussing the research of Kylene Beers, so let's end our list of what not to do with her findings. As Kylene noted, "My research shows that while avid readers want the teacher or librarian to do a read-and-tease and then let them finish the book on their own, reluctant readers often want the teacher (librarian) to read aloud the entire book. Why? Because avid readers easily visualize the text, but reluctant readers often complain that they can't 'see it' as they read. Hearing the

text read aloud (by a good reader) helps them visualize—and therefore connect better. Another example: reluctant readers often prefer nonfiction, especially short works with lots of visual support. Avid readers are more comfortable with fiction or nonfiction and like longer works."

3.9 HOW DO WE ENGAGE RELUCTANT READERS TO TALK WITH TEACHERS/LIBRARIANS ABOUT THEIR READING?

Two rules for this one:

1. This is *not* a test! Ever!
2. There are *no* wrong answers.

Reluctant readers are so accustomed to being graded or judged or assessed on their responses to their assigned reading that they've long ago learned to keep their mouths shut. They are terrified of getting the wrong answer; of displeasing the teacher/librarian; and, perhaps most importantly, of looking "stupid" to themselves and their peers. We've had reluctant readers who've told us, "I can't talk about this book because then everyone will know how dumb I am." Therefore, your first task is to make your RRs feel safe. We repeat: safety is everything. Often RRs have been humiliated beyond their limits of endurance in class and have grasped the idea that no words are good words. If you gently persuade them that there are no "bad" consequences for speaking their minds, you open up the world to them and restore their damaged sense of self-worth. The idea that there are no wrong answers may be the most crackpot idea they've ever heard, but once you convince them it's true, they'll talk and talk and talk. RRs who are math or science inclined are particularly loath to believe that any answer or comment they make has value. In their world, there is one right answer and you work toward it until you get it. Reiterate to them that there is no formula for talking about books, anymore than there's a formula for talking about our friends, our parents, our enemies, our heroes, and all the other people in life we find reflected in books. In fact, reluctant readers may discover an intellectual freedom they've never known: the right to explore human beings and their "infinite variety" in any way they choose. Talk about them, write about them, draw pictures of them, compose poems about them, yell about them, ask about them, pass judgment on them, offer sympathy or love or outrage: it's all there for them if they'll just believe their considerations of a book are just as good as anyone else's. Enthusiasm is a highly contagious disease. If you want your reluctant readers to talk with you about a book, offer them a forum where they can listen to how it's done. Remember: there are no rules.

If you can arrange it, small groups are the key (safety in numbers). Perhaps you could create a small "story time" (only don't call it that) for teen RRs. What do children love best about the library? When someone reads to them. It may be a surprise to learn that this love of aural learning never actually goes away. For years, Patricia had an entire class of reluctant readers, but she could get them to read almost anything she thought appropriate if she read the first couple of chapters out loud to them. Eschewing their desks, they would lounge around on the floor, relax, and very soon become rapt. They *loved* being read to, and it gave them a running start for their own journey with the book. At least once a month she brought in a stack of books and read a chapter from each one, just to give them an idea about what they might like to choose for independent reading. She soon discovered that the advanced English students were jealous. They weren't getting the benefits that the RR class was, and they wanted to know why. So she started reading to them too, occasionally, and they were also delighted. Read to students as if you were each of the characters, laugh when you find something funny and give them a chance to laugh to, pause after a striking passage and give them a chance to respond, and you'll be amazed how fast RRs' attitudes about reading change. This is not "spoon-feeding"; rather, it is unlocking the doors of literacy and joy and exploration. Remember that for today's teens, this is the nation of IPod—they are used to listening, and they like it.

Let your RRs talk to each other. Their respect for their peers' opinions is worth its weight in book gold. If you can arrange a book circle in your library or class, occasionally devote the entire time to having the members discuss what books they have found they liked, or even loved. Stress that this is not a book-report session. Many RRs still have bad dreams about having to do book reports and the corresponding methods they used to avoid them. In this space, they can say whatever they want, as long as they have a recommendation. They may speak for five minutes or ten seconds; the point here is to furnish them with a safe forum for talking about why they liked a book. Not just, "I liked it," but what made them feel that way. Allow others to ask questions or make comments. If a member has no book to comment on, fine. Try again another day. What you're trying to impose on your RRs is that you, and everyone else present, have respect for their opinions, whatever they may be. As RRs so often feel that their opinions about any book-related idea are worthless, you may find yourself restoring to health their views of themselves.

3.10 HOW CAN TEACHERS/LIBRARIANS USE TOOLS LIKE NOVELIST TO ENCOURAGE RELUCTANT READERS?

NoveList, the online database used by so many libraries across the country, offers much much more than call numbers and author names; programs like these are a virtual journey through every shelf in the place, with reviews, recommendations, special sections for teachers, and favorite-writer lists from professional authors. Whether you are a librarian, a teacher, or a parent with a library card, here's a teaching device that is endlessly useful and diverting.

Patricia used NoveList like candy for her RR class. After conferring with the school librarian and gaining his agreement to close the library for two periods on a designated day, her class of reluctant readers overran the school library and felt for the first time that they had a right to be there.

The class was composed of fifteen young women, all haters of any reading material—anytime, anywhere. They were allergic to the library. Many could be described as extroverts, used to voicing their opinions rather loudly; their personalities were the kind that give some library patrons the itch, and they'd known for all their years in school that "their kind" is not always welcome in the school or public library. Therefore, the idea of spending an entire afternoon in the "Room of Silence and Books" was met with skepticism at best, outright refusal at worst. They prepared for a palace revolution, and Patricia scrambled for the ambassadorial prowess necessary to counter their vociferous objections. After being assured that no one would mind if they talked out loud or, worse, ran through the hallowed shelves, they grudgingly agreed to give it a try.

Venturing (some for the first time in their lives) into the school's excellent library, they did agree that the computers were cool (reading a screen doesn't count as reading for RRs) and that while the library is an alien land and probably dangerous, it beat sitting in a classroom on a Friday afternoon. First, they ran through the shelves, yelling at the top of their voices. They stood on the tables and jumped up and down. One of them did somersaults down the main avenue of shelving. When they were finally convinced that the library was theirs for the rest of the day and that no one was going to scold them, they sat and launched the computers.

These girls—not known for their patience for explanatory instruction—were hooked by NoveList in the first minute. They toured the site with very little guidance, with a steady stream of straightforward commentary.

"Oh, man. Look at this. You can print up a list and take it with you. Cool."

"Yeah, look at my list—147 books in one category, and the computer did all the work for me!"

"Hey, I never heard of this book, but the title sounds spooky. The description sounds spooky, too. Is it okay if I read this book?"

Soon, the online catalog had rendered teacher and librarian superfluous. The fifteen reluctant readers (some with severe reading difficulties), fingers flying, were racing each other to see who could come up with the best list of prospective reads. Patricia had lured them into the library, but NoveList had kept them there. But would this computer tool reach beyond the lists it had generated for the RRs? Would anything but romance novels prevail with these reluctant clients? One week later, these "I Hate Reading" readers were deep into exploring the following titles:

1. *The Horse Whisperer* by Nicholas Evans
2. *Practical Magic* by Alice Hoffman
3. *She's Come Undone* by Wally Lamb
4. *The Scarlet Pimpernel* by Baroness Orczy
5. *Bastard out of Carolina* by Dorothy Allison
6. *Billy Bathgate* by E. L. Doctorow
7. *Ellen Foster* by Kaye Gibbons
8. *Murdered Sleep* by Thomas D. Davis

They kept their printouts in notebooks, the beginnings of their own reader advisory journals. Would they continue to maintain them after graduation? One of the students wrote to me during the summer break:

"I found five books that seem interesting to me and that I plan on reading before college. I will never be lonely again. That trip to the library made me want to read again."

Several of those RRs said before the close of the semester, "When can we go to the library again? I had so much fun there!"

Patricia regarded these responses as casual miracles and gave all the credit to NoveList. The key to the whole enterprise, however, was making the RRs feel that the library was in their power rather than the other way around, and that they had nothing but freedom to pursue, or not to pursue, the books on their lists. Parents and teachers can achieve similar results with field trips to the bookstore. Patricia conducted several of these trips during her tenure in the regular classroom; after talking with the community-relations director of the local franchise of a large bookstore chain, a group of students brought their parents to the store, where they were give ninety minutes to pull any books off any shelves, sit on the floor in the stacks, and read until they found something they wanted to buy. The community-relations director met the group at the door, welcomed everyone, and said he'd be around if anyone party had questions or problems finding anything. This impressed on the RRs that the bookstore, just like the library, was a safe place, and one in which their presence would be embraced and appreciated. At the end of the browsing, the group met in the coffee shop downstairs for refreshments and to compare purchases. For the several students without funds for this outing, we opened the Bank of the Teacher for quiet contributions. If you combine books with the promise of time out of school and food (with teenagers, food is always an irresistible draw), you might be surprised how much more attractive an afternoon of reading can be to an RR. The added advantage to this venture was to get parents involved, who were delighted that their offspring thought book shopping was something to be excited about. Many of them assured their children that yes, certainly, they could come back to the bookstore when they finished reading their purchases of the day.

Chapter 4

What Kinds of Books Work?

> "My books aren't quiet and I think that's a great way to grab reluctant readers."
>
> Joyce Sweeney

4.1 WHAT WILL RELUCTANT READERS READ?

We're almost there, so get your pencils ready, but before discussing materials that will appeal to reluctant readers, we need to present four caveats up front.

4.1a Four Caveats

1. **There is no magic bullet** or slam dunk that will work with all, even most, reluctant readers. The only reading materials that reluctant readers will read are the ones that they will read. That stated, this section is going to make generalizations about the sorts of materials that experience, and in some cases research, has shown will appeal to reluctant readers. Part 2, however, provides a list of "turnaround titles"—that is, book mentioned by our experts for turning nonreaders into readers—but this work is about building relationships with nonreaders rather than handing them a book off a list that somebody else recommended.

2. **This is not the place for titles.** The second part of this book is packed with lists of specific titles; this part is about describing what might attract a reluctant reader to a particular format/genre, general comments about that format/genre, and some representative titles. (Note: We've written about these issues before in all three editions of *Connecting Young Adults and Libraries* as well as in *A Core Collection for Young Adults*.) Since what may appeal to a reluctant teen reader may, of course,

appeal to any teen reader, there's going to be some overlap. We apologize in advance for any duplication.

3. One of the assumptions guiding the work as a whole is that **"reading is reading is reading"**—that is, to change the paradigm about nonliterary and non–school-assigned reading by any teen from, "well, at least they're reading something" to "they're reading." In part, this is because we believe that reading is the end in itself. Of course, reading one book is not the end; reading another book, then another, and then another is the end. Yes, there is value in moving a reluctant reader up those reading ladders discussed earlier, but there's as much value in moving that reluctant reader from her first book to her second book to her third book. The real goal is not just that the teen read one book but that he become a self-defined reader. And since it is during the teen years that adult habits are often defined, the ultimate end is to move teens from a self-identified reluctant reader to a self-motivated lifelong reader. We want teens to stop thinking of reading as something they have to do but instead something they want to do. We want them to choose to read for pleasure. It's really that simple . . .

4. . . . and that difficult, for it follows that if reading is reading is reading, than any reading material will do. If we say it's not about the classics, the "Best Books," or even books, then it stands to reason that reading magazines should "count" as reading. **If we place no value judgments on materials and thus on the reader, then shouldn't anything and everything be allowed?** By this reasoning, if we really want to get teen boys to read, every library should purchase *Maxim, King, Playboy,* and other magazines of that ilk. If we want boys to read in class, we should get rid of Twain's *Letters from the Earth* and replace it with *Letters to Penthouse.* Rather than buying series paperbacks, let's go down to the Velvet Touch XXX bookstore and pick up a stack of porno paperbacks. That would get reluctant readers reading, no? But we don't. We'll not even bother with the obvious reasons we don't and look instead at the goal. Yes, these things constitute reading for pleasure, for sure, but they're not what we're discussing here. Instructions on how to make a bomb, a hate-literature pamphlet, and a "slam Web site" are also reading. We've got to back away from an absolute position either way and admit that there are lines we need to draw. We would argue that the lines right now are drawn too close (reading equals school reading and/or fiction), and we've got to move them so that reading includes comic books, nonfiction, even an Eastbay catalog, but perhaps not a catalog from Vivid Video. We want kids to read in part because we believe in reading as a "social good," and if the reading materials are antisocial, that pretty much defeats the purpose.

4.1b Twenty-Four Gems

1. **Books—realistic teen fiction.** Relevance and readability matter most. While there are certainly reluctant readers who will become absorbed in science fiction and fantasy, for many who read fiction, it is realistic teen fiction than presents the best entry. For the reluctant reader, the best teen fiction is not that which paints the prettiest pictures with the most sparkling imagery, but that which holds up the best mirror to their lives. One obstacle for reluctant readers that we've mentioned throughout—including in the opening quote by the fifteen-year-old boy—is that reading needs to be about something the teen cares about. Since many teens care deeply about figuring out their own lives, books that provide an honest reflection of the adolescent experience are a good bet. A young Latino male might indeed "find himself" in a novel by Sarah Dessen, but there's a better chance that young man will read the works of Gary Soto. It's a tough thing; we don't want to stereotype readers—if it's a young black male, hand him a Walter Dean Myers novel and think problem solved—but we must realize that reluctant readers need books that are easy for them to read. And we mean this not so much in terms of sentence structure but in terms of what they can succeed with. A young African American girl might fall in love with the works of Richard Peck, but it's more likely she'll find success, and herself, in the works of Janet McDonald, Nikki Grimes, Sharon Flake, or Jacqueline Woodson. Woodson herself noted, "I think what matters most to young people is being able to see some part of themselves reflected in the story. When they pick up a book and recognize something, *anything,* it makes them feel like they matter and like the book cares about them. It legitimizes them." Yet for all the good stuff about teen fiction, for many reluctant readers, it still has to be plot driven. Most nonreaders care about what happens, not why it happens or the internal musings of the characters.

"What makes a good book for a reluctant reader? A book with a voice and a story that is genuine to young adults. I don't see reluctant readers as 'poor' readers, but readers who are not often interested in books. For them reading is an occasional choice, so when I write a 'young adult' book, I'm also making a choice to connect with them in an honest, and non-condescending way."

Jack Gantos

2. **Books—genre teen fiction.** For a period of time in the late 1980s through the mid-1990s, the horror genre was thriving in books for teens. Diane Hoh; Christopher Pike; and, in particular, R. L. Stine were writing scary books that reluctant readers read without fear. In our early work on Stine, the constant theme of parents/teachers was that while they were delighted that teens were reading, they wished they were reading something of more quality. We've made the argument before that Stine's books are of tremendous quality, and that's not the focus here; instead, the issue at hand is the appeal of genre fiction to reluctant readers. What genre fiction does for reluctant readers is offer them a safe box, since they know either instinctively or through limited reading experience that certain genres have certain rules. Books with rules are easier to follow, are less likely to disappoint, and allow a reluctant reader to focus on the story and the story alone. Most genre fiction—in particular horror and mystery—are very plot driven; it's not about character but about action. As Stine once noted, his characters are too busy running for their lives to learn anything. And while the type of action might be different in other genres, such as romance, science fiction, or fantasy, the importance of plot, stock character and situations, and expected payoff still remains. We'll talk about the Harry Potter phenomenon in more detail at the end of this chapter, but we'll advance a point here. While there are certainly plenty of nonreaders who became readers because of Harry Potter, we'd argue from our experience (there seems to be no research on the subject) that those are exceptions, not rules. On the surface, the Potter books are everything a reluctant reader hates: long, loaded with characters, set in an imaginary world, and a genre that "avid readers" seem more comfortable tackling. Yet digging deeper, it would become obvious once they got the first page open that the book succeeds both as genre fiction and as realistic fiction in portraying the life and times of an adolescent very much like themselves in many ways, with the exception of the wizardry.

3. **Books—fiction just for reluctant readers.** One of the most well-known series comes from Orca Books. Called Orca Soundings, these books, as noted by Tori Jensen, are "short (very key) straightforward, have *great* covers, and cover very relevant teen issues." And all of that is no accident, as noted by Orca's Andrew Wooldridge, who wrote us that "the only instructions I give authors are to keep the story within a certain word count. Our Orca Soundings and Orca Currents titles are all between 14,000 and 16,000 words long. Other guidelines: first-person narrative and a linear plot. Beyond that I try and give feedback as the author progresses. We have no word list. The main criteria is . . . compelling and

convincing story, believable characters, and respect for the reader. The cover treatment is also incredibly important. If the intended audience is turned off by the cover, they definitely will not read it." The hallmarks of the Orca books are those previously noted for fiction for reluctant readers. Wooldridge noted that "we ask for first-person narratives and linear plots, fewer characters so as to avoid confusing the reader, no flashbacks or changes of perspective, and lots of dialogue." What makes Orca and a similar series—the Bluford High series from Townsend Press (one of the few series featuring African American characters)—special is the intention to publish books just for the reluctant reader market. As Wooldridge noted, "I think Orca Soundings is a new trend in books for reluctant teen readers—quality books for this demographic that do not talk down to the reader."

4. **Books—series fiction.** As mentioned, series fiction (and by that we mean numbered titles that come out if not monthly then on a regular basis, rather than fantasy sagas such as Redwall or even Harry Potter) offers a great deal to reluctant readers. With series books, size matters. Most series books are in paperback and small; thus, they can be easily hidden from view and quickly read if the reader is hooked. With so many reluctant readers of all types mentioning time as a critical roadblock to more reading, series fiction titles are almost always quick reads, loaded with hooks to pull readers through the 200-plus pages at a breakneck pace. Most series books are genre fiction, and so readers get all of those advantages coupled with something vital in the YA world: branding. A hot brand attracts attention (Gossip Girls, anyone?) and therefore adds a coolness factor to reading, which may appeal to some reluctant readers. More important, however, is dependability. The classic story told by Dr. Kylene Beers is about the young man who, when told the library had so many good books, replied "which ones"—meaning the kid knew better than to think that every book was a good one. Given that some reluctant readers become reluctant because they've tried or been forced to read so many bad books, the search for a good book is always there. Like McDonald's or Burger King, the series books offer a carefully prepared-to-formula, test-marketed, dependable if somewhat bland experience. Series fiction works for reluctant readers as well as nonreluctant readers. One of the greatest fallacies is that series fiction actually retards reading; however, all the research—not to mention the anecdotal experience of hundreds of avid-reading librarians raised on Nancy Drew—proves otherwise. The biggest boom for reaching reluctant readers would be a twenty-first-century Goosebumps—a series that would be so hot, so popular, that even nonreaders would

read it just because it was there. And once they did, most would be hooked. For a short period of time, *Buffy the Vampire Slayer* TV tie-in books captured a similar audience, which shows how other media can encourage reading, even as TV/movies/the Web take away available reading time. Although series fiction suffered a post *Fear Street* slump, it seems—according to Lora Bruggeman—to be posed for a comeback, as "in the past couple of years, publishers have gotten better with publishing popular fiction for teens, like the Gossip Girl, A-List, and Stormbreaker series."

5. **Books—adult fiction.** Here's a strange thing we've seen: teens who consider themselves reluctant readers yet will read 400-plus-page tomes by such best-selling authors as Michael Crichton, John Grisham, and James Patterson, or double the pages and make it Stephen King. Related to this are the many nonreading teens who'll come to a book after seeing the movie. Even though these teens don't think they like to read, they've already been hooked by the story—*Jurassic Park* comes to mind as the best example of this—and will pick up the book. They know the story and want to re-experience it. Many teens report that after years of nonreading, a book based on a movie led them back to reading. The world of adult fiction contains all the subgenres we've touched on, such as series fiction (romance series or action adventure titles like *The Executioner*) and genre fiction. In genre fiction, hard-suspense tales like those of James Patterson, which are page-turning, plot-driven romps, seem the best bet. Something interesting is at work here. Some teens reject reading throughout junior high and the start of high school because they see it as something adults want them to do: the drive for independence overwhelms all else. But by their junior or senior year, most have moved beyond that knee-jerk developmental response and instead see reading as a grown-up thing to do. Thus, late in their teen years, they often start reading books their parents have around the house. For many nonreading teens of color, its not Walter Dean Myers that they're getting hooked on but adult fiction best-selling authors like Eric Jerome Dickey, Omar Tyree, and Zane.

6. **Books—urban fiction.** While there is certainly a small group of writers writing YA fiction for teens of color, the real action is in the adult field. The past few years have seen an explosion in what the trade has called "ghetto literature." Much of it is self-published, and it is a far cry from the PG-13 action found in Walter Dean Myers. As Jamie Watson noted, "African American titles are also very popular with teens of all races. The adult books, such as *B-More Careful* and the Zane titles, may

be full of sex and drugs, but so are the rap lyrics that are #1 on the charts. This is a world that fascinates teens, and reluctant readers are no exception. I've worked with many girls who tell me they only read things from Triple Crown Productions." Yet it is also true that because of the content, these books are not likely to be found in school libraries, and many public libraries won't carry them either (or don't replace them if they are not returned). Yet as Miranda Doyle noted, if you really want to reach nonreaders, you must "buy the books, magazines, graphic novels, etc., that they really want to read, even if those materials are controversial, edgy, or otherwise inappropriate."

7. **Books—short fiction.** If one of the stock excuses of every reluctant reader is about books being too long, then short stores are the obvious answer. They also answer many of the other obstacles: no time, no interest, and poor skills. Perhaps twenty years ago there were a handful of short-story collections aimed just at teens, and many of those were still classic collections, which seemed more like textbooks than real books. That changed when Don Gallo pulled together stories for his first collection, *Sixteen,* published in 1984. This was a book meant for readers, not teachers; it contained new stories from young-adult writers, not old stories from dead white men. While there are certainly other - short-story collections by other editors, Gallo's collections remain the standard and the most accessible for reluctant readers. His collections include:

- *Sixteen*—the first ever anthology of original short stories for teenagers written by a variety of authors who write for young adults. One of YALSA's 100 Best of the Best Books published between 1966 and 1999.
- *Visions*—The second ever collection of new short stories for teens.
- *Join In*—Seventeen multiethnic short stories about the lives of contemporary American teenagers whose ethnic backgrounds are Vietnamese, Chinese, Puerto Rican, Cuban, Mexican, Pueblo Indian, Japanese, Lebanese, Laotian, and African American.
- *Ultimate Sports*—In this collection of sixteen stories, both male and female teens engage in a variety of sports, including basketball, football, track, cross-country, sailing, scuba diving, boxing, wrestling, racquetball, triathlon, and the ultimate sport of the future.
- *No Easy Answers*—These sixteen short stories about character development depict teenagers facing situations that test their moral strength as they deal with such issues as computer blackmail, drug use, pregnancy, gang violence, and peer pressure.

- *On the Fringe*—Eleven stories focus on the experiences of teenage outsiders struggling with peer pressure, conformity, personal identity, popularity, and harassment.
- *Destination Unexpected*—Ten stories about teenagers who go on some kind of journey where they learn something about themselves as well as about a part of the wider world.
- *First Crossing*—Stories about teen immigrants from Mexico, China, Romania, Haiti, Korea, Kazakhstan, Sweden, Venezuela, Cambodia, and Palestine, and their experiences adjusting to American life.
- *What Are You Afraid Of?* Stories about phobias—coming in spring 2006.

Seven non-Gallo collections of particular interest to reluctant readers are:

- *Dirty Laundry: Stories about Family Secrets,* edited by Lisa Rowe Fraustino. Viking, 1998. An excellent variety of stories about such things as plagiarism, abortion, child abuse, mental illness, and transgender acceptance by authors such as Richard Peck, Bruce Coville, Chris Crutcher, Rita Williams-Garcia, and M. E. Kerr.
- *Every Man for Himself: Ten Stories about Being a Guy,* edited by Nancy Mercado. Dial, 2005. A variety of life lessons from the pens of Ron Koertge, David Levithan, David Lubar, Walter Dean Myers, Rene Saldana Jr., Terry Trueman, and other writers.

"Any good book is a good book for reluctant readers. I'm not being glib. It just turns out that though I'm a voracious reader and never go anywhere without two books (just in case one isn't any good), my tastes mesh pretty well with those of many reluctant readers. I like a strong plot, I like lots of dialogue, and I like restraint in description."

David Lubar

- *Love and Sex: Ten Stories of Truth,* edited by Michael Cart. Simon & Schuster, 2001. These stories about teen sexuality range from the hilarious ("Extra Virgin" by Joan Bauer) to the thought provoking ("The Cure for Curtis" by Chris Lynch), with several that include explicit descriptions of hetero- and homosexual activities.
- *One Hot Second: Stories about Desire,* edited by Cathy Young. Knopf, June 2002. Stories about first love and first times, by writers such as Sarah Dessen and Nancy Garden.
- *On the Edge: Stories at the Brink,* edited by Lois Duncan. Simon & Schuster, 2000. A dozen new stories from writers such as Alden R.

Carter, Terry Davis, Margaret Peterson Haddix, and Ellen Wittlinger about teenagers on various edges: the edge of sanity, the edge of a family, the edge of a ravine, the edge of annihilation.

- *13: Thirteen Stories That Capture the Agony and Ecstasy of Being Thirteen,* edited by James Howe. Atheneum, 2003. The title says it all—by writers such as Bruce Coville, Alex Sanchez, Lori Aurelia Williams, Ron Koertge, Meg Cabot, and Rachel Vail.
- *Twelve Shots: Outstanding Short Stories about Guns,* edited by Harry Mazer. Delacorte, 1997. In addition to stories about violence and the threat of violence, there are stories of personal discovery, friendship, and even humor in this powerful collection, written by Chris Lynch, Richard Peck, Walter Dean Myers, and others.

Finally, individual authors such as Sharon Flake, Walter Dean Myers, and Chris Crutcher have put together collections of their own stories. Like the rest of these collections, these are fine fodder for reading aloud, for sharing with teachers, and for turning a nonreader onto an author he or she might connect with and thus want to read a longer work from.

8. **Books—children's books** (picture, chapter, and easy readers). This is a tough one. Reluctant readers don't want to read baby books, even if that happens to be where their reading skills would take them. While some reluctant teen readers will return to childhood favorites, such as Dr. Seuss, there are certainly other options. Two authors really stand out: Dav Pilkey and Jon Scieszka. Both pen picture books as well as chapter books. And while you won't see a lot of reluctant teen readers showing off their *Captain Underpants* books to classmates, they will read them. Same with Scieszka's picture-book favs like *Stinky Cheese Man* as well as his middle grade series Time Warp Trio. Series fiction at the elementary school level is abundant and often tied in with other media. Even easy readers, where many teen remedial readers are forced to go due to lack of skills, are now rich in movie tie-ins and reliable, more contemporary series as opposed to Frog and Toad. While we certainly don't want to be actively putting children's books in the hands of teens (unless they ask for them), there's nothing wrong with having them around our libraries and classrooms. Even purely pictorial books like *I Spy* prove a point: there is pleasure to be had in the act of opening this thing with covers and pages in between. That's a lesson that readers learned and nonreaders often missed or, after years of schooling, have learned is a lie. Author John Coy noted, "I think the old belief that once readers reach a certain age they are no longer interested in picture books is no longer valid. Students who have grown up with the

mix of text and illustration on the Web are comfortable with a wide variety of combinations of words and pictures and this includes picture books if they address their genuine interests."

"It's worth noting that most men prefer reading nonfiction. (Only 17 percent of novels sold are sold to men.) We shouldn't be surprised, then, when reluctant reader boys choose the *Guinness Book of Records* over *Bridge to Terabithia*. They emulate their fathers."

Paul Kropp

---

9. **Books—nonfiction** (general). The key here is to talk with teens about their interests, then match them with good nonfiction. "Good" means high interest, not always best reviewed. Former Quick Picks chair Lora Bruggeman noted, "We found that a lot of the nonfiction books were much more popular that the fiction. I think that the top ten lists were made up of more nonfiction than fiction also." Lets look at some other facts about nonfiction. After reviewing years of reading interest-survey research, there is a clear and unmistakable preference for nonfiction among male readers. This is true from surveys of fourth graders to those of high school students and to those in between. Boys prefer nonfiction, and while not all boys are reluctant readers and not all reluctant readers are boys, these same surveys tell us that males are more likely not to read for pleasure. Researching reading and at-risk teens is a focus of Teri Lesesne, who noted, "In my seven-year study of at-risk teens, one of the observations I have been able to verify year after year is that nonfiction matters to these less-than-enthusiastic readers. Even though some of them read nonfiction regularly, they do not see themselves as readers because nonfiction is not as valued in the English classroom." So the facts about nonfiction are these: it reaches reluctant readers, it reaches nonreaders, it reaches poor readers, it reaches at-risk kids, it reaches boys, and it makes up some of teens' favorite books. Nonfiction helps kids define their identity; broadens their intellectual horizons; allows nonreaders to enjoy books, if only through looking at pictures and reading captions; develops their special interests with an eye to lifelong learning; and, in personal narratives, allows them to find themselves on the page. Nonfiction allows teens to respond in all the same ways as fiction: laugh, cry, emote, and grow. Even more than fiction, however, nonfiction can result in social activity. Books of jokes, oversize sports books, and sex books cry out for passing around and reading aloud. Nonfiction reading leads to discussion, debate, and destruction.

Destruction is a good indicator of interest level. Which is stolen more—fiction or nonfiction? We would assume most libraries spend a lot more time and money replacing the sex books than the Richard Peck catalog. One reason for this is simple: while teens may read fiction only for the "good parts," this is common with nonfiction. As Marina Claudio-Perez noted, "With the limited time the teens have, rarely would they have the time to finish the book. With nonfiction, it doesn't matter, as the readers don't have to find the end that is necessary for fiction. With nonfiction, they find the end in every page, with the new things, pictures and concepts, they discover." Nonfiction is custom-fit for tighter schedules: for reading on buses, before bed, between classes, or even during TV commercials. Thus, nonfiction's appeal to the reluctant reader is obvious, but a growing market in every school and public library is the teen that is new to reading English. No matter how good a novel like *Last Chance Texaco* or even *The Outsiders* is, for someone struggling with vocabulary, nonfiction is more inviting. Nonfiction for new teen readers serves the same function as easy readers to children: big margins, simple text, and good illustrations. All of these can be used to hook readers by laying books out on library tables, setting them next to computers, or showing/telling during booktalks. As Kat Kan noted, "When I booktalked in schools and encountered teens who said they didn't like to read, I used fun nonfiction books—urban legends, dumb criminal-type stories, *The Top 10 of Everything*. Those sorts of nonfiction ended up being popular, and when the teens did show up in my library, they asked for those books—you know, the one you read with all the stupid crimes."

10. **Books—nonfiction biography.** The book called *Child Called It* was cited over and over again as a "turnaround" book by librarians we interviewed. Also high on the list were other biography or personal-narrative teen titles (we'll talk about pop culture bios shortly). The attraction of nonreading teens to these stories should be obvious: relevance. While they may not be able to imagine a different world or even a fictional one much like their own, many reluctant teen readers can grasp the concrete details, dialogue, and hard dilemmas faced by the young people in books such as these. While some would argue that *Go Ask Alice* and the other Beatrice Sparks "as told to" books belong in fiction, they really fit within this genre. Books about teens in trouble, such as gang stories like *Monster*, or about overcoming physical obstacles, like *Autobiography of a Face*, may engage the most reluctant of readers as they fantasize, empathize, and become totally engaged with the crisis the real-life character faces.

11. **Books—nonfiction illustration heavy books.** There are really two types: the books by DK (and all their imitators) and classic coffee-table books. The appeal of DK books to reluctant readers should be obvious: high interest, lots of illustrations compared to little text, and great covers. In libraries, these books belong on display. While DK first started with books heavy in the sciences, which may not be a real reluctant reader pull, it's gotten heavily involved in pop-culture offerings, such as books on movies and comic-book heroes. The idea is to take what kids know—for example, the *Star Wars* movie—and capture it in book form. An even better example of this are books that are more photographic essays than informational texts. Mary Ann Harlan calls these oversized, meant-more-for-browsing-than-close-reading "gateway books." She noted that "When I can get kids to take picture books (I'm thinking of the *VX* book on last year's Quick Picks list), I can usually build up credibility to get them to take something else." The idea is to show teens that they can succeed with the book format; that the physical act of looking at something on a printed page, then turning the page, is a good one.

12. **Books—nonfiction informational books in series.** This is the area in which you'll find the most books written just for the "hi lo" market, as it used to be called: high interest/low vocabulary. Publishers such as Lerner, Enslow, Rosen, and Capstone dominate this market. While many of the titles are used by students for educational reasons, there is certainly a high appeal to reluctant teen readers looking for recreational reading. Concerning the books his company publishes, Adam Lerner noted, "We continually strive to build understanding of where reluctant readers are coming from, what interests them, what will draw their attention. We've been successful with the usual reluctant reader topics—sports, vehicles, and such—because we've also given a great deal of attention to the design techniques, with bold colors and striking images that live up to young readers' expectations. Kids are bombarded with bold, dynamic graphic treatments through TV, video games, and magazines." One of the lists in part 2 comprises books that read like magazines and with good reason. Lerner further noted that "when we acquire books with high-interest topics that will appeal to reluctant readers, we want to be sure the authors can write in compelling ways to hold these readers' attention. Our editors do work with the authors to ensure the texts are readable and understandable for the intended grade level. Word lists don't work well for either reluctant or struggling readers. For example, a word list would level a four-syllable word like 'motorcycle' or 'carburetor'

quite high, yet if the reader is into vehicle topics, these words aren't difficult for them. Instead, we craft a text to read smoothly and easily, ensuring that we hold readers' attention. . . . We believe heavy and interesting use of big pictures often with full bleeds greatly appeals to these readers. We also ensure that information is presented in digestible bits and that the interior text is easy to navigate. The text needs to 'breathe' as well but not necessarily within the static 'white space' traditionally associated with reluctant reader design." The reason for this shift in thinking is simple: the impact of the Internet—which is graphic heavy—provides instant information and can always be more current than any book title. That's not necessarily a bad thing; instead, it's a lesson for publishers. As Lerner noted, "Their broad exposure to the media has increased their sophistication immensely. We need to find ways to 'sell' the idea of books to kids, and we need to provide engaging, well-designed books that will draw them in and deliver information in a way that appeals to them." Like many publishers in the teen market, Lerner looks to "connect with the people 'in the trenches' of this situation—the librarians, teachers, and researchers who study firsthand what turns kids off about reading, and how to turn them back on. We also make it a point to maintain more informal, but still important, direct contact with kids to gauge their ever changing interests." Mark Enslow, president of Enslow Publishers, noted, "A good book for reluctant readers (RRs) is a high interest book, with a great cover and a reading level of fourth grade or lower. We at Enslow target the middle school and high school RRs. We tend to use the same authors over and over again that can pull off writing for the RR. We ask them to be sure to create a compelling first chapter, some text that is really exciting, good nonfiction." He added, "We at Enslow feel a responsibility to publish for RRs. We understand their reluctance to dive into the book format. However, we want to reward young readers with an exciting read about a topic they care about." There are adult nonfiction equivalents: the dummy series and its imitators. It's a real shame that publishers choose to use terms like "dummies" and "idiots," which may certainly repel reluctant readers who don't like the implication. Yet these books do have appeal, as many of them are about high-interest subjects, and while the vocabulary may not be controlled, the way the text is presented often is. Rather than straight text, most of these books feature a high degree of illustrations coupled with bullet lists, sidebars, and other nonstandard methods of presenting information.

13. **Books—nonfiction pop goes the culture.** But it's not always the informational book series, produced by library-friendly publishers, that bring kids to nonfiction. As Lora Bruggeman noted, "In the nonfiction leisure teen collection, probably 70 percent of the books weren't reviewed in library journals for teens or weren't reviewed at all in library journals." The hottest stuff is too hot to get reviewed, or by the time it is, it's stone cold. Teens create popular culture, which has been true since the 1950s, and in the twenty-first century, this trend is not going away. With studies showing more teenagers in the United States than ever before, in the next few years, this phenomenon will only increase. Nonfiction paperbacks about music, TV, movies, and sports respond to the very culture kids are creating. Erin Helmrich noted, "My collection of teen's popular interests is one of the strengths of the collection, and I know the teens appreciate it." The push toward reality shows that started with MTV's *Real World* continues: kids are interested in real lives as much as made-up ones. We need to view other media not as a roadblock to reading but as an on-ramp. As Jamie Watson noted, "I've generally had the most excitement with popular nonfiction. Especially books about pop culture figures. Poetry doesn't work with my reluctant readers at all, unless it's by Alicia Keys and called 'lyrics'—then they can't get enough! Say the word 'biography' and you won't get any attention, but show them the book *Unbelievable: The Life, Death and Afterlife of the Notorious B.I.G.* and you'll be surprised at how many teens will read a 400-page book."

14. **Books—graphic novels.** The past few years have seen an explosion of interest in this area and thus a lot of professional writing, so we'll be brief. A graphic novel is a self-contained story that uses a combination of text and art to articulate plot. It is equivalent in content to a long short story or short novel and in some ways a larger version of a comic book. Graphic novels can be studied as art, with discussions of their illustrations. They can be studied as literature and art, with attention to form and content. Graphic novels require students to not only decode text but also follow its flow and grasp the essentials of narrative, mood, character, or plot through images, and then meld parts into a unified whole. Graphic novels are popular because they offer a quick, visual format that is attractive to a generation of teens that has become visually oriented with media. In addition, the nonlinear format appeals to those more accustomed to reading hypertext on a computer screen than traditional linear text. Most of the character development comes not through introspection but through action and dialogue.

The dialogue text in word-balloon bites appears to teens to be more like real conversation. The description is left more to the artist, thus the story can focus on plot, dialogue, and action. Because of movies or other media, many of the characters are not new to readers. Finally, graphic novels usually come in paperback format and often come in a series, providing continuity and familiarity. Unlike any other previous generation, today's teens are comfortable with nontext visual media and are therefore more at ease "reading" the combination of words and pictures used in the graphic-style format to tell a story. Graphic novels contribute to the development of both visual and verbal literacy. Visual learners can connect with graphic novels in a way that they cannot with text-only books. But take note: not all reluctant readers will or even can read graphic novels; not all graphic novels are for reluctant readers. We would argue that any teen who is a regular graphic-novel reader is an avid reader who has just chosen a different type of reading material. Michele Gorman, one of the top experts in the nation on graphic novels, reminds us, "Based on my experience, I would say that graphic novels as a format appeal to not only reluctant readers, but English as a second language students, on-grade level readers, and readers with strong language and solid reading skills. However, having said that, I think it is safe to say that graphic novels do appeal to a certain number of reluctant readers who are hesitant to read because they have faced failure in the past with the reading process. Graphic novels, comic books, and even magazines offer simple sentence structure and visual clues that help the young reader decipher the text. They also offer fast-paced action, conflict, and heroic endeavors—all things that can easily pull a reluctant reader into the story."

15. **Books—collected comics.** "I'm no Super Genius, or are I?" says Homer Simpson, and it doesn't take a super genius to know the appeal of collected comics to reluctant readers. Again, these are characters they know from either television or newspaper comic strips. From the silliness of *Garfield* to the political edginess of the *Boondocks,* collected comics offer reluctant readers the chance to laugh out loud, something rarely found in most fiction. While some collected comics tell a story, most are merely reprints of previously published strips or comic books. In fact, some have very little narrative at all because they are merely collections of very, very short stories—for example, *School Is Hell* by Matt Groening. Although it is an older title, it represents the best of the humor genre. Like a graphic novel, such a title has reoccurring characters and themes, but there is no real narrative.

Collections like these provide libraries with something that teens ask for over and over: humor. Is it any secret that teens like to laugh? No, but our humor selections don't always fit the bill. While there are some truly funny novels, fiction is not the answer for every reader. If the entire graphic-format movement has taught us anything it's to recognize and then respect the range of reading experiences.

16. **Books—Manga.** Manga (pronounced *maynga*) is the Japanese word for comic book or graphic novel. Traditionally, manga is produced in black-and-white, on fairly coarse paper—a format for the masses. Manga comes in a variety of genres: romance, horror, science fiction, drama, military stories, and sports. Most manga is in serial format, with most titles having multiple volumes. Anime (pronounced *ann-ee-may*) is the film equivalent of this genre. Manga that's been reproduced from the original Japanese series is put together from right to left. To an American reader, it appears that the book has been put together backward. Manga is most popular with American teenagers and older children; although some manga is published for the adult market, the vast majority of its fans are teens and tweens. In some areas, Japanese culture is very different from American. What is an acceptable level of nudity and sexuality for teenagers in Japan may be very different from what is acceptable in your community or at your school. The following is a statement from Tokyopop, the leading manga publisher in the United States: "There are notable cultural differences in many titles. These may include but are not limited to crude humor, nudity, ambiguous sexuality and gender roles, and fashion that may be considered unusual. These issues are deemed acceptable to Japanese readers and are a part of what makes Tokyopop manga authentic, popular, and cool with young people in the USA." And as Kimberly Paone noted, "In my library, the largest amount of progress I've seen with reluctant readers has come through graphic novels—especially manga. Teens who for years said they didn't have time to read or they didn't like to read are now consuming manga in enormous amounts."

17. **Books—poetry.** The poetry of Tupac, Ashanti, and Alicia Keys were all noted by librarians as "turnaround books"—and for good reason. Teens know these people and want to read their words, as opposed to those of dead white English guys. The connection between rap and poetry is profound, and books—or lyrics Web sites—serve as another huge attraction to the reluctant reader. Just as important is the growing number of books featuring the poetry of teens, such as those in the Teen Ink series. We believe that readers write and writers read, so

in addition to promoting teen-produced poetry, libraries and teachers should encourage students to write; what better way to get students hooked on words than letting them express themselves through the printed page. Another type of poetry of interest to teens are verse novels, such as those by Mel Glenn. Because they read as poems, for some reluctant teen readers, they are much easier than straight narrative. Note, however, that not all verse books work for reluctant readers, because many—such as *Realm of Possibility* by David Leviathan—are very deliberately literary. On the other side of the street is *Where the Sidewalks Ends*, which no classroom or library serving teens should be without.

18. **Magazines and newspapers.** The quote at the start of the book tells it all: magazines are where it's at for many reluctant readers, particularly boys. We've written a great deal about the appeal of magazines to all teens, so to briefly review: *Sixteen* and other fanzines were on top of the *Beverly Hills 90210* or *NSYNC fads long before book publishers could rush out titles, and conversely, they drop fads just as fast. Old news is no news to many young adults, so the very nature of magazines makes them perfect for reluctant teen readers. Most teen magazines, and even those adult titles of interest to teens, have two things in common: they are long on currency and short on pages without ads. Given that the one reason many teens, especially boys, don't read books is simply physical—it means sitting still for too long—magazines are the perfect alternative. They can be read quickly in between classes or under a teacher's glance. This is not surprising as magazines are visual, which is a huge drawing card for the stereotypical members of the MTV generation. Magazines appeal to the short attention spans and busy schedules of many young adults. Readers who find books challenging will find in most YA magazines simple vocabulary, lots of pictures, and short articles. Because of these factors, magazines much more so than books are seen by all teens as a social plus. A teenage boy who gets "caught" with a book by his friends/peers in certain circles gets "nerded" out. The same kid seen with a magazine is asked to share it. There is not the same negative stigma attached to reading magazines as to reading books, in part because magazines can be about what is hot and now. A teen interested in rap music might be lucky to find ten books in the library on this subject. But a library could meet this interest monthly with a magazine subscription. As young adults grow older they begin to develop special interests, which magazines can better respond to than books. The whole notion of magazines is to find a special-interest group and

provide a product for them to buy. As Teri Lesesne noted, "I would say that periodicals (magazines) are undervalued by many educators when it comes to motivating reluctant readers because somehow reading those types of materials is not deemed real 'reading.'" Much the same, reading newspapers is taken for granted as a reading activity. It is also the area in which librarians and teachers have a real ally: newspapers are scared to death that young people are not reading them; thus, many have developed programs (such as Newspapers in Schools) that provide papers, curriculum, and other materials to encourage the reading of newspapers. Not just the local daily paper should be available to teen readers, but also alternative papers as well as *USA Today*. With its excellent sports and entertainment coverage, not to mention its technique of reducing the world to pie chart form, *USA Today* was meant for reluctant adult readers, and thus works well with teens. All that said, not everyone concurs with using magazines. Librarian Amy Cheney, who works with teens in correctional facilities, noted, "Sometimes I find magazines are a determent to reading. Kids don't 'graduate' from magazines to books, but rather just wait for the next issue of whatever it is to get into. If that's not available, they aren't as willing to try something else."

19. **Tabloids.** Who can resist the dish or dirt on some celebrity as outlined in the *Star*? Who doesn't want to know what Bat Boy has been up to in the *Weekly World News*? Tabloids are placed by the checkout at the grocery store along with the candy: we know it's not good for us, yet we can't look away. Thus, reluctant teen readers might easily find within the pages of tabloids text they will read, which sometimes even includes book excerpts.

20. **Comic books.** We've talked about graphic novels, but what about monthly comic books provided by the same vendors as magazines? Why would a school or public library want to provide comic books to attract reluctant readers? Here you have a format that is inexpensive, is popular with hard-to-reach male readers, generates circulation, takes up little space, and weeds itself. Plus, it meets the needs of customers, in particular teen and preteen boys. Yes, adults read comics and so do girls of all ages, but the core audience for comics are coming-of-age males. What is the pull of comic books for young men in the making? The answers are varied and certainly depend on circumstances, but a lot of it relates to basic adolescent development. The "fantastic four" core themes of adolescence are independence, excitement, identity, and acceptance. Comics go four for

four. First, comics—because they are easy to read and because they are inexpensive—are a format that reinforces a teen's independence. Add onto that the anti-comic stance of many adults and the rugged individualism of comic-book superheroes, and it becomes obvious how this format fulfills that first core developmental need. Second, saying that comics are exciting is stating the obvious, so the question is, Why is managing excitement so important to teen boys? It's not just about the mind but about a body changing, growing, and flexing. Third, what teen boy doesn't want to be a superhero? Who wouldn't want to beat up the bad buys, do the right things, and be adored? Comic books are just as much fantasy literature as a Harry Potter novel, except these heroes wear capes rather than glasses. Comics are total wish-fulfillment fodder. Most superheroes have two identities; most teen boys have that as well. The part they show at school and at home, and the part they show when among their friends. Finally, acceptance is a little more complicated, but events in schools in recent years involving teen boys show how desperate boys are to be accepted, especially those who are outside of the mainstream in some way. When a library collects comics, it is showing that it accepts teens who have different reading tastes and interests than others. Comics also send a message to poor, reluctant, or new readers that the library is about having a positive experience. If that happens with a Richard Peck novel, that is fine; if it happens with *X-Men #207*, that is fine as well. So what is the holdup? Libraries often view services to teens, which would embrace collecting graphic formats, as "special" and outside of their normal mission. What this demonstrates is a radical inconsistency of changing formats due to the changing needs of our customers. Teens like comic books because, as described, the developmental changes occurring in their lives cause them to look for formats that meet those core needs of independence, excitement, identity, and acceptance. Collecting comic books, then, is not about doing anything special for teens; it's about doing the same thing we do for other customer segments. Embracing comics is yet another way for libraries to serve teens by connecting with the popular culture that connects teens to each other. Popularity of the subject and the format should be enough reason to collect graphic formats; however, there is one more element that seems to be the crux of the issue: respect the stereotype of the comic-book reader is largely a negative one: a semi-literate juvenile delinquent who isn't smart enough to read "real books." Like most stereotypes, this flies straight in the face of the facts, but no matter. Librarians may embrace this stereotype because they themselves were not comic-book readers; they don't know any comic-book readers; they don't understand comic-book readers; and it does not jibe with their view of what reading is or should be. We all used to say about comics and graphic novels and even series books that "at least they are reading something." As we shift our focus to the outcomes of reading among teenagers and the need to respect the teen experience as a cornerstone to successful young-adult shifts, we come to realize two things. First, that reading is an end, not a means; that the value comes not from what the critics or the librarians think about a particular book or format, but from what it does for the teen reader. The outcome, the positive experience, is what matters. But for those who can't stretch that far and believe that the sole purpose of comics is to get kids to read quality literature (which is harder to define than "graphic novel") they need to realize that the "something" they want kids to move beyond is pretty damn good in and of itself.

21. **Catalogs.** Maybe you're with us so far, but catalogs? Are catalogs from Victoria's Secret, Eastbay, or Crutchfield on anyone's radar as reading material? Probably not, and that's a shame, because these catalogs—which teens mostly flip through to look at the pictures and/or models but not read any of the text—represent another type of experience. Remember, most reluctant readers have learned something about reading: they don't like it because it is not fun and brings them no pleasure. They simply do not associate the act of turning the pages of a printed piece enjoyable. Catalogs—yes, catalogs—can help create the relationship between page flipping and pleasure. It's not the grail by any means, but it's something.

22. **Text on a computer.** Another book in and of itself. Does reading e-mail, IMs, or the captions on the BET Web page count as reading? What if any role does technology play in motivating unmotivated readers? There are certainly connections to be made with other reading materials and technology. For example, teens who visit the WWE Web site will almost certainly check out or at least look through the WWE magazine or a WWE produced wrestling biography. They might even check out those drab Chelsea House "the wrestlers known as" series, but they are certainly not going to go from being computer users to being readers of *Wrestling Sturbridge*—not just because it's fiction (after all, if these kids were fiction readers, they wouldn't be new customers), but because they didn't see it on TV. Steve Austin is on TV; Rich Wallace isn't. Kids are already in the tent—the computer

has gotten them there—but nonfiction books about the very topics they are looking up can keep them there. Then they begin to discover reading as pleasure, not as torture, and for many, the world of fiction opens up to them. If one of the missions of libraries is to get and keep kids reading so that they will become lifelong learners and take that bridge to adult reading, then books that speak to their passions will help with that task.

23. **Audiobooks.** Some might argue that this isn't reading, but we disagree. Listening to an audiotape is an interaction with text, albeit in a much different way. The elements that make up reading remain: a reader must still imagine the characters, the place, and the action. Since time is an issue for many teens, the portability of audiobooks allows teens to read in places and at times that wouldn't accommodate a book. What works best for some readers is using the text and the tape together. As Nancy Levin told us, "Books on tape coupled with the actual book and/or movie make a great bridge to reading for a reluctant reader." Francisca Goldsmith noted that another advantage of the audio format might be "perceived time crunches, and the fact that silent pleasure reading is passive physically." She explained, "I think audiobooks help with this, as well as with those who really need to be physically active to feel engaged—very possible to do while listening." While our focus here is on kids who can read but choose not to, we should mention the success of audiobooks with teens who have reading difficulties. Audiobooks with the text at hand is a tremendous tool for helping struggling readers learn to read better. Classroom teacher Laura Gajdostik noted, "Audiobooks are magical with my students who experience difficulties in learning (students with special needs and students 'at-risk' of not graduating—i.e., students with an IEP plan and STRIVE 'at-risk' students). I have had enormous success using audiobooks with these populations of students."

24. **DVDs/movies.** Like audiobooks with struggling readers, DVDs can be used with unmotivated readers to excite them about the story. If you ask avid teen readers about their reading history, many will tell you that one of the first adult novels they read outside of school was a book that had recently been turned into a movie. Use movies to got them interested, then link them back with books—but not just the novel the movie was based on. Nonfiction about the subject of the movie, magazines, and Web pages can be used to expand on the ideas in the movie. A good movie pulls the reader into a story; we should use that to move readers to stories and facts in printed form.

4.2 TEN REASONS THAT YOUNG ADULTS LIKE NONFICTION

1. They are fascinated with facts.
2. They are developing special interests.
3. They are developing intellectual curiosity.
4. They have short attention spans.
5. They want to look at pictures/visuals.
6. They view nonfiction as socially acceptable.
7. They find fiction difficult.
8. They like "real life" stories, such as personal narratives.
9. Nonfiction is relevant to their lives.
10. Nonfiction inspires lifelong learning.

4.3 TEN REASONS THAT YOUNG ADULTS LIKE FICTION

1. It shows YAs being independent from adults.
2. It reassures them that they are "normal."
3. It presents role models.
4. It demonstrates problem solving in action.
5. It allows them to feel like they are winners/overcoming odds.
6. It displays relationships of all sorts.
7. It captures the intensity and uncertainty of their lives.
8. It helps them develop a socially responsible behavior.
9. It explores the lives of other teenagers.
10. It is fun!

> "I think a good book for reluctant readers includes a compelling plot; a main character they can recognize, relate to, and care about; and a vocabulary that makes sense to them."
>
> Catherine Atkins

4.4 WHAT ARE QUALITIES IN A BOOK THAT WILL HOOK MANY RELUCTANT READERS?

The most obvious is a book that "doesn't suck," but what does that mean? This selection criteria is in part from YALSA's Quick Picks for Reluctant Young Adult Readers Committee and lays out what attributes librarians should look for in books to appeal to nonreaders.

Physical Appearance

- Cover: catchy, action-oriented, attractive, appealing, good blurb
- Print style: sufficiently large for enjoyable reading
- Format: appropriate and appealing balance of text and white space
- Artwork/illustrations: enticing, realistic, demonstrated diversity

Style

- Clear writing that easily communicates without long convoluted sentences of sophisticated vocabulary
- Acceptable literary quality and effectiveness of presentation
- Simple vocabulary but not noticeably controlled

Fiction

- High interest "hook" in first ten pages
- Well-defined characters and not too many of them
- Sufficient plot to sustain interest
- Plotlines developed through dialogue and action rather than descriptive text
- Familiar themes with emotional appeal for teenagers
- Believable treatment
- Single point of view
- Touches of humor when appropriate
- Told in chronological order—not too many flashbacks

> "You really only have the first few pages to reel in a nonreader, so that first page in particular is make or break, and should optimally reflect action as well as a distinct and recognizable teen voice."
>
> Rachel Cohn

Certainly, not every book that is good for reluctant readers fits this bill; however, if you run almost any of the turnaround titles through these lists, you'll see they score on almost every point. As an example of fiction, let's look at *Things Change*, written by one of this book's coauthors.

Things Change tells the story of sixteen-year-old Johanna, one of the best students in her class, who develops a passionate attachment to troubled seventeen-year-old Paul and finds her plans for the future changing in unexpected ways. In many expected ways, however, this book fits the profile:

- High interest "hook" in first ten pages: The first line of the book is "I want you to kiss me." Enough said.
- Well-defined characters and not too many of them: Paul and Johanna are the two leads of the story with three supporting players: two best friends and one of the best friend's girlfriends. While there are some adults in the story, it is mainly a story about teen life and times.
- Sufficient plot to sustain interest: The story is basic: girl meets boy, girl loves boy, girl loses boy; the twist is that boy hits girl. The book is about the physical side of teen romance, which includes both sexual intimacy and physical violence. Once Paul turns violent, the plot switches from that of a young girl falling in love to how and when Johanna can get out and stay out of an abusive relationship.
- Plotlines developed through dialogue and action rather than descriptive text: The book is very dialogue heavy, perhaps too much so to give readers a real sense of place and context.
- Familiar themes with emotional appeal for teenagers: Sadly, the story resonates with lots of readers—particularly teen girls—since violence is involved in almost 10 percent of teen relationships. The story is also about Johanna's journey from innocence to experience, in part by declaring her independence from her parents; that struggle is *the* conflict of adolescence.
- Believable treatment: Almost all the reviews of this book, not to mention all the e-mails from readers, show that this is the power of the story—these are characters and situations that are real to many teens.
- Single point of view: *Things Change* does not fit here; it uses two voices to tell the story.
- Touches of humor when appropriate: Yes—unless you ask the reviewer from *School Library Journal.*
- Told in chronological order—not too many flashbacks: While the book is primarily told in the present, many of the scenes with Paul feature flashbacks, so again, not a perfect fit.

Things Change isn't a typical reluctant-reader book in part because the main character herself is a reader (her nickname is "Books"), but it seems to work. As high school teacher Delores Digiacomo noted, "One of my male nonreaders was sitting in the hallway while an almost nonreader (also male) was reading aloud. They were hanging on every word and trying desperately to finish the book in time for the discussion. I almost cried to think that they had finally found something that made them want to read. When everyone had finished the book, the discussion was lively and animated, and the book had appealed to both males and females, something that is a bit rare for this age group."

If you go through the titles listed in the "Turnaround Titles" section, you'll probably find that most fit. But we offer two other quick lists to consider. Since one of the reasons teens don't like to read is that they can't find books that interest them, its constructive to recall what *all* teens like in books. When teens say a book is good, it means lots of things, but in many cases it means they've made a connection with the book; in fiction, they've related to the character. Teen reading is often as much about the readers themselves as about the words on the page.

4.5 WHAT'S THE ROLE OF INTELLECTUAL FREEDOM?

> "A certain amount of the usual four-letter-words are also required to catch and hold a reluctant reader's attention; and this, too, becomes a balancing act for an author, because too many such words (or sometimes just *one* of the stronger words) will either keep a book out of a school library or get it banned later on . . . which has happened with several of my books."
>
> Jess Mowry

Inherent in this book (and in our beliefs) is the idea that reluctant readers must be allowed to choose their own reading materials whenever possible. Giving teenagers the right to select their own material is scary for adults of all kinds, and teachers and librarians are no exception. It is our job to encourage teenagers to read and to enjoy reading, but not to select recreational reading materials for them nor to pass judgment on the titles they select. Reading-material selection is one of very few areas in their lives in which teenagers can have the freedom (a freedom that is developmentally necessary) to explore various identities, lifestyles, and personal interests. If they know nothing about how other people are living their lives, how can we expect them to make decisions about living their own? We cannot control these explorations (and, consequently, the reading choices that support them) any more than we can control whether or not they pierce their tongue, get a tattoo, or dye their hair blue. We might prefer they read books we determine to be more "appropriate," just as we would prefer they keep their natural hair color, but we can't (and shouldn't) make that decision for them. Parents of individual teenagers are the only ones who should act "parental" in guiding their teens to materials they find appropriate. (And everyone who works with teenagers knows that just because their parents find it inappropriate doesn't mean that teenagers won't read it. In fact, it usually means just the opposite.)

There are many titles that teenagers want to read that we might find personally questionable or even offensive. If we can't keep some of these titles in our school library, we must refer that student to the public library. If we're in a public library and can't keep these titles in our teen or young-adult area, we can certainly keep them in our adult area and refer teens to that section when they're looking for the title. For educators advocating for teens and reading, we often stand in the way of adults who want to control what teens read and even what they think. As youth advocates, it is our role to stand up for teenagers—reluctant readers or not—and the materials they want.

Recognizing teenagers as having the ability to select materials for themselves is scary. They might get bad ideas; they might not learn what we want them to learn; they might make bad choices; they might read about things and people we don't approve of; they might ask us hard questions. But by giving them the benefit of the doubt, providing a variety of materials from which they can choose, and answering those hard questions, they just might start getting some ideas of their own.

4.6 DOES A THIN BOOK ALWAYS MEAN AN EASY BOOK FOR RELUCTANT READERS?

> "The book cannot be intimidating in size. . . . This is not to say that novels for reluctant readers must be bone-head simple; rather, I'm speaking more of the overall style of the book. We all know books that are deeply layered in meaning—for example, *The Old Man and the Sea*—yet at first glance appear thin and very simple. A better word than 'simple' might be elemental—pared down to the essential elements of narrative, but with a worthwhile plot— that's my idea of a novel for the reluctant reader."
>
> Will Weaver

Former YALSA president Deborah Taylor cuts right to the heart of it, noting, "Many teachers and librarians don't take the time to find out why reluctant readers are reluctant. I've observed that some teachers and librarians believe that any easy or short book will work without considering teen interest." Many teens also think thin equals easy. You can disabuse them of this notion easily; just hand them a copy of Joseph Conrad's *Heart of Darkness,* the first volume of Proust's *Remembrance of Things Past,* or Chris Lynch's *Free Will.* One of the greatest gifts you can give your reluctant reader patron or student is to divorce them from their conviction that thin=easy and long=hard. Another useful equation: Length does not equal language, and it's all about the language, isn't it? While reluctant readers tend to cling to the problematic certainty that they can't judge books by their covers (although many do) but by their number of pages, it's understandable that they have come to assess books this way. Most young-adult novels are quite short by industry standards, and it's easy for the young adults in question to apply the litmus test of length when they're accustomed to regard the short YA works as easy reading and the longer, more adult books as difficult. How many times have we heard a reluctant reader complain: "But this book is *so* long! I'll never finish it; it's more than I can do. I'll get depressed [angry, impatient, etc.] if I try to read this."

There are useful responses to such fears, some founded and some not.

1. If this book is easier reading than the shorter ones you've attempted in the past, you might find you'll complete it much more quickly than you think.

2. The story in this book is so cool, you're going to wish you could keep on reading when it ends. (Expect raised brows and rolling eyes, but your RRs may give you the benefit of the doubt.)

3. There is no time-limit law. If you need a month or a year, it doesn't matter, as long as you enjoy what you read. You can check out a library book and then renew it. If you love it, make a trip to Half-Price Books or Amazon.com and buy the book. You can spend the rest of your life exploring the pages if you like. (The idea of buying a book for pleasure may strike RRs with the same likelihood as the moon sprouting wings and flying into the sun, but once they get the hang of it, they generally enjoy the novelty of it—pun intentional.) The sixth book in the Harry Potter series is 652 pages long. The only complaint we've heard from its readers is that they were left hanging at the end and want the rest of the story *right now!* If your RRs like the tale of the half-blood prince, you may find it handy to point out that other long books can be just as mesmerizing. Well, almost. Observe that Christopher Paolini's *Eragon* is 544 pages, and the second in his trilogy, *Eldest,* is 704. Paolini's novels are filled with "foreign" words of his own creation and scores of character names and places, yet his books sell and sell and sell. Reluctant readers aren't afraid of long books; they're only afraid of long books that bore or confuse them. Jonathan Stroud's Bartimaeus trilogy weighs in at 464 pages for the first volume, 574 for the second, and 512 for the third. You may point out to an RR who's read all three tomes that he or she has 1,550 pages to his reading credit. You can add up the Harry Potter saga if you want to be really impressive: 3,650 so far. And as one reader wrote on Amazon.com: "If book 7 is the last book (and I believe it will be), I hope it is 5,000 pages."

4.7 WHY DON'T TEENS—NOT JUST RELUCTANT READERS—READ THE CLASSICS?

> "I think a good book for reluctant readers need to be fast-paced. Keep it moving. Not a lot of long descriptive passages, or philosophical musings. Excitement! Also, a main character they can relate to."
>
> William Sleator

1. The main characters are not teenagers.
2. The events, problems, and plots are not related to today's teens.
3. The classics have complicated plotlines.
4. The point of view is not from an adolescent's perspective.
5. The dialogue does not reflect teenage speech.
6. The language exceeds the level of understanding of most teenagers.
7. The pace is too slow, and they are too long.
8. Teenagers have experienced outmoded and uninspiring methods of teaching this literature.
9. The format—that is, cover, type style and size, white space—is unappealing to teens.
10. Teenagers generally have no choice in deciding to read a classic, instead, it is assigned.

4.8 WHAT CLASSIC TITLES ARE ACCESSIBLE TO EVEN THE MOST RELUCTANT OF READERS?

If we define "classic" a little more broadly than the usual catalogue books by DEWM—that is, dead European white men (and a few notable dead American white men, as well)—there are many literary works that reluctant readers can discover with joy. Oprah caught on to this and helped turn a nation back into readers, and we can do the same with reluctant teens. Here are some titles that have been road-tested with adolescents resistant to books and found not wanting, but wanted.

Flowers for Algernon, by Daniel Keyes. The story of Charlie Gordon—a man with an IQ of 68, who undergoes experimental neurosurgery and emerges a genius—has never failed with my students. They find it fascinating because of the first-person narrative, which shifts gradually from a poorly spelled, ill-punctuated diary full of simple sentences and simpler thoughts to a beautifully written reflection on philosophy, love, science, loss, and the absolute unfairness of it all, as the results of the operation begin to reverse themselves. As Charlie's brain diminishes, he works frantically to find the flaw in the science that gave him intelligence only temporarily, and the suspense of his search heightens the reluctant reader's determination to read to the end. Teens feel Charlie's losses: his mind, his burgeoning love affair with Alice Kinnian, his new life as a "normal" person, and—perhaps worst of all—his old life and friends. When Charlie's IQ plummets, he is the clichéd man without a country. He has no life to stay in and no life to go back to. His displacement, combined with his extraordinarily sweet nature and hope in spite of it all, evokes in reluctant readers anger, sadness, and a desire to discuss the complexity of what they have read.

I Know Why the Caged Bird Sings, by Maya Angelou. The book the *New York Times* called "simultaneously touching and comic" has lost none of its power in the thirty-six years since its original publication. Part autobiography, part memoir, part bildungsroman, Angelou's stories of growing up with her younger brother Bailey in Stamps, Arkansas, in the segregated 1930s compels reluctant readers of any race. Angelou has mastered the style of writing history as if it were fiction, and one of the happiest aspects of her technique is that individual chapters may be consumed as short stories. One needn't tackle the whole book at once. As she confronts the reality of racism for the first time, the horrors of early sexual abuse, and the challenges of growing up in deep poverty during the Depression, Angelou retains her honesty, her strength of spirit, and even her humor. *I Know Why the Caged Bird Sings* has something for everyone, and we've known few reluctant readers who didn't agree.

Welcome to the Monkey House, by Kurt Vonnegut. Perhaps less well known than his celebrated novels, this collection of short stories is ideal for the reluctant reader. First, they are short. Second, several do not carry the science fiction tinge of many of his books (for the sci-fi avoiders among you), but they're still crammed with delightfully odd characters and wonderful irony. Many of the stories are forty or fifty years old, which serves as a catalyst for a little history lesson; "The Hyannis Port Story," for instance, serves up references to John Kennedy, Robert Kennedy, Pierre Salinger (Bobby and Pierre "can't play golf for sour apples"), Nikita Khrushchev, and Barry Goldwater. "More Stately Mansions" will appeal to all teens who have ever wanted to redecorate their rooms and been thwarted in their attempts. "Adam," a very short story of a Holocaust survivor whose wife has just had a baby, is wrenching for a number of reasons. The new father, Heinz Knechtmann (repeatedly addressed as "Mr. Netman" by tired doctors and bored bartenders), has no one to call with the wonderful news; his entire family, and his wife's, are dead. The patrons at the bar where he goes to celebrate are jealous he's had a son; one has seven daughters and the other eight. How can they be joyful with just another girl? they wonder—a concept Heinz fails to appreciate. All the stories in this collection are brimming with irony, history, comedy, and sadness; at least some will appeal to any kind of reluctant reader, who are welcomed into Vonnegut's imagination, as well as his Monkey House.

One Flew over the Cuckoo's Nest, by Ken Kesey. The tale of Randall Mc-Murphy and his war on Nurse Ratched in the psychiatric ward of an Oregon state hospital rightfully brought critics to call Kesey "a great new American novelist," and the decades after its publication have only proven them right. As a metaphor for a sane man trapped in an insane world, the book is hilarious and disturbing at the same time. Reluctant readers will enjoy the revolt against authority, especially as the authority is basically evil, and find great interest in Kesey's broad range of secondary characters. The first chapter can be confusing for the inexperienced reader because it is told from the Chief's point of view, and he's having a psychotic breakdown at the time he's telling it. Just tell your reluctant teens that the narrator is sometimes (but not always) going to sound very odd, and they'll be well forewarned.

Ragtime, by E. L. Doctorow. One of the first novels to combine fiction characters with historical figures, *Ragtime* is almost hypnotic in its originality. Henry Ford, Emma Goldman, J. P. Morgan, Sigmund Freud, Evelyn Nesbit, Emiliano Zapata, Robert Peary, and Stanford White are among the famous names crossing paths with the fictional Coalhouse Walker Jr., perhaps the greatest composer of ragtime music who ever lived. Music, mayhem, architecture, baseball, murder, and anarchy all have their time and place in this wonderful story, which lays itself out in a linear narrative for those reluctant readers who hate, as one of my students once put it, "jumping back and forth and up and down till you don't know where you are in the book."

Jane Eyre, by Charlotte Bronte. Despite its great length and occasional lapses into French, Charlotte Bronte's masterpiece has often been a huge hit with my reluctant readers, particularly girls. Young women who find technically simpler books a challenge somehow latch on to Jane's Cinderella life right from her days as an abused ward in Gateshead, to her years as an tortured student in the Lowood School, to her life-shattering romance with Edward Rochester in Thornfield. The mystery, the Gothic overtones, the changes in Jane as she overcomes her hatred for those who once made her wretched, and her role as

Rochester's salvation appeal mightily to many a reluctant reader from ninth grade up.

Pride and Prejudice, by Jane Austen. You'd be surprised how many reluctant readers (mostly girls) leap into the story of Lizzy Bennet and Fitzwilliam Darcy when they won't go near less-complex novels. Lizzy, her sisters and parents, and the "neighbors" with whom they become involved are such vivid characters that teen readers forget they're in another country two centuries ago and plow right into the plots of the Money-Grubbing Mother, the Ridiculous Sister, and the Proud Suitor, never quite realizing that Austen's plots aren't really plots at all but more like set pieces in which to allow her characters to enjoy and regret the great range of human folly.

Ordinary People, by Judith Guest. Because the central character in this novel is a teenage boy, teens tend to love this story, even if they cannot identify with upper-middle-class tragedy unfolding in the Chicago suburbs. Conrad Jarret's return from a psychiatric hospital following the accidental death of his older brother and his subsequent struggle with school, friends, girls, a loveless mother, and his own horrible repressed memories are the stuff of teen angst, and they get it from the first paragraph. If your reluctant reader has heard the rumor that *Ordinary People* has actually been (shudder) required reading in some curricula, hasten to assure them that it's still a cool read.

The Lottery and Other Stories, by Shirley Jackson. Before there was Stephen King and Dean Koontz, there was Shirley Jackson. A master of horror without the clichés and gore of many modern blood-spattering writers, Jackson's work became "classic" almost as soon as it was published. Long included in high school English texts before a wave of censorship rendered it "evil," the title story still packs a serious punch, and many reluctant readers have come to me with the same question: "Does the last line mean what I think it does?" Hand them "The Lottery" and, voila! you are met with a reluctant reader eager to talk about his reading. The other stories in the collection offer the same subtle horror, as much psychological as physical. They haven't lost their power in the fifty-six years they've been in print.

Shane, by Jack Schafer. In a sparse, terse style, this short novel explores the relationship between the Starrett family and an enigmatic stranger named Shane in the American West of 1889. The Starrett's young son, Bob, narrates a story of nobility, mystery, violence, sacrifice, fate, and the manner in which one's past can continue to haunt despite all efforts to escape it. Bob's innocent point of view, particularly in recounting the unrealized love affair between his mother, Marion, and Shane, creates dramatic irony, with the reader understanding more than the child. While this book's interest is certainly not limited to boys, they may appreciate the fact that most of the action is conducted by males.

The Custom of the Country, by Edith Wharton. Okay, it's long, but it's a Gilded Age soap opera, with the bad girl winning all the boys and leaving a trail of shattered lives in her wake. Undine Spragg is the mother of all barracudas we so love to hate in tales of domestic war, and while the novel reveals her as a monster of selfishness and dishonor, is it fun to read? Totally!

Other winners in the Reluctant Reader Classics Countdown: Short stories by O. Henry, Guy de Maupassant, Roald Dahl, Eudora Welty, Flannery O'Connor, Raymond Carver, Ernest Hemingway, F. Scott Fitzgerald, and William Faulkner; *In Cold Blood,* by Truman Capote; *The Handmaid's Tale,* by Margaret Atwood; *Lincoln,* by Gore Vidal; *The Bluest Eye,* by Toni Morrison; *Steppenwolf,* by Herman Hesse; *On the Road,* by Jack Kerouac; *The Fountainhead,* by Ayn Rand (just tell them to skip Roark's courtroom speech after the first two pages); and *The Catcher in the Rye,* by J. D. Salinger—even after nearly sixty years, reluctant readers can still identify with Holden Caulfield, who hates school, phonies, and sometimes himself.

4.9 WHAT'S THE PULL OF HARRY POTTER? DID ROWLING REALLY HOOK NONREADERS, AND IF SO, HOW?

In a documentary about the events of 9–11, a five-year-old boy looked directly into the camera and said, "The bad men learned to fly airplanes in America. Why would they kill Americans if they learned to fly from Americans?" We live in a dangerous world, and the danger is all the more frightening because it is so often hard to understand. In her Harry Potter series, J. K. Rowling creates a world as full of danger as any and gives the answer to the unanswerable: Why do people do evil things? Because they are evil. And how do the good defeat them? With magic. The appeal of Harry Potter to children, adults, and reluctant readers of all ages is escape. Here's a world in which a spell and a magic wand can flout the enemy, while our hero struggles with homework, a puerile aunt and uncle, the confusions of first love, the joys of friendship, and the thrill of competitive sports. Readers who come from nonnuclear families can identify with Harry's longing for a real family and his touching relationship with Dumbledore, the headmaster at Hogwarts School. Teens struggling to find their "place" in life can identify with a boy who has great talents but is not always sure what to do with them. Everyone knows someone like Hermione, the over-achieving student; Ron, the sweet-natured best friend beleaguered by his parents' limited resources; Malfoy, the school bully; and Snape, the teacher we all had and hated at one time or another. For mystery lovers, there is mystery. For romance mavens, there is the promise of Harry and Ginny, Ron and Hermione. Would you like monsters? Hagrid keeps any number of them, all interesting and all creepy. Government corruption your cup of tea? Check. How about the internecine politics of running a school? You've got it. And who among us has never wished we could at some time and place become invisible? There's Harry with his invisibility cloak enabling him to eavesdrop at the drop of a—well, cloak. English teachers love the novel of development, in which the protagonist learns the life lessons necessary for becoming a mature human being. Those lessons are rampant in every one of Rowling's six novels and, we presume, will be forthcoming in the seventh. Rowling's imagination is apparently limitless, whether describing magic animals, wizards with all-too-human foibles, gallantry, grieving, or triumphs. While the plots are linear (so dear to the reluctant reader's heart), there are frequent flashbacks and sometimes flashforwards—after all, there's magic at work here. The point is that Rowling entrusts her readers to follow her wherever she goes, and they do. We've talked to Harry Potter devotees from nine to sixty, and they can all quote chapter and verse from any of the books at any time. It is astonishing the level of detail reluctant readers can embrace when the stories are as well constructed, coherent, and creative as these are. Rowling once said she was riding on a train when in her mind she saw Harry Potter complete: the boy, his name, his appearance, his spirit, everything. Rather like Athena springing from the head of Zeus, the character of Harry came full-blown from the head of J. K. Rowling. She renders him that clearly to her readers, and that's the irresistible draw of him: his adventures will never invoke the dreaded words "I don't get it" but invariably create that wonderful question, "Have you read it yet? I'm dying to talk about it with you." You may recall a phenomenon of the nineteenth century, when New Yorkers lined the docks waiting for ships to bring the latest installment of Dickens's *The Old Curiosity Shop,* calling out frantically, "Is Little Nell still alive?" (Consider that Dickens and Rowling share a genius for tag names: Kit Nubbles, Dick Swiveller, and Quilp, compared to Dudley Dursley, Lord Voldemort, Professor Snape, and Dumbledore.) There are parallels between those anxious readers and the lines at bookshops around the world when Rowling's latest installment finally arrives. Perhaps she has returned us to a time when reading was not just a pleasure but an adventure, a social enterprise, and a glorious escape from our own troubling world.

4.10 HOW DO WE MOTIVATE RELUCTANT READERS UP THE LADDER FROM EASY READING TO MORE CHALLENGING MATERIAL?

The way to move up any ladder is one step at a time. What do we do with RRs who fall in love with R. L. Stine and want to read everything he's written? Let them, for heaven's sake! Like life, however, reading is often a series of transactions, of bargains, of "trading up." If your R. L. Stine lover has ploughed through six or eight of the Stine oeuvre, then you might suggest Stephen King for the next rung on the reading ladder. Some of his work is excellent and thought provoking. *The Stand,* for example, while long, is character driven, and the scenes are short and change often. King's motif in the novel is that of William Butler Yeats's "The Second Coming." That's a good third step. Once the RR has consumed *The Stand,* he will already understand the context of the poem, and Yeats's short masterpiece is a wonderful vehicle for discussion of allusion. (This is not theory; it's been road-tested in an RR classroom.) It's not too far a leap, if the RR is really getting into making deals with the devil, to move on to books still more challenging. *The Turn of the Screw* is an example, but you must lead your RR through this one chapter at a time, with constant conversation and references to the books she's already read. Literature does not exist in a vacuum, and once RRs understand the concept, they start lighting up with the excitement that comes with making connections.

Stine's appeal is understandable. He's spooky, and spooky is always fascinating. One of the most widely read books of the last four years is *The DaVinci Code,* which combines the puzzle with the spooky with the mysteries of ancient history. Its prose is not particularly brilliant, but the story moves like a freight train, and millions of readers who take pride in their collections of Charles Dickens or William Faulkner have kept the book on the best-seller list to this day. If sophisticated readers want to take a mental vacation with Dan Brown, why not let your RRs take a shot at him? If they don't like the book, move on to another. One caveat about moving up the reading ladder: sometimes those rungs are slippery. Rather than let your patron or student fall when your suggestion doesn't work, catch them with another idea. They will get to the top of their abilities sooner or later. Really, they will.

Perhaps the best advice in this area comes from author Neil Gaiman, who encourages everyone (on his ALA poster) to "Read. Read everything. Read the things they say are good for you, and the things they claim are junk. You'll find out what you need to find. Just Read."

VOICES FROM THE FIELD

"It is easy to bring in the big readers—they are here at the library already. I did a training at a library that said they only served honor students in their community, as that was all that came in to the library. I was sad for them, because my job has been so enriched by working with reluctant readers. The book circulation has definitely risen as we cater to more specific teen interests, but I also see the community and my work from so many facets now."

—Amy Alessio

"Many school librarians engage students in the selection of books for the Media Center; however, most use the AP English students. The ones who already like to read, know the books are a 'oh, so pleasant to work with.' I worked with the school social worker and decided to take his anger management group to a local bookstore to select books for us. None had ever been to a bookstore and most admitted they didn't care for reading. When we got to the bookstore, they were given a brief intro to books the staff thought they might like, then they spent a good hour searching for books and computing how they could best spend the funds allotted to them! The student we were warned to watch because it was certain he would cause a problem found *The Coldest Winter Ever,* which he had never read, sat in a chair, and read the entire time we were at the bookstore. Most of these students had never been in the school Media Center; however, after this afternoon selecting and having lunch together, we began a very positive relationships based on books! If you use students who don't like to read to pick the books, they'll pick books other reluctant readers will pick up!"

—Edith Campbell

"99% of the youth I work with in the correctional facility are nonreaders. Many become readers when they are here and are incarcerated. However, being locked in a cell with nothing to do often isn't enough to encourage them to read. They need encouragement, inspiration, and attention along with books that are new. Of all the genres, I find that addressing a youth's ethnic/racial background, horror and books such as the Bluford series to be of most help."

—Amy Cheney

"Some kids have been so beaten down by English teachers and school that they simply rebel against anything school pushes. That cycle of poverty in socioeconomics applies in a way to education.

Kids who are impoverished readers and/or learners are trapped in a downward spiral that sucks them away from reading. Lack of family support is a factor. Lack of model readers is a factor. Lack of access to books and reading materials is a factor. Lack of reading skills and school skills are factors. Learning disabilities are factors. Misplaced gender identification (i.e., a boy who desperately wants to be macho and who believes that real men don't read books) is a factor. Kids trapped in this alliterate/illiterate cycle has as good a chance of escaping it as a second generation, chronic welfare recipient does. I also think that some kids (my son was one) have never learned that there are different ways to read. Despite my efforts to convince him that aesthetic approaches to reading are OK, my son read EVERYTHING efferently, thus he read his AP physics textbook in exactly the same way he read *Les Miserables*. He'd never had a teacher who taught him that we read some books or texts simply for pleasure."

—Chris Crowe

"One of the most counterproductive things we do is pushing the same type of books on them that they have already decided they don't like probably won't work. If they have been forced to read a lot of award-winning fiction, for example, suggesting a book that just won an award probably won't go over well, even if it's a great book."

—Miranda Doyle

"I think a reluctant reader just has not found the right book to appeal to him or her. Careful reader's advisory and evaluation of the teens reading skills will put the right book in the right hands at the right time."

—Beth Gallaway

"What doesn't work is saying 'I *loved* this book!' to a teen one has never seen before is not going to persuade him or her to read the book. Whether I am 28 or 52—I am still an adult to that teen and just because I *loved* a book doesn't mean it's a good book or the right book for that particular teen. I think, too often, librarians trying to reach reluctant teens jump in and start making suggestions without asking questions about the teen's interest. Remember that this is not the time to talk about what you like, but ask questions to find out what kind of book the teen might like."

—Michele Gorman

"When faced with teens who say they don't like to read and won't admit to reading anything 'ever', I have found that tossing a copy *of*

365 Birthdays Interpreted or *The Portable Book of Birthdays* into their midst will have them pouncing on a book, reading aloud with friends, discussing. Even the most 'anti-reading' teen will not be able to resist looking up his or her day to see if the book offers insight or is completely—utterly—totally off the mark."

—Mari Hardacre

"In general, I think a lot of less active readers want something they already know: maybe their friends are reading it, or there's a movie, or a collection from a magazine, that sort of thing. I think people like that guarantee that it won't be a waste of time to read it, and an unfamiliar subject/title has more potential to be not fun."

—Jessy Griffith

"Each reluctant reader wants the same thing we all want in a good book: something that meets our needs and/or interests at the moment. Laurie Halse Anderson talks about reluctant readers as being more discriminating readers rather than reluctant. I think there is some truth to that. I will basically read almost anything, especially if stranded somewhere with time on my hands and no books. The same is certainly not true for the reluctant reader."

—Teri Lesesne

"Many reluctant readers have problems affecting their fluency or comprehension. Would you want to spend time with something that is in a language you just don't understand?"

—Nancy Levin

"Attaching massive projects and reading 'requirements' to any kind of reading is punitive and makes reading a chore. Most kids would rather do the dishes! Traditional book reports have got to go. I mean, Oprah's Book Club is such a smashing success because she and the audience discuss, connect, and relate in writing and verbally. I doubt it would have worked if she told audience members that their success in life depended upon a tome-length dissection of the role of symbolism in _____ (fill in the blank)."

—Jenny McBride

"I feel like lots of teenagers have no idea what great reading material is available—fiction, nonfiction, poetry, magazine, graphic novels, etc. If they knew, either they'd be reading or at least they'd have a positive feeling about reading. All too often reading just means dreaded school assignments of some sort. I can live with the idea that some teens don't read for pleasure, sometimes because they're so busy.

I just hate the idea that they would read if only they knew. . . . I find it heartbreaking that so many English teachers choose to—or have—assign only the same things we adults read years ago in school, as if nothing good had been published since. We'd create a lot more teen readers and a lot more lifelong readers if we could get more teachers to use YA books in assignments and suggest them for supplemental reading."

—Kathleen Odean

"A colleague commented once how she hated going shopping for any clothes—there are too many choices, you have to try on everything, no one is around to help you but she sees clothes on people that she likes but she can never find them herself. I told her you just described what an RR feels like in the library. Too many choices, you have to read/know about the book to figure out if you will like it and no one is there to help you (perception, of course!) My favorite store is one in which the person helping me understands what I like and knows a bit about me and listens to what I say about certain clothes, remembers what I liked in the past, doesn't just give me a bunch of stuff, rather picks out what she thinks suits me. That is how I try to help RR's find books. It may take longer but I think the outcome is better all around."

—Patricia Suellentrop

"I believe boys are more reluctant than girls because they lag behind girls in brain development, so when all kids are asked to become in-dependent readers boys are starting off behind. It is harder for them, and difficult for them to see the girls advancing ahead of them, and so there is discouragement, a bit of shame, and a whole lot of frustration. We educators don't always recognize this deficiency, and we measure reading attainment rather than development, so we end up reinforcing boys' uneasiness about their reading abilities. The other big reason—boys lack role models. Very few people involved with reading—children's librarians, child care workers, elementary teachers—are male, and men read very differently then women. You may have noticed, when men read they tend to do so in isolation (alone in their rooms, hidden behind a newspaper, listening to an audiobook in the car), while women tend to read in social groups (book clubs). Hard for boys to find role models there."

—Michael Sullivan

"When I worked at Enoch Pratt, in urban Baltimore, I wasn't at all surprised by the popularity of urban fiction, rap bios, etc. But this is not a 'black thing'. This is the dominant youth culture right now, and it transcends race and economic stature. I've had more kids read *The Wu-Tang Manual,* the above poetry books, the Allen Iverson bio, the Notorious BIG books, the Omarion bio, then all the other reluctant reads put together. Again, I want to stress it is not a BLACK thing it is a YOUTH culture thing. It is also wonderful. I have seen, in my lifetime, race become a much smaller issue among young people, and I attribute it 95% to rap music. All kids love it and it has broken down barriers that nothing else had been able to do."

—Jamie Watson

"In too many classrooms, we've reduced all reading experiences to efferent experiences. If I'm reading *Charlotte's Web* to be able to answer the discussion guide questions, then I'm reading to find those answers, not to experience the laughs and tears that Wilbur experiences. Kids who come to school having been read to a lot prior to first grade generally walk into school with an aesthetic stance firmly in place. They understand that reading is about experiencing. Kids who lack those early reading experiences don't have any stance—efferent or aesthetic. So, they develop the one that school experiences promote—and that's generally an efferent stance."

—Kylene Beers

Part II.   Titles That Work

FOREWORD TO PART II BY MEL GLENN

Perhaps it would not be too sardonic to say that many teens and preteens have the reading attention span of advanced fleas. Besieged by all manner of technological wizardry, our young readers exist in an altered state of sensory overload.

Between the IPod, computer, movies, TV, and a whole array of Game Boys, and who knows, Game Girls, reading is often the last horse in the race for a teenager's leisure attention. ("What? I should read for fun? I've got too much stuff to do.") Would it be fair to say that nearly all teens are reluctant readers, more accustomed to sound and sight bites than to the joys of curling up in the corner with a good book?

How, then, to grab them?

In a story, we have to grab 'em early in terms of character, action, and maybe a little bit of mystery. The opening of my book, *Who Killed Mr. Chippendale?*, starts with the murder of a teacher on page 5. I am not suggesting that all books need to have a killer, but the hook, like for a song, has to be planted early.

I don't want to "write down" to kids, but I think my prose is naturally not very complicated or overly sophisticated reflecting, no doubt, both teen language and my own personal immersion in their world having taught for over thirty years in the New York City public school system.

Teenagers, reluctant or not, live double lives: the happy teenage chatter surrounding an outer shell of coolness, and the emotional pit inside of conflicted feelings of doubts and insecurities. Their emotions, contrary to some public opinion, do not run the gamut from A to A. They feel acute pain and joy, going from elation to despair, and back to pumped up, in the blink of an eye.

Good writing, then, can provide the affirmation of "Hey, I am not alone in an indifferent universe." It is the bright light of words that can illuminate the dark corners of the heart.

And if I can reach that corner, so can countless other YA authors, actors, librarians, teachers, and parents. The word just has to get out, preferably on the wings of mass media, because if it does not, reading for pleasure will place last in the Leisure Time Sweepstakes Derby. With a little creative energy, not to mention the infusion of a little money, reading can move to the front of the pack, thereby cementing its rightful place linking the written word with the endless possibilities of imagination.

This part is divided into five chapters. First is a list of "turnaround" books, with all disclaimers noted. Second is a series of fiction lists, followed by the third part, a series of nonfiction lists. Next is the graphic novel section, which also contains manga. The fifth section is cleverly dubbed "other lists" and contains a variety of "best" lists as well as a list of read-alikes, featuring both fiction and nonfiction. We hope these lists are helpful, but rather than being an end, they should serve as a beginning—a beginning to developing your own lists, putting together book talks, preparing recommendations for teachers, and organizing displays. It's up to you to keep current by using the Young Adult Library Services Association's Quick Picks list and other sources, and—most importantly—by purchasing replacement copies of every book stolen, marked missing, or in high demand. These books have proven appeal and thus are books you should always have on the shelf. What's most important, however, is not knowing which titles work but understanding why these titles work.

A few remarks about using these lists: Most of the titles were in-print as of fall 2005, and all of the ordering information came from *Books in Print* (online edition), but they may not all be available by the time you are reading this. Most, but not all, of these lists are annotated. The annotations are original or taken from the CIP. The grade-level recommendations are suggested interest level, not reading level. As this is not just a straight alphabetical listing of titles but rather short usable lists, we have included an author/title index as part of this book's overall index to provide access.

If you would like any of these lists for use in your library but don't feel like retyping them, just e-mail us at connectingya@yahoo.com; we'll send you up to five lists via e-mail.

> "The difference between 'I love this book!' and 'This is a great book' is a narrow one—and both, of course, can be true—but one shares, while the other seems to impose. Enthusiasm is an accelerant!"
>
> Kathe Koja

Turnaround Titles—Fifty-Seven Varieties of Great Reading Experiences

As part of every interview, we asked, "What one book—fiction, nonfiction, adult, teen, or picture book—do you think could be a 'turnaround' book, which would turn a nonreader into a reader?" Most everyone's reply was similar to that of Kylene Beers, who noted:

> I don't think there is one turnaround book. That reduces a love of reading to a silver bullet—or in this case a magic book. Reluctant readers come to reading reluctantly. For a while they'll be book-at-a-time readers—readers who will read the book we put into their hand but they won't seek out the next good book on their own. Gradually, with support and encouragement, they'll move toward a stance that says, "This reading thing is good—good enough that I'll seek a book out on my own." Maybe that's the turnaround book—the book that the kid on his own finds that he enjoys.

Further, Michele Gorman reminds us that it's not about lists, but listening:

> I don't think there is any one book that can automatically turn a nonreader into a reader. What I do think is possible is that we, as librarians, can help shed the light on reading as an enjoyable way to spend some time if we get to know our young patrons, ask solid questions about a person's likes and dislikes, pay attention to their responses, and then make good recommendations based on the

information we just received versus the latest award winner, what we read and liked last week, or what got a starred review in the professional journal. I also think it's important that we remember that all kids are not like we were—in fact, most are not and most will not become librarians. They may never be big readers, but a positive library experience may keep a reluctant teen reader from becoming an alliterate adult.

They're both totally right, but still . . . people want a list. So with these quotes as disclaimers and knowing its about relationships, not reading lists, we present the following list of turnaround titles. These are not, then, magic-bullet books but books that individual librarians reported individual successes with concerning individual teens. This doesn't mean they will necessarily work for your teens, but these are really good books. You'll find just about all of them included—and annotated—in the lists that follow. The "(M)" notes a title for a more mature or older reader.

1. Anderson, Laurie Halse. *Speak.*
2. Ashanti. *Foolish/Unfoolish.*
3. Banks, Russell. *Rule of the Bone.* **(M)**
4. Brunvand, Jan Harold. *Big Book of Urban Legends.*
5. Burgess, Melvin. *Doing It.* **(M)**
6. Card, Orson Scott. *Ender's Game.*
7. Chbosky, Stephen. *Perks of Being a Wallflower.* **(M)**
8. Cisneros, Sandra. *House on Mango Street.*
9. Curtis, Christopher Paul. *The Watsons Go to Birmingham—1963.*
10. Drooker, Eric. *Blood Song.*
11. Flake, Sharon. *Skin I'm In.*
12. Flake, Sharon. *Who Am I without Him.*
13. Flinn, Alex. *Breathing Underwater.*
14. Foley, Mick. *Have a Nice Day.* **(M)**
15. Gantos, Jack. *Hole in My Life.*
16. Giles, Gail. *Playing in Traffic.*
17. Giles, Gail. *Shattering Glass.*
18. Glenn, Mel. *Class Dismissed.*
19. Going, K. L. *Fat Kid Rules the World.*
20. Groening, Matt. *Simpsons* comics (any).
21. Hinton, S. E. *Outsiders.*
22. Holmes, Shannon. *B-More Careful.* **(M)**
23. Johnson, Angela. *First Part Last.*
24. Keyes, Alice. *Tears for Water.*

25. Korman, Gordon. *Son of the Mob.*
26. Lubar, David. *Hidden Talents.*
27. McCall, Nathan. *Makes Me Wanna Holler.*
28. McDonald, Janet. *Spellbound.*
29. Mowry, Jess. *Way Past Cool.*
30. Myers, Walter Dean. *Monster.*
31. Nixon, Joan Lowery. *Whispers from the Dead.*
32. Paolini, Christopher. *Eragon.*
33. Paulsen, Gary. *Harris and Me.*
34. Paulsen, Gary. *Hatchet.*
35. Pelzer, David. *Child Called It.*
36. Porter, Connie Rose. *Imani All Mine.*
37. Rodriquez, Louis. *Always Running.* **(M)**
38. Rowling, J. K. *Harry Potter* (any).
39. Sachar, Louis. *Holes.*
40. Shakur, Sanyika. *Monster: The Autobiography of an L.A. Gang Member.* **(M)**
41. Shakur, Tupac. *Rose That Grew from Concrete.*
42. Shan, Darren. Cirque Du Freak series.
43. Sleator, William. *Interstellar Pig.*
44. Smith, Jeff. *Bone.*
45. Souljah, Sister. *Coldest Winter Ever.* **(M)**
46. Sparks, Beatrice. *Go Ask Alice.*
47. Stine, R. L. *Dangerous Girls.*
48. Strasser, Todd. *Give a Boy a Gun.*
49. Tillage, Leon Walter. *Leon's Story.*
50. Trueman, Terry. *Stuck in Neutral.*
51. Tyree, Omar. *Flyy Girl.* **(M)**
52. Vibe magazine staff. *Tupac.*
53. Volponi, Paul. *Black and White.*
54. Werlin, Nancy. *Killer's Cousin.*
55. Williams, Stanley "Tookie." *Life in Prison.*
56. Woods, Teri. *Dutch.* **(M)**
57. Woodson, Jacqueline. *Miracle's Boys.*

"In the process of writing, all I'm thinking about is the story. I'm not aware of anything else around me. It's like a spell sort of, where I'm just trying to get into the heads of my characters and understand what their story is trying to say."

Jacqueline Woodson

Fiction

MYSTERY, ACTION, AND SUSPENSE

Alten, Steve. *Meg: A Novel of Deep Terror*. Bantam, 1998. 352p. $6.99 (0-553-57910-X). Grades 9 and up.

On a top-secret dive into the Pacific Ocean's deepest canyon, Jonas Taylor finds himself face-to-face with terror.

Avi. *Wolf Rider: A Tale of Terror*. Simon & Schuster/Pulse, 1993. 202p. $5.99 (0-0204-1513-3). Grades 6 and up.

After receiving an apparent crank call from a man claiming to have committed murder, fifteen-year-old Andy finds his close relationship with his father crumbling as he struggles to make everyone believe him.

Beale, Fleur. *I Am Not Esther*. Hyperion, 2004. 256p. $6.99 (0-7868-1673-2). Grades 7 and up.

After her mother unexpectedly leaves her with her uncle's family—members of a fanatical Christian cult—Kirby tries to learn what has become of her mother and struggles to cope with the repressiveness of her new surroundings and to maintain her own identity.

Bloor, Edward. *Tangerine*. Scholastic, 2001. 294p. $5.99 (0-4392-8603-4). Grades 6 and up.

Twelve-year-old Paul, who lives in the shadow of his football-hero brother Erik, fights for the right to play soccer despite his near blindness and slowly begins to remember the incident that damaged his eyesight.

Cooney, Caroline. *The Face on the Milk Carton*. Laurel Leaf, 1994 reprint. 220p. $6.99 (0-440-22065-3). Grades 6 and up.

Recognizing herself as the missing child on a school milk carton, Janie is compelled to investigate and has to choose between her love for the people she has always known as her parents and needing to learn the truth.

Cooney, Caroline. *The Voice on the Radio.* Laurel Leaf, 1998. 220p. $5.99 (0-440-21977-9). Grades 6 and up.

Fifteen-year-old Janie feels devastated when she discovers that her boyfriend has betrayed her and her family through his college radio program.

Cooney, Caroline. *What Janie Found.* Laurel Leaf, 2000. 235p. $5.99 (0-440-22772-0). Grades 6 and up.

When Janie's father suffers a severe stroke, her happily established life is suddenly shaken as she must now help her mother through this difficult time—both emotionally and financially.

Cooney, Caroline. *Whatever Happened to Janie.* Laurel Leaf, 1994 reprint. 224p. $5.99 (0-440-21924-8). Grades 6 and up.

Suffering an identity crisis after reuniting with her biological family, Janie realizes that the past twelve years cannot be brought back, and is torn between the Spring family's desire for justice and her love for the Johnsons.

Duncan, Lois. *Daughters of Eve.* Laurel Leaf, 1990 reprint. 266p. $5.50 (0-44-091864-2). Grades 7 and up.

As the club sponsor for the Daughters of Eve at Modesta High, Irene Stark, a popular and dedicated teacher, uses feminist philosophy to manipulate the girls' lives in a bizarre plan to avenge past injustices.

Duncan, Lois. *Don't Look Behind You.* Laurel Leaf, 1990 reprint. 179p. $5.50 (0-44-020729-0). Grades 7 and up.

April's father's job as an undercover FBI agent forces the family to move far from home and assume new identities as part of the Federal Witness Security Program, and April must leave everything that she loves.

Duncan, Lois. *Down a Dark Hall.* Laurel Leaf, 1997 reprint. 150p. $5.99 (0-44-091805-7). Grades 7 and up.

Kit Gordy and three other students at an exclusive boarding school for girls find themselves part of a terrifying experiment.

Duncan, Lois. *I Know What You Did Last Summer.* Laurel Leaf, 1999 reprint. 250p. $5.99 (0-44-022844-1). Grades 7 and up.

Four teenagers try to conceal their responsibility for a hit-and-run accident while being pursued by a mystery figure seeking revenge.

Duncan, Lois. *Killing Mr. Griffin.* Laurel Leaf, 1993 reprint. 165p. $5.99 (0-44-094515-1). Grades 7 and up.

A joke about killing the toughest teacher in school, the one who demands the most and gives the lowest grades, becomes a topic of serious discussion among the boys at the local hangout.

Duncan, Lois. *Ransom*. Laurel Leaf, 1993 reprint. 144p. $5.99 (0-44-097292-2). Grades 7 and up.

Five teenagers are kidnapped from their school bus and held for ransom by two men who have already killed old Mr. Godfrey, their regular bus driver.

Duncan, Lois. *They Never Came Home*. Laurel Leaf, 1992 reprint. 183p. $5.99 (0-44-020780-0). Grades 7 and up.

When two youths fail to return home from a weekend camping trip, a nightmare of terror begins for their families.

Duncan, Lois. *The Twisted Window*. Laurel Leaf, 1991 reprint. 216p. $5.50 (0-44-020184-5). Grades 7 and up.

Tracy, a high school junior, becomes embroiled in the problems of a strange boy, who asks her assistance in "snatching" his half-sister from her father, who has allegedly kidnapped her.

Forsyth, Christine. *Adrenaline High*. James Lorimer, 2003. 126p. $4.99 (1-55028-792-3). Grades 7 and up.

Real-life issues, including drug dealing and domestic violence, combine in a mystery as sixteen-year-old D'Arcey Dufresne and her loyal companions team up to help a classmate in need.

Giles, Gail. *Dead Girls Don't Write Letters*. Simon Pulse, 2004. 128p. $6.99 (0-689-86624-0). Grades 7 and up.

Things had been getting a little better until Sunny got a letter from her dead sister. That more or less ruined her day.

Haddix, Margaret Peterson. *Running Out of Time*. Aladdin, 1997. 192p. $4.99 (0-689-81236-1). Grades 6 and up.

Living on a historical site where the time is the 1840s, Jessie escapes into the present. This book now has a renewed interest since the release of the movie *The Village*, which bears some striking similarities.

Hartinger, Brent. *Last Chance Texaco*. HarperCollins, 2004. 240p. $15.99 (0-06-050912-0). Grades 9 and up.

Troubled teen Lucy Pitt struggles to fit in as a new tenant at a last-chance foster home.

"I believe that good writing is clear writing. There should never be a moment when the reader has to stop and say, 'Okay, what just happened?' or reread the paragraph."

Brent Hartinger

Horowitz, Anthony. Alex Rider series. Puffin, 2003–2005. Grades 6 and up.

Working as a secret agent for Britain's most exclusive agency, Alex Rider battles international terrorists, rebellious teenagers, and arch-villains—all with appropriately cool spy gadgets.

> *Stormbreaker.* 234p. $5.99 (0-14-240165-X).
> *Point Blank.* 304p. $5.99 (0-14-240164-1).
> *Skeleton Key.* 288p. $5.99 (0-14-240102-1).
> *Eagle Strike.* 352p. $5.99 (0-14-240292-3).
> *Scorpia.* 312p. $17.99 (0-3992-4151-5).

Lawrence, Iain. *The Wreckers.* Random House, 1999. 224p. $5.50 (0-440-41545-4). Grades 6 and up.

John Spencer narrowly escapes with his life after the ship on which he is traveling with his father, the owner, is wrecked off the Cornish coast, lured to its destruction by a gang seeking to plunder its cargo.

Madison, Bennett. *Lulu Dark Can See through Walls.* Penguin/Razorbill, 2005. 248p. $9.99 (1-5951-4010-7). Grades 7 and up.

When someone steals her purse and her identity, high-school junior and reluctant girl sleuth Lulu Dark investigates.

McNamee, Graham. *Acceleration.* Random House, 2003. 224p. $15.95 (0-385-73119-1). Grades 8 and up.

"It's like the Hardy boys meet Hannibal Lecter."

Naylor, Phyllis Reynolds. *Sang Spell.* Simon & Schuster/Simon Pulse, 2000. 212p. $4.99 (0-689-82006-2). Grades 6 and up.

When his mother is killed in an automobile accident, high-schooler Josh decides to hitchhike across the country, and finds himself trapped in a mysterious village somewhere in the Appalachian Mountains among a group of people who call themselves Melungeons.

Nixon, Joan Lowery. *The Kidnapping of Christina Lattimore.* Harcourt, 2004. 185p. $5.95 (0-15-205031-0). Grades 6 and up.

A teenage girl is kidnapped but, when freed, is accused of masterminding the scheme to extort money from her wealthy grandmother.

Peretti, Frank. *Nightmare Academy* (Veritas Project, No. 2). Tommy Nelson, 2003. 320p. $8.99 (1-4003-0340-0). Grades 6 and up.

A frightening thrill ride that takes a realistic look at right and wrong, as Elijah and Elisha seek to find the truth behind the mysterious disappearance of two runaways. From one of the best-selling Christian novelists in the United States.

Plum-Ucci, Carol. *The Body of Christopher Creed*. Hyperion, 2001. 331p. $6.99 (0-786-81641-4). Grades 8 and up.

When the town freak leaves after years of being bullied, Torey Adams delves into the mystery and uncovers truths that may be simply too hard for him to handle.

Qualey, Marsha. *Close to a Killer*. Delacorte, 2000. 208p. $5.95 (0-440-22763-1). Grades 7 and up.

Two prominent city residents have been murdered, and Barrie knew both of them. But does she know their killer?

Qualey, Marsha. *Thin Ice*. Random House, 1999. 242p. $4.99 (0-440-22037-8). Grades 7 and up.

Arden refuses to believe that her older brother died in a snowmobile accident.

Roberts, Willo Davis. *Twisted Summer*. Simon Pulse, 1998. 189p. $4.99 (0-689-80600-0). Grades 7 and up.

Cici is devastated when she learns that her friend Brody is being considered the prime suspect in the murder of a young girl in town and begins her own search to find the real murderer, an investigation that puts her in danger.

Sachar, Louis. *Holes*. Random House, 2003. 233p. $6.50 (0-440-41946-8). Grades 6 and up.

Stanley Yelnats is under a curse—a curse that began with his no-good-dirty-rotten-pig-stealing-great-great-grandfather and has since followed generations of Yelnats.

Springer, Nancy. *Blood Trail*. Holiday House, 2003. 112p. $16.95 (0-8234-1723-9). Grades 6 and up.

After his best friend is murdered, seventeen-year-old Booger realizes he is the only one who has any idea who may have committed the crime—but he doesn't dare tell anyone.

Tanzman, Carol. *Shadow Place*. Roaring Brook Press, 2004. 192p. $15.95 (0-7613-1588-8). Grades 6 and up.

Fourteen-year-old Lissa, sworn to secrecy but worried about her lifelong friend's weird behavior and increasing hostility toward his abusive father, learns in a chat room that he intends to buy a gun.

Werlin, Nancy. *The Killer's Cousin*. Dell, 2000. 240p. $5.99 (0-440-22751-8). Grades 8 and up.

Acquitted of murder, David tries to start a new life in Boston.

Westerfeld, Scott. *So Yesterday*. Penguin/Razorbill, 2004. 225p. $16.99 (1-59514-000-X). Grades 7 and up.

Trend spotter and fashion expert Hunter Braque must use all of his cool hunting talents to find a big-money client who has mysteriously disappeared.

Zindel, Paul. *Night of the Bat.* Hyperion, 2003. 144p. $5.99 (0-7868-1226-5). Grades 6 and up.

Teenage Jake joins his father on an expedition to study bats in the Brazilian rain forest and finds the project menaced by a giant brain-eating bat.

Zindel, Paul. *Rats.* Hyperion, 2000. 176p. $4.99 (0-7868-1225-7). Grades 6 and up.

Thriller about rats who escape from a dump on New York City's Staten Island and the courageous teenager who stops the rodents from taking over the city.

Zindel, Paul. *Reef of Death.* 1998. Hyperion, 2002. 177p. $5.99 (0-7868-1309-1). Grades 6 and up.

P. C. McPhee hops a plane to Australia to help his uncle solve an offshore mystery involving something huge and fierce and hungry in the water.

SCIENCE FICTION AND FANTASY

Colfer, Eoin. *Artemis Fowl.* Miramax, 2002. 304p. $7.99 (0-7868-1707-0). Grades 7 and up.

When a twelve-year-old evil genius tries to restore his family fortune by capturing a fairy and demanding a ransom in gold, the fairies fight back with magic, technology, and a particularly nasty troll.

Shusterman, Neal. *Downsiders.* Simon & Schuster, 2001. 256p. $4.99 (0-689-83969-3). Grades 7 and up.

Talon lives Downside, underneath New York City.

Sleator, William. *House of Stairs.* Puffin, 1991. 176p. $5.99 (0-1403-4580-9). Grades 6 and up.

Five sixteen-year-old orphans of widely varying personalities are placed in a house of endless stairs as subjects for a psychological experiment on conditioned human response.

Westerfeld, Scott. *The Uglies.* Simon & Schuster/Simon Pulse, 2005. 448p. $6.99 (0-6898-6538-4). Grades 7 and up.

In a future where people are divided up into "uglies" and "pretties," Tally Youngblood must decide if she should run away with her new friend. The sequel *Pretties* was released in November 2005.

Weyn, Suzanne. *The Bar Code Tattoo.* Scholastic, 2004. 252p. $5.99 (0-439-39562-3). Grades 7 and up.

When you turn seventeen, you get a bar code tattoo. It's a rite of passage. It's the be-all and end-all of identity. Everybody does it, but what if you say no? What if you don't want to become just a code?

White, Andrea. *Surviving Antarctica: Reality TV 2083*. HarperCollins, 2005. 356p. $15.99 (0-06-055454-1). Grades 7 and up.

In the year 2083, five fourteen-year-olds who were deprived by chance of the opportunity to continue their educations reenact Scott's 1910–1913 expedition to the South Pole as contestants on a reality television show, secretly aided by a Department of Entertainment employee.

SUPERNATURAL

Anderson, M. T. *Thirsty*. Candlewick, 2003. 256p. $6.99 (0-7636-2014-9). Grades 7 and up.

Chris has tried water, milk, and juice, but only blood will quench his thirst.

Atwater-Rhodes, Amelia. *In the Forests of the Night*. Laurel Leaf, 2000. 147p. $5.50 (0-440-22816-6). Grades 8 and up.

First of multiple titles about supernatural topics, written by a teenager. Other titles include *Demon in My View, Shattered Mirror, Midnight Predator, Hawksong,* and *Snakecharm.*

Duncan, Lois. *A Gift of Magic*. Laurel Leaf, 1999 reprint. 230p. $5.50 (0-44-022847-6). Grades 7 and up.

A young girl gifted with remarkable powers of extrasensory perception struggles to come to terms with her unusual ability.

Duncan, Lois. *Locked in Time*. Laurel Leaf, 1986. 168p. $5.99 (0-44-094942-4). Grades 7 and up.

When Nore Robbins visits her new stepmother, brother, and sister in Louisiana, she is unnerved by the feeling of evil and eerie threats that pervades the plantation.

Duncan, Lois. *Stranger with My Face*. Laurel Leaf, 1990 reprint. 235p. $5.50 (0-44-098356-8). Grades 7 and up.

Laurie thinks she is being spied on and is then dropped by several friends as a result of things they say she was seen doing but which she does not recall.

Duncan, Lois. *Summer of Fear*. Laurel Leaf, 1992 reprint. 219p. $5.99 (0-44-098324-X). Grades 7 and up.

Soon after the arrival of her cousin Julia, insidious occurrences begin that convince Rachel that Julia is a witch who must be stopped before her monstrous plan can be effected.

Duncan, Lois. *The Third Eye*. Laurel Leaf, 1991 reprint. 220p. $5.50 (0-44-098720-2). Grades 7 and up.

Karen struggles to find the courage to use her psychic gifts to help people, especially when she realizes that the lives of twelve people depend on her help.

Kindl, Patricia. *Owl in Love*. Houghton Mifflin, 2004. 208p. $6.99 (0-618-43910-2). Grades 7 and up.

Part bird of prey, part teenage girl in love, and now part stalker, Owl Tycho's life is complicated.

Klause, Annette Curtis. *Blood and Chocolate*. Dell, 1999. 288p. $5.99 (0-440-22668-6). Grades 10 and up.

Vivian Gandillon relishes the change—the sweet, fierce ache—that carries her from girl to wolf.

Klause, Annette Curtis. *The Silver Kiss*. Laurel Leaf, 1992. 224p. $5.50 (0-440-21346-0). Grades 8 and up.

A teenage girl, beset with personal problems, meets a silver-haired boy who is a vampire.

Naylor, Phyllis Reynolds. *Jade Green: A Ghost Story*. Simon Pulse, 2001. 176p. $4.99 (0-689-82002-X). Grades 7 and up.

While living with her uncle in a house haunted by the ghost of a young woman, recently orphaned Judith Sparrow wonders if her one small transgression causes mysterious happenings.

Nixon, Joan Lowery. *A Deadly Game of Magic*. Harcourt, 2004 reprint. 228p. $5.95 (0-15-205030-2). Grades 7 and up.

Lisa and three friends are trapped in a strange house in which a magician starts performing terrifying tricks, one of which is murder.

Nixon, Joan Lowery. *The Séance*. Harcourt, 2004 reprint. 210p. $5.95 (0-15-205029-9). Grades 6 and up.

A séance begun as a game when a young girl insists that she can communicate with the dead ends in murder when the lights suddenly go out and one of the participants vanishes.

Shusterman, Neal. *Dread Locks: Dark Fusion, Book One*. Dutton, 2005. 164p. $15.99 (0-525-47554-0). Grades 7 and up.

Accustomed to a carefree existence, fourteen-year-old Parker Baer meets the girl next door and finds his life taking a menacing turn as he begins to absorb some of her terrible powers.

Sleator, William. *The Boy Who Couldn't Die*. Abrams/Amulet, 2004. 174p. $16.95 (0-81094-824-9). Grades 6 and up.

When his best friend dies in a plane crash, sixteen-year-old Ken has a ritual performed that will make him invulnerable, but he soon learns that he had good reason to be suspicious of the woman he paid to lock his soul away.

Stine, R. L. *Dangerous Girls*. Avon, 2004. 320p. $5.99 (0-06-053082-0). Grades 8 and up.

Destiny Weller and her twin sister, Livvy, return from their summer vacation with an overpowering thirst—an inhuman desire to drink blood.

Stine, R. L. *The Taste of Night: Dangerous Girls 2*. HarperCollins, 2004. 240p. $14.99 (0-06-059616-3). Grades 9 and up.

Livvy Weller wants her twin sister, Destiny, to join her on the darker side as a vampire, but Destiny is determined to restore Livvy to her human condition and bring her back home to their family.

"I think it starts with the title, actually. I spend a *lot* of time dreaming up intriguing, irresistible book titles. Then I think you have to give kids a good idea of where the book is going to take them in the first chapter or two."

R. L. Stine

Watson, Jude. *Premonitions*. Scholastic, 2004. 241p. $6.99 (0-439-60995-X). Grades 6 and up.

Haunted by premonitions ever since she was a young child, Grace finds she must rely on her unwanted gift when her best friend suddenly disappears.

HUMOR

Anderson, M. T. Burger. *Wuss*. Candlewick, 2001. 192p. $6.99 (0-763-61567-6). Grades 7 and up.

Hoping to shed his loser image, Anthony plans revenge on a bully, which results in a war between two competing fast-food restaurants—Burger Queen and O'Dermott's.

Bauer, Joan. *Squashed*. Penguin, 2001. 192p. $5.99 (0-698-11917-7). Grades 7 and up.

As sixteen-year-old Ellie pursues her two goals—growing the biggest pumpkin in Iowa and losing twenty pounds—she strengthens her relationship with her father and meets a young man with interests similar to her own.

Clarke, Miranda. *Night of a Thousand Boyfriends: A Date with Destiny Adventure*. Quirk Books, 2003. 144p. $7.95 (1-931686-35-1). Grades 9 and up.

In the style of choose-your-own adventure, the reader is a single woman in New York, looking for a decent date.

Gantos, Jack. *Joey Pigza Swallowed the Key.* HarperTrophy, 2000. 160p. $5.99 (0-06-440833-7). Grades 6 and up.

To the constant disappointment of mother and teachers, Joey has trouble paying attention and controlling his mood swings when his prescription medications wear off and he starts getting worked up and acting wired.

Howe, Norma. *The Adventures of Blue Avenger.* HarperCollins, 2000. 240p. $6.99 (0-06-447225-6). Grades 8 and up.

On his sixteenth birthday, David Schumacher decides to change his name to Blue Avenger, hoping to find a way to make a difference in his Oakland neighborhood and in the world.

Korman, Gordon. *No More Dead Dogs.* Hyperion, 2002. 192p. $5.99 (0-7868-1601-5). Grades 6 and up.

Eighth-grade football hero Wallace gets detention and is sentenced to attend rehearsals of the school play, where, in spite of himself, he becomes wrapped up in the production.

Korman, Gordon. *Son of the Mob.* Hyperion, 2004. 272p. $5.99 (0-7868-1593-0). Grades 7 and up.

There is just one thing that really sets Vince Luca apart from other kids—his father happens to be the head of a powerful crime organization.

Lynch, Chris. *Slot Machine.* HarperTrophy, 1996. 256p. $5.95 (0-06-447140-3). Grades 7 and up.

For Elvin Bishop—fourteen, overweight, and a self-proclaimed nonathlete—a summer sports "retreat" is more like the twenty-one trials of hell.

Paulsen, Gary. *Harris and Me: A Summer Remembered.* Dell, 1995. 160p. $5.50 (0-440-40994-2). Grades 6 and up.

A humorous story in which the narrator often gets the blame for mischief caused by troublemaker Harris.

Paulsen, Gary. *How Angel Peterson Got His Name: And Other Outrageous Tales about Extreme Sports.* Random House, 2004. 128p. $5.50 (0-440-22935-9). Grades 6 and up.

When you grow up in a small town in the north woods, you have to make your own excitement; these are true stories from Gary Paulsen's childhood in Minnesota.

Peck, Richard. *A Long Way from Chicago.* Puffin, 1998. 148p. $5.99 (1-424-0110-2). Grades 6 and up.

A boy recounts his annual summer trips to rural Illinois with his sister during the Great Depression to visit their larger-than-life grandmother.

Rees, Douglas. *Vampire High*. Delacorte, 2003. 240p. $15.95 (0-385-73117-5). Grades 7 and up.

When his family moves from California to New Sodom, Massachusetts, and Cody enters Vlad Dracul Magnet School, many things seem strange.

Sachar, Louis. *Sideways Stories from Wayside School*. Avon, 1993. 124p. $5.99 (0-380-69871-4). Grades 6 and up.

Thirty different stories describe the strange things that happen at Wayside School, an architectural accident that was built sideways, thirty stories high, with one classroom on each floor. Great as a read-aloud.

Scieszka, Jon. *True Story of the Three Little Pigs by A. Wolf*. Puffin, 1996. Unpaged. $6.99 (0-14-054451-8). Grades 6 and up.

When Alexander Wolf is framed, he seeks justice and tells his own version of "The Three Little Pigs."

> "Humor goes a long way in making a book accessible. But on top of all that, it has to be a good piece of fiction, too."
>
> Lauren Myracle

SPORTS

Deuker, Carl. *High Heat*. HarperCollins/Trophy, 2005 reprint. 250p. $5.99 (0-06-057248-5). Grades 7 and up.

When sophomore Shane Hunter's father is arrested for money laundering at his Lexus dealership, the star pitcher's life of affluence and private school begins to fall apart.

Deuker, Carl. *Night Hoops*. HarperCollins/Trophy, 2001. 250p. $5.99 (0-06-447275-2). Grades 7 and up.

While trying to prove that he is good enough to be on his high school's varsity basketball team, Nick must also deal with his parents' divorce and the erratic behavior of a troubled classmate who lives across the street.

JOURNALS AND LETTERS

Avi. *Nothing but the Truth: A Documentary Novel*. Scholastic, 2004. 192p. $9.95 (0-439-32730-X). Grades 6 and up.

A ninth grader's suspension for singing "The Star-Spangled Banner" during homeroom becomes a national news story.

Bauer, Cat. *Harley Like a Person.* Winslow Press, 2000. 248p. $5.95 (1-58837-005-4). Grades 9 and up.

Fourteen-year-old Harley, an artistic teenager living with her alcoholic father and angry mother, suspects that she is adopted and begins a search for her biological parents.

Cabot, Meg. *Boy Meets Girl.* HarperCollins/Avon, 2004. 400p. $13.95 (0-06-008545-2). Grades 10 and up.

Twentysomething Kate Mackenzie, who works and lives in New York City, hates her boss and has just broken up with her longtime boyfriend because he can't commit.

Cabot, Meg. *The Boy Next Door.* HarperCollins/Avon, 2002. 384p. $13.95 (0-06-009619-5). Grades 10 and up.

Melissa Fuller, twentysomething scandalmonger for a New York newspaper, is nicer than most Manhattanites, since she hails from a small town in Illinois.

Chbosky, Stephen. *The Perks of Being a Wallflower.* Pocket/MTV, 1999. 256p. $13 (0-671-02734-4). Grades 10 and up.

Outsider Charlie writes about his freshman year in high school; his new, insightful, bohemian friends; his defiance of conformity; and his evolution into a man of action.

Danziger, Paula, and Ann M. Martin. *P.S. Longer Letter Later.* Scholastic, 1999. 234p. $5.99 (0-590-213-113). Grades 6 and up.

Twelve-year-old best friends Elizabeth and Tara-Starr continue their friendship through letter writing after Tara-Starr's family moves to another state.

Danziger, Paula, and Ann M. Martin. *Snail Mail No More.* Scholastic, 2001. 320p. $5.99 (0-439-06336-1). Grades 6 and up.

Now that they live in different cities, thirteen-year-olds Tara and Elizabeth use e-mail to "talk" about everything that is occurring in their lives.

Haddix, Margaret Peterson. *Don't You Dare Read This, Mrs. Dunphrey.* Simon Pulse, 2004. 128p. $4.99 (0-689-87102-3). Grades 8 and up.

An abused and neglected teenager pours her heart into a journal for English class.

Marsden, John. *Letters from the Inside.* Dell, 1996. 160p. $4.99 (0-440-21951-5). Grades 8 and up.

Through the mail, Mandy and Tracey become fast friends, but what are the secrets hidden between the lines of their cheerful letters?

McCafferty, Megan. *Sloppy Firsts*. Crown, 2001. 304p. $11.95 (0-609-80790-0). Grades 9 and up.

When her best friend, Hope, moves away from Pineville, New Jersey, sixteen-year-old Jessica Darling is devastated.

Myracle, Lauren. *TTYL*. Abrams/Amulet, 2004. 224p. $15.95 (0-8109-4821-4). Grades 6 and up.

Chronicles, in the form of e-mail messages, the day-to-day experiences, feelings, and plans of three friends—Zoe, Maddie, and Angela—as they begin tenth grade.

Sparks, Beatrice, ed. *Almost Lost: The True Story of an Anonymous Teenager's Life on the Streets*. Avon, 1996. 240p. $4.99 (0-380-78341-X). Grades 8 and up.

The story of a depressed teenage boy discusses the events that led to his leaving home, his struggle to survive on the streets, and his fight with self-hatred.

Sparks, Beatrice, ed. *Annie's Baby: The Diary of Anonymous, a Pregnant Teenager*. Avon, 1998. 256p. $5.99 (0-380-79141-2). Grades 8 and up.

In diary format, this is the story of fourteen-year-old Annie, her love for an abusive rich boyfriend, and her rape and subsequent pregnancy.

Sparks, Beatrice, ed. *Go Ask Alice*. Simon Pulse, 1998. 185p. $5.99 (0-689-81785-1). Grades 9 and up.

The real-life diary of a teenager whose life is dominated by her drug problems follows her experiences from her indoctrination into the world of drugs to three weeks before her death.

Sparks, Beatrice, ed. *It Happened to Nancy*. Flare, 1994. 241p. $5.95 (0-380-77315-5). Grades 8 and up.

A teenage victim of AIDS recounts her battle with the disease in her diary, describing her first love, the night she was date-raped, her diagnosis of AIDS, and her thoughts and dreams.

Sparks, Beatrice, ed. *Kim: Empty Inside: Diary of an Anonymous Teenager*. Avon, 2002. 165p. $5.99 (0-380-81460-9). Grades 8 and up.

Seventeen-year-old Kim, feeling the pressure of maintaining an A average to stay on her college gymnastics team, becomes obsessive about her weight and develops anorexia.

Sparks, Beatrice, ed. *Treacherous Love: The Diary of an Anonymous Teenager*. Avon, 2000. 164p. $5.99 (0-380-80862-5). Grades 8 and up.

Fourteen-year-old Jennie reveals in her diary how abandoned she feels until she gets special attention from the charismatic substitute math teacher, Mr. Johnstone, whose feelings for her develop into a dangerous relationship.

Yolen, Jane, and Bruce Coville. *Armageddon Summer*. Harcourt, 1999. 272p. $5.99 (0-15-202268-6). Grades 7 and up.

The world will end on Thursday, July 27, 2000. At least that's what Reverend Beelson has told his congregation. Meanwhile, Marina and Jed have found love.

REALISTIC PROBLEMS

"A good book for a reluctant reader should have lots of dialogue—realistic, 'teen speak' dialogue. It should deal with issues not often discussed, but which are important to teens. The opinions of publishers, parents, librarians, teachers, and booksellers should all come second to the opinions of the readers, and readers should be enabled in the sincere belief that this is a book written for them, that they are reading out of choice, not responsibility."

Shelly Stoehr

Anderson, Laurie. *Speak*. Penguin/Puffin, 2001. 208p. $8.99 (0-1413-1088-X). Grades 8 and up.

A high school freshman goes mute after she is raped by a popular senior at a summer party, and she refuses to reveal the reason behind her refusal to speak.

Atkins, Catherine. *When Jeff Comes Home*. Penguin/Puffin, 2001. 231p. $6.99 (0-698-11915-0). Grades 8 and up.

Sixteen-year-old Jeff, returning home after having been kidnapped and held prisoner for three years, must face family, friends, and school and the widespread assumption that he engaged in sexual activity with his kidnapper.

Bechard, Margaret. *Hanging on to Max*. Simon Pulse, 2004. 208p. $3.99 (0-7613-2574-3). Grades 7 and up.

A high school senior copes with the challenges of taking care of a baby while trying to get a diploma and maintain a social life.

Bunting, Eve. *Blackwater*. HarperCollins, 2000. 160p. $5.99 (0-06-440890-6). Grades 6 and up.

Thirteen-year-old Brodie Lynch was ready for the perfect summer of adventure when a harmless prank goes too far, changing everything forever.

Burgess, Melvin. *Smack*. HarperCollins/Avon, 1999. 293p. $6.99 (0-380-73223-8). Grades 9 and up. (M)

After running away from their troubled homes, two English teenagers move in with a group of squatters in the port city of Bristol and try to find ways to support their growing addiction to heroin.

Cadnum, Michael. *Rundown*. Penguin/Puffin, 2001. 176p. $6.99 (0-14-131087-1). Grades 9 and up.

Jennifer Thayer went for a run, threw herself down a hill, and then filed a false police report, claiming that she fought off a rapist.

Cohn, Rachel. *Gingerbread*. Simon Pulse, 2004. 176p. $3.99 (0-689-84337-2). Grades 8 and up.

After getting tossed from her posh boarding school, wild, willful, and coffee-addicted Cyd Charisse returns to San Francisco to live with her parents.

Coman, Carolyn. *What Jamie Saw*. Puffin, 1997. 128p. $5.99 (0-14-038335-2). Grades 6 and up.

Having fled to a family friend's hillside trailer after his mother's boyfriend tried to throw his baby sister against a wall, nine-year-old Jamie finds himself living an existence full of uncertainty and fear.

Cooney, Caroline. *The Terrorist*. Scholastic, 1999. 198p. $5.99 (0-590-22854-4). Grades 8 and up.

Sixteen-year-old Laura, an American living in London, tries to find the person responsible for the death of her younger brother, Billy, who has been killed by a terrorist bomb.

Creech, Sharon. *Walk Two Moons*. HarperCollins/Trophy, 1996. 280p. $6.99 (0-06-4405-176). Grades 6 and up.

On a long car trip, thirteen-year-old Salamanca Tree Hiddle tells her grandparents the story of a friend who copes with a lunatic and the disappearance of her mother—a tale that reflects Sal's own experience with abandonment.

Curtis, Christopher Paul. *Bucking the Sarge*. Random House/Wendy Lamb, 2004. 259p. $15.95 (0385323077). Grades 8 and up.

Fourteen-year-old Luther dreams of going to college but gets increasingly involved in his mother's shady business dealings.

Draper, Sharon M. *Darkness before Dawn*. Simon Pulse, 2002. 288p. $5.99 (0-689-85134-0). Grades 7 and up.

Recovering from the recent suicide of her ex-boyfriend, senior class president Keisha Montgomery finds herself attracted to a dangerous, older man.

Draper, Sharon. *Forged by Fire.* Simon Pulse, 1998. 160p. $4.99 (0-689-81851-3). Grades 7 and up.

When his loving aunt dies, Gerald is suddenly thrust into a new home filled with anger and abuse.

Draper, Sharon. *Tears of a Tiger.* Simon Pulse, 1996. 192p. $5.99 (0-689-80698-1). Grades 7 and up.

A high school basketball star struggles with guilt and depression following a drunk-driving accident that killed his best friend.

Ewing, Lynne. *Party Girl.* Random House, 1999. 128p. $4.99 (0-375-80210-X).

Is it possible for Kara to dream of a future while she's living a nightmare of gang violence and drive-by killings?

Ferris, Jean. *Bad.* Farrar, Straus and Giroux, 2001. 192p. $5.95 (0-374-40475-5). Grades 8 and up.

In an attempt to please her friends, sixteen-year-old Dallas goes along with their plan to rob a convenience store and is sentenced to six months in a girls' rehabilitation center.

Flake, Sharon. *Begging for Change.* Hyperion, 2004. 256p. $5.99 (0-7868-1405-5). Grades 6 and up.

An impoverished teen, obsessed with getting money any way she can to build a nest egg for her and her mother, gets herself into trouble.

Flake, Sharon G. *The Skin I'm In.* Hyperion, 2000. 176p. $5.99 (0-7868-1307-5). Grades 7 and up.

In her inner-city middle school, Maleeka Madison is picked on by classmates because she is poorly dressed, is darker than the others, and gets good grades.

Flinn, Alex. *Breaking Point.* HarperCollins, 2003. $6.99 (0-06-447371-6). Grades 8 and up.

Fifteen-year-old Paul enters an exclusive private school and falls under the spell of a charismatic boy who may be using him.

Flinn, Alex. *Breathing Underwater.* HarperCollins, 2002. 272p. $7.99 (0-06-447257-4). Grades 9 and up.

Sent to counseling for hitting his girlfriend, Caitlin, and ordered to keep a journal, sixteen-year-old Nick recounts his relationship with Caitlin, examines his controlling behavior and anger, and describes living with his abusive father.

Flinn, Alex. *Nothing to Lose.* HarperCollins/Avon, 2005. $6.99 (0-06-051752-2). Grades 8 and up.

After running away, Michael returns home when his mother goes on trial for killing his stepfather.

Frank, E. R. *America*. Simon Pulse, 2003. 256p. $7.99 (0-689-85772-1). Grades 10 and up. (M)

Fifteen-year-old America finds himself in a treatment facility after a suicide attempt and alternates between the present—mostly his therapy sessions with Dr. B.—and the past.

Griffin, Adele. *Amandine*. Disney, 2003. 208p. $6.99 (0-7868-1441-1). Grades 6 and up.

Her first week at a new school, shy, plain Delia befriends Amandine, not anticipating the dangerous turns their friendship would take.

Grimes, Nikki. *Bronx Masquerade*. Penguin/Puffin, 2003. 176p. $5.99 (0-8037-2569-8). Grades 7 and up.

When Wesley Boone writes a poem for his high school English class and reads it aloud, poetry-slam style, he kicks off a revolution.

Hautman, Pete. *Sweetblood*. Simon & Schuster, 2004. 242p. $5.99 (0689873247). Grades 8 and up.

Lucy Szabo, former "good girl" and good student, becomes involved with a group of "proto vampires" she meets online.

Hinton, S. E. *The Outsiders*. Penguin/Puffin, 1997 reprint. 192p. $6.99 (0-14-038572-X). Grades 7 and up.

Two rival gangs—the "haves" and "have-nots"—fight it out on the streets of an Oklahoma city.

Hopkins, Ellen. *Crank*. Simon Pulse, 2004. 544p. $6.99 (0-689-86519-8). Grades 10 and up. (M)

Kristina Georgia Snow is the perfect daughter: gifted high school junior, quiet, never any trouble. But on a trip to visit her absentee father, Kristina disappears and Bree, the exact opposite of Kristina, takes her place.

Hrdlitschka, Shelley. *Dancing Naked*. Orca, 2002. 240p. $6.95 (1-55143-210-2). Grades 8 and up.

Sixteen-year-old Kia's life is about to change forever when she learns she is pregnant.

Hrdlitschka, Shelley. *Kat's Fall*. Orca, 2004. 176p. $7.95 (1-55143-312-5). Grades 7 and up.

Darcy Frasier, fifteen, has grown up with the responsibility of caring for himself and his eleven-year-old sister, who is deaf and suffers from epileptic seizures.

Johnson, Angela. *The First Part Last*. Simon & Schuster, 2005. 144p. $5.99 (0-689-84923-0). Grades 9 and up.

Bobby's restless, impulsive—a classic urban teenager. But the thing that makes him different is that he's going to be a father.

Jones, Patrick. *Things Change*. Walker, 2004. 224p. $16.95 (0-8027-8901-3). Grades 9 and up.

Sixteen-year-old Johanna, one of the best students in her class, develops a passionate attachment for troubled seventeen-year-old Paul and finds her plans for the future changing in unexpected ways.

Klass, David. *You Don't Know Me*. HarperCollins, 2002. 352p. $6.95 (0-06-447378-3). Grades 8 and up.

Fourteen-year-old John creates alternative realities in his mind as he tries to deal with his mother's abusive boyfriend; his crush on a beautiful, but shallow classmate; and other problems at school.

Koertge, Ron. *Stoner + Spaz*. Candlewick Press, 2002. 176p. $15.99 (0-7636-1608-7). Grades 8 and up.

A troubled youth with cerebral palsy struggles toward self-acceptance with the help of a drug-addicted young woman.

Koja, Kathe. *Blue Mirror*. Farrar, Straus and Giroux, 2004. 128p. $16.00 (0-374-30849-7). Grades 8 and up.

Seventeen-year-old loner Maggy Klass, who frequently seeks refuge from her alcoholic mother's apartment by sitting and drawing in a local café, becomes involved in a destructive relationship with a charismatic homeless youth named Cole.

Koss, Amy Goldman. *The Girls*. Penguin/Puffin, 2002. 128p. $5.99 (0-14-230033-0). Grades 7 and up.

Each of the girls in a middle-school clique reveals the strong, manipulative hold one of the members exerts on the others, and the hurt and self-doubt that it causes them.

Levenkron, Steven. *The Best Little Girl in the World*. Warner, 1981 reprint. 253p. $6.99 (0-44-635-865-7). Grades 8 and up.

Francesca, a model daughter and student, begins losing large amounts of weight and refuses to eat in this composite of case histories of teenage girls suffering from anorexia nervosa.

Levenkron, Steven. *The Luckiest Girl in the World*. Penguin, 1998 reprint. 188p. $13.00 (0-14-026-625-9). Grades 8 and up.

Katie Roskova—a beautiful, talented, and intelligent teenager with a future as a figure-skating champion—struggles to cope with the pressures of her life by cutting herself.

Luna, Louisa. *Brave New Girl*. MTV Books, 2001. 197p. $11.95 (0-74-340-786-5). Grades 10 and up. (M)

An outcast at school, misunderstood by her parents, and mourning the disappearance of her older brother, fourteen-year-old Doreen seeks solace in her music until her sister's boyfriend forces her to confront new feelings about the world around her.

McCormick, Patricia. *Cut*. Scholastic/Push, 2002. 160p. $6.99 (0-439-32459-9). Grades 8 and up.

A family trauma lands Callie at Sea Pines, a psychiatric treatment facility, where she must learn to overcome her self-destructive obsession with cutting herself.

McDonald, Janet. *Brother Hood*. Farrar, Straus and Giroux, 2004. 176p. (0-374-30995-7). Grades 7 and up.

Sixteen-year-old Nate, an academically gifted student who attends an exclusive private boarding school, straddles two cultures as he returns home for occasional visits to see his family and "gangsta crew" in Harlem, New York.

McDonald, Janet. *Chill Wind*. Farrar, Straus and Giroux, 2002. 134p. (0-374-39958-1). Grades 7 and up.

Afraid that she will have nowhere to go when her welfare checks are stopped, nineteen-year-old high school dropout Aisha tries to figure out how she can support herself and her two young children in New York City.

McDonald, Janet. *Spellbound*. Speak, 2003. 138p. $5.99 (0-142-50193-X). Grades 7 and up.

Raven, a teenage mother and high school dropout, is determined to enter college by winning a spelling bee.

McDonald, Janet. *Twists and Turns*. Farrar, Straus and Giroux, 2003. 144p. $18.95 (0-374-39955-7). Grades 8 and up.

With the help of a couple of successful friends, eighteen- and nineteen-year-old Teesha and Keeba try to capitalize on their talents by opening a hair salon in the run-down Brooklyn housing project where they live.

"What I have discovered from corresponding with my own reluctant readers who send e-mail via my Web site projectgirl.com is that they like stories and characters they can relate to or identify with, and they appreciate dialogue written in a language they themselves speak. A good story, of course, is essential, but how it is told seems to go a long way in inspiring reluctant readers."

Janet McDonald

McNamee, Graham. *Hate You*. Random House, 2000. 128p. $5.50 (0-440-22762-3). Grades 7 and up.

Nursing hatred for the father who choked her and damaged her voice as a child, seventeen-year-old Alice writes songs she feels she cannot sing and seeks to reconcile her feelings for herself and her father.

Mikaelsen, Ben. *Touching Spirit Bear*. HarperCollins/Trophy, 2002. 241p. $5.99 (0-06-073-400-0). Grades 9 and up.

After his anger erupts into violence, Cole, in order to avoid going to prison, agrees to participate in a sentencing alternative based on the Native American Circle Justice and is sent to a remote Alaskan Island, where an encounter with a huge Spirit Bear changes his life.

"Hooking the reader is everything. We live in a fast-paced Nintendo world where there has to be immediate gratification. If a book starts slowly, often the reader will set the book down and never return. If this happens, how good the book is remains academic."

                                                                    Ben Mikaelsen

---

Myers, Walter Dean. *Crystal*. HarperCollins/Trophy, 2002 reprint. 196p. $5.99 (0064473120). Grades 8 and up.

Fifteen-year-old Crystal has difficulty trying to reconcile her personal and school life with the sexy, sophisticated persona her career as a quickly advancing high-fashion model has forced on her.

Myers, Walter Dean. *Monster*. HarperCollins, 1999. 304p. $6.99 (0-06-440731-4). Grades 8 and up.

While on trial as an accomplice to a murder, sixteen-year-old Steve Harmon records his experiences in prison and in the courtroom in the form of a film script, as he tries to come to terms with the course his life has taken.

Myers, Walter Dean. *Scorpions*. HarperCollins/Trophy, 1990. 216p. $5.99 (0-06-447066-0). Grades 8 and up.

After reluctantly taking on the leadership of the Harlem gang the Scorpions, Jamal finds that his enemies treat him with respect when he acquires a gun—until a tragedy occurs.

Myers, Walter Dean. *Shooter*. HarperCollins/Amistad, 2005. 223p. $6.99 (0064472906). Grades 7 and up.

After his friend goes on a shooting rampage at school, Cameron must re-examine his life and place in the world.

Myers, Walter Dean. *Slam!* Scholastic, 1998. 266p. $5.99 (0-59-048668-3). Grades 8 and up.

Sixteen-year-old Slam Harris is counting on his noteworthy basketball talents to get him out of the inner city and give him a chance to succeed in life, but his coach sees things differently.

Peters, Julie Anne. *Define "Normal."* Little, Brown, 2003. 208p. $5.95 (0-316-73489-6). Grades 6 and up.

When she agrees to meet with Jasmine as a peer counselor at their middle school, Antonia never dreams that this girl with the black lipstick and pierced eyebrow will end up helping her deal with the serious problems she faces at home and become a good friend.

Philbrick, Rodman. *Freak the Mighty.* Scholastic, 2001. 176p. $4.99 (0-439-28606-9). Grades 7 and up.

Two eighth-grade misfits—one physically impaired, the other with a learning disability—become fast friends.

Sapphire, Ramona Lofton. *Push: A Novel.* Knopf, 1997. 192p. $11.95 (0-679-76675-8). Grades 10 and up. (M)

Precious Jones, sixteen years old and pregnant by her father with her second child, meets a determined and highly radical teacher who takes her on a journey of transformation and redemption.

Sister Souljah. *The Coldest Winter Ever: A Novel.* Simon & Schuster, 2001. 320p. $13.95 (0-7434-2681-9). Grades 10 and up. (M)

Winter Santiaga thinks she has it all: money, the latest designer styles, a great body, and the respect of the neighborhood. All that changes when her father moves the family.

Smith, Roland. *Zach's Lie.* Hyperion, 2003. 224p. $5.99 (0-7868-0617-6). Grades 7 and up.

When Jack Osborne is befriended by his school's custodian and a Basque girl, he begins to adjust to his family's sudden move to Elko, Nevada, after entering the Witness Security Program.

Sones, Sonya. *One of Those Hideous Books Where the Mother Dies.* Simon & Schuster, 2004. 272p. $15.95 (0-689-84169-8). Grades 7 and up.

Fifteen-year-old Ruby Milliken leaves her best friend, her boyfriend, her aunt, and her mother's grave in Boston and reluctantly flies to Los Angeles to live with her father, a famous movie star.

Sones, Sonya. *What My Mother Doesn't Know.* Simon Pulse, 2004. 272p. $3.99 (0-689-84114-0). Grades 7 and up.

Sophie describes her relationships with a series of boys as she searches for Mr. Right.

Soto, Gary. *The Afterlife*. Harcourt, 2003. 176p. $16.00 (0-15-204774-3). Grades 8 and up.

A senior at East Fresno High School lives on as a ghost after his brutal murder in the restroom of a club where he had gone to dance.

Spinelli, Jerry. *Maniac Magee*. Little, Brown, 1999. 192p. $6.99 (0-316-80906-3). Grades 6 and up.

Orphaned as an infant, Jerry Magee is reared by his feuding aunt and uncle until he runs away at age eight.

Spinelli, Jerry. *Wringer*. HarperTrophy, 2004. 256p. $6.50 (0-06-059282-6). Grades 6 and up.

In Palmer's hometown, ten-year-old boys are awarded the time-honored privilege of becoming "wringers." Wringers are boys who break the necks of wounded birds in the town's annual pigeon shoot.

Strasser, Todd. *Can't Get There from Here*. Simon & Schuster, 2004. 208p. $15.95 (0-8118-4033-6). Grades 7 and up.

Tired of being hungry, cold, and dirty from living on the streets of New York City with a tribe of other homeless teenagers who are dying, a girl named Maybe ponders her future.

Strasser, Todd. *Give a Boy a Gun*. Simon & Schuster/Simon Pulse, 2002. 208p. $5.99 (0-689-84893-5). Grades 7 and up.

Events leading up to a night of terror at a high school dance are told from the point of view of various people involved.

Stratton, Allan. *Chanda's Secrets*. Annick Press/Firefly, 2004. 193p. $19.95 (155037835X). Grades 8 and up.

Chanda struggles with the deaths of those around her and the shame of being molested as she continues her education and cares for her siblings and friend Esther, amid the poverty and AIDS epidemic that plague her African homeland.

Trueman, Terry. *Stuck in Neutral*. HarperTempest, 2001. 128p. $6.95 (0-06-447213-2). Grades 8 and up.

Fourteen-year-old Shawn McDaniel, who suffers from severe cerebral palsy and cannot function, relates his perceptions of his life, as he believes his father is planning to kill him.

Vizzini, Ned. *Be More Chill*. Hyperion/Miramax, 2004. 304p. $16.95 (0-7868-0995-7). Grades 9 and up.

Badly in need of self-confidence and a change of image, high school nerd Jeremy Heere swallows a pill-sized supercomputer that is supposed to help him get whatever he wants.

Wallace, Rich. *Playing without the Ball*. Random House, 2002. 224p. $5.50 (0-440-22972-3). Grades 8 and up.

Feeling abandoned by his parents, seventeen-year-old Jay finds hope for the future in a church-sponsored basketball team and a female friend.

Williams-Garcia, Rita. *Like Sisters on the Homefront*. Penguin/Puffin, 1998. 176p. $5.99 (0-14-038561-4). Grades 8 and up.

When Gayle gets into trouble with her boyfriend, her mother sends the street-smart fourteen-year-old and her baby, Jose, down to Georgia to live with Uncle Luther and his family.

Wittlinger, Ellen. *The Long Night of Leo and Bree*. Simon & Schuster, 2003. 128p. $6.99 (0-689-86335-7). Grades 9 and up.

On the anniversary of his sister's murder, Leo—tormented by his mother's insane accusations and his own waking nightmares—kidnaps a wealthy girl intending to kill her, but instead their long night together helps them both face their futures.

Wolff, Virginia. *Make Lemonade*. Scholastic, 2003. 208p. $5.99 (0-590-48141-X). Grades 8 and up.

LaVaughn needed a part-time job; what she got was a baby-sitting gig with Jolly, an unwed teen mother.

Woods, Brenda. *Emako Blue*. Penguin Putnam, 2004. 128p. $15.99 (0-399-24006-3). Grades 7 and up.

Monterey, Savannah, Jamal, and Eddie never had much to do with each other until Emako Blue shows up at chorus practice, but just as the lives of the five Los Angeles high school students become intertwined, tragedy tears them apart.

SHORT STORIES

Appelt, Kathi. *Kissing Tennessee and Other Stories from the Stardust Dance*. Harcourt, 2004. 132p. $5.95 (0-15-205127-9). Grades 6 and up.

Eight graduating eighth graders relate the stories of love and heartbreak that have brought them to Dogwood Junior High's magical Stardust Dance.

Cart, Michael. *Rush Hour: Sin*. Random House/Dell, 2004. $9.95 (0385730314). Grades 10 and up. (M)

Original stories, essays, and art around the general topic of sin.

Crutcher, Chris. *Athletic Shorts: Six Short Stories*. HarperCollins, 2002. 208p. $6.99 (0-06-050783-7).

Athletes face up to more than sports in these tales of love and death, bigotry and heroism, and real people doing the best they can, even when that best is not enough.

Duncan, Lois, ed. *Night Terrors: Stories of Shadow and Substance.* Simon Pulse, 1997. 192p. $5.99 (0-689-80724-4). Grades 6 and up.
Eleven original stories about ghosts, gangs, murders, and monsters.

Flake, Sharon. *Who Am I without Him? A Short Story Collection about Girls and the Boys in Their Lives.* Hyperion, 2004. 176p. $15.99 (0-7868-0693-1). Grades 7 and up.
Ten stories of teens and their often-painful romantic struggles.

Gallo, Don, ed. *First Crossing: Stories about Teen Immigrants.* Candlewick, 2004. 240p. $16.99 (0-7636-2249-4). Grades 8 and up.
Stories of recent Mexican, Venezuelan, Kazakh, Chinese, Romanian, Palestinian, Swedish, Korean, Haitian, and Cambodian immigrants reveal what it is like to face prejudice, language barriers, and homesickness along with common teenage feelings and needs.

Gallo, Don. *No Easy Answers: Short Stories about Teenagers Making Tough Choices.* Random House, 1999. 323p. $6.50 (0440413052). Grades 7 and up.
Stories about teenagers in situations that test their moral and ethical characters.

Holt, David, and Bill Mooney. *Spiders in the Hairdo: Modern Urban Legends.* August House, 1999. 109p. $7.95 (0-87483-525-9). Grades 6 and up.
This collection of urban legends—weird, cruel, outrageous, and haunting—presents some of the tabloids of living folklore.

McCafferty, Megan, ed. *Sixteen: Stories about That Sweet and Bitter Birthday.* Crown/Three Rivers Press, 2004. 336p. $10.95 (1-4000-5270-X). Grades 9 and up.
A compilation of short stories inspired by all the angst, melodrama, and wonderment of being sixteen.

Myers, Walter Dean. *145th Street: Short Stories.* Random House, 2001. 160p. $5.50 (0-440-22916-2). Grades 7 and up.
A wrenchingly honest collection of urban stories set on one block of 145th Street.

Nixon, Joan Lowery. *Ghost Town: Seven Ghostly Stories.* Random House, 2002. 147p. $4.99 (0-440-41603-5). Grades 6 and up.

A collection of stories about eerie encounters in various ghost towns across the United States, with each story accompanied by an afterword about the actual town on which the story is based.

Paulsen, Gary. *My Life in Dog Years*. Random House, 1999. 144p. $5.50 (0-440-41471-7). Grades 6 and up.

Gary Paulsen has owned dozens of unforgettable and amazing dogs. Each chapter of this book tells the story of one special dog.

Schwartz, Alvin. *Scary Stories to Tell in the Dark*. Trophy Press, 1986. 111p. $5.99 (0-06-440-170-7). Grades 6 and up.

The first of Schwartz's three books of stories based on the oral traditions of American folklore.

RELATIONSHIPS

Brian, Kate. *The Princess and the Pauper*. Simon Pulse, 2004. 272p. $5.99 (0-689-87042-6). Grades 7 and up.

When sixteen-year-old Julia of Los Angeles and sixteen-year-old Princess Carina of Vineland switch places, Julia dances at the ball with the incredible Markus and Carina escapes rigid protocol to spend time with a rock star.

Cabot, Meg. All American Girl series. HarperCollins, 2003–2005. Grades 7 and up.

A sophomore girl stops a presidential assassination attempt, is appointed teen ambassador to the United Nations, and catches the eye of the very cute first son.

All American Girl. 416p. $6.99 (0-06-447277-9).
Ready or Not. 283p. $15.99 (0-06-072450-1).

Davidson, Dana. *Jason and Kyra*. Hyperion/Jump at the Sun, 2004. 336p. $16.99 (0-7868-1851-4). Grades 7 and up.

Sixteen-year-old Jason is gorgeous, smart, graceful on the basketball court, and dating popular, beautiful Lisa, but Jason falls for Kyra—his nonconformist, highly academic research partner from his AP English class.

Draper, Sharon. *Romiette and Julio*. Simon & Schuster/Simon Pulse, 2001. 320p. $5.99 (0-689-84209-0). Grades 7 and up.

Romiette—an African American girl—and Julio—a Hispanic boy—fall in love on the Internet and find themselves being harassed by a gang whose members object to interracial dating.

King, Stephen. *Nightmares and Dreamscapes.* New American Library/Signet, 1997. 692p. $7.99 (0451180232). Grades 9 and up.

Twenty short works by the author include stories about vampires and detectives, as well as nonfiction.

Krulik, Nancy. *Newly Wed.* Simon & Schuster, 2005. 204p. $5.99 (0-689-87660-2). Grades 9 and up.

After meeting through an online dating service, Jesse and Jen agree to write about their first year of marriage for the service's Web site, but when the glow of the honeymoon wanes, they find married life more than they bargained for.

Mackler, Carolyn. *The Earth, My Butt, and Other Big Round Things.* Candlewick, 2003. 256p. $15.99 (0-7636-1952-2). Grades 8 and up.

Feeling like she does not fit in with the other members of her family, fifteen-year-old Virginia tries to deal with her self-image and her first physical relationship.

Mackler, Carolyn. *Vegan Virgin Valentine.* Candlewick, 2004. 240p. $16.99 (0-7636-2155-2). Grades 8 and up.

Mara's niece, who is only one year younger, moves in, bringing conflict between the two teenagers because of their opposite personalities.

Manning, Sarra. *Guitar Girl.* Dutton, 2004. 224p. $15.99 (0-525-47234-7). Grades 7 and up.

Seventeen-year-old Molly Montgomery never planned on becoming famous. Starting a band with her best mates, Jane and Tara, was just a way to have some fun.

Myracle, Lauren. *Rhymes with Witches.* Abrams, 2005. 209p. $16.95 (0-8109-5859-7). Grades 9 and up.

The Bitches rule the school—and now Jane is one of them.

FICTION SERIES

Abbott, Hailey. Summer Boys series. Scholastic, 2003. $8.99 ea. Grades 8 and up.

Cousins Ella, Beth, and Jamie are at their family's beach house, and they're gearing up for the wildest time of their lives.

Summer Boys. 224p. (0-439-54020-8).
Next Summer. 240p. (0-439-75540-9).

Asai, Carrie. Samurai Girl series. Simon Pulse, 2003–2004. $6.99 ea. Grades 7 and up.

Nineteen-year-old Heaven flees her arranged marriage after her brother is murdered by a ninja.

The Book of the Sword. 287p. (0-689-85948-1).
The Book of the Shadow. 224p. (0-689-85949-X).
The Book of the Pearl. 271p. (0-689-86432-9).
The Book of the Wind. 224p. (0-689-86433-7).
The Book of the Flame. 210p. (0-689-86713-1).
The Book of the Heart. 240p. (0-689-86712-3).

Burke, Morgan. The Party Room trilogy. Simon Pulse, 2005. $5.99 ea. Grades 7 and up.
  Who is murdering prep-school students at Manhattan's hottest night spot?

Get It Started. 272p. (0-689-87225-9).
After Hours. 256p. (0-689-87226-7).
Last Call. 272p. (0-689-87227-5).

Butcher, A. J. Spy High series. Little, Brown, 2004–2005. $6.99 ea. Grades 8 and up.
  As students at a special high school that trains them to be secret agents, six teenagers struggle to complete the training exercises as a team before being sent out into the field to sink or swim.

Mission One. 224p. (0-316-73760-7).
Chaos Rising. 240p. (0-316-73765-8).
Serpent Scenario. 224p. (0-316-7376-6).
Paranoia Plot. 240p. (0-316-76260-1).
Blood Relations. 240p. (0-316-78092-8).

Cabot, Meg. The Mediator series. HarperCollins/Avon, 2003–2005. $6.99 ea. Grades 7 and up.
  Sixteen-year-old Susannah Simon is a mediator for the dead, and she also happens to be in love with Jesse—a nineteenth-century ghost.

Haunted. 288p. (0-06-0751-649).
Shadowland. 304p. (0-06-0725-125).
Ninth Key. 304p. (0-06-0725-125).
Reunion. 304p. (0-06-0725-133).
Darkest Hour. 280p. (0-06-0725-141).

Chandler, Elizabeth. Dark Secrets series. Simon Pulse, 2002–2005. $5.99 ea. Grades 7 and up.
  Female heroines must unravel secrets of all kinds.

Back Door of Midnight. 224p. (0-689-86642-9).
The Deep End of Fear. 320p. (0-689-85259-2).
Don't Tell. 228p. (0-7434-0029-1).
Legacy of Lies. 192p. (0-7434-0028-3).
No Time to Die. 224p. (0-7434-0030-5).

Cusick, Richie Tankersley. The Unseen series. Penguin/Razorbill, 2005. $6.99 ea. Grades 7 and up.

After a horrifying encounter in a graveyard, Lucy cannot shake the feeling that she is being watched, but she is unwilling to trust the one person who might be able to help her.

It Begins. 304p. (0-14-2404-632).
Rest in Peace. 288p. (0-14-2404-640).

Dean, Zoey. The A List series. Little, Brown, 2003–2005. $8.99 ea. Grades 9 and up.

Anna Percy leaves Manhattan to spend the second half of her senior year with her father in Los Angeles and quickly becomes involved in the lives of the rich and famous.

The A List. 228p. (0-316-73435-7).
Girls on Film. 256p. (0-316-73475-6).
Blonde Ambition. 240p. (0-316-73474-8).
Tall Cool One. 250p. (0-316-73508-6).
Back in Black. 304p. (0-316-01092-8).

De la Cruz, Melissa. The Au Pairs series. Simon & Schuster, 2004–2005. Grades 9 and up.

Sun and sea, hot parties, hot guys, and the promise of $10,000 for taking care of four overprivileged, undersupervised kids.

The Au Pairs. 304p. $8.99 (0-689-87319-0).
Skinny Dipping. 304p. $14.95 (1-4169-0382-8).

Ewing, Lynne. Daughters of the Moon series. Hyperion, 2000–2004. $9.99 ea. Grades 7 and up.

Four girls with unusual powers must form together to fight the evil Atrox.

Goddess of the Night. 294p. (0-7868-0653-2).
Into the Cold Fire. 264p. (0-7868-0654-0).
Night Shade. 275p. (0-7868-0708-3).
The Secret Scroll. 268p. (0-7868-0709-1).
The Sacrifice. 269p. (0-7868-0706-7).
The Lost One. 274p. (0-7868-0707-5).

Moon Demon. 289p. (0-7868-0849-7).
Possession. 275p. (0-7868-0850-0).
The Choice. 275p. (0-7868-0851-9).
The Talisman. 288p. (0-7868-1878-6).
The Prophecy. 288p. (0-7868-1891-3).
The Becoming. 275p. (0-7868-1892-1).

Ewing, Lynne. Sons of the Dark series. Hyperion, 2004–2005. $9.99 ea. Grades 7 and up.

Having escaped slavery in the parallel universe of Nefandus, fifteen-year-old Obie must return to retrieve his mother's rune stones in order to fulfill his destiny in modern-day Los Angeles as one of the four Sons of the Dark.

Barbarian. 272p. (0-7868-1811-5).
Escape. 270p. (0-7868-1812-3).
Outcast. 272p. (0-7868-1813-1).
Night Sun. 270p. (0-7868-1814-X).

Golden, Christopher. Body of Evidence series. Simon Pulse, 1999–2004. $4.99 ea. Grades 9 and up.

Jenna Blake, a student at a college outside of Boston, accepts a job as an administrative assistant to the medical examiner at the local hospital.

Body Bags. 272p. (0-671-03492-8).
Thief of Hearts. 245p. (0-671-03493-6).
Soul Survivor. 232p. (0-671-03494-4).
Meets the Eye. 256p. (0-671-03495-2).
Head Games. 232p. (0-671-77582-0).
Brain Trust. 242p. (0-671-77585-5).
Last Breath. 304p. (0-689-86526-0).

Haddix, Margaret Peterson. Shadow Children series. Grades 6 and up.

In a future where the Population Police enforce the law limiting a family to only two children, "thirds" must hide together to stay alive.

Among the Hidden. Aladdin, 2000. 153p. $5.99 (0-689-82475-0).
Among the Impostors. Aladdin, 2002. 165p. $5.99 (0-689-83908-1).
Among the Betrayed. Aladdin, 2003. 170p. $5.99 (0-689-83909-X).
Among the Barons. Aladdin, 2004. 182p. $5.99 (0-689-83910-3).
Among the Brave. Simon & Schuster, 2004. 145p. $15.95 (0-689-85794-2).
Among the Enemy. Simon & Schuster, 2005. 224p. $15.95 (0-689-85796-9).

Harrison, Lisi. The Clique series. Little, Brown, 2004–2005. $9.99 ea. Grades 6 and up.

After Massie steals her only friend, Claire strikes back.

The Clique. 208p. (0-316-70129-7).
Best Friends for Never. 208p. (0-316-70131-9).
Revenge of the Wannabes. 304p. (0-316-70133-5).
Invasion of the Boy Snatchers. 256p. (0-316-70134-3).

Hopkins, Cathy. Mates, Dates series. Simon Pulse, 2003–2005. $5.99 ea. Grades 6 and up.

Lucy, Izzie, and Nesta are fourteen-year-old Londoners with all kinds of troubles with boys, self-confidence, friends, and enemies.

Mates, Dates, and Cosmic Kisses. 208p. (0-689-85545-1).
Mates, Dates, and Designer Divas. 208p. (0-689-85546-X).
Mates, Dates, and Inflatable Bras. 160p. (0-689-85544-3).
Mates, Dates, and Sleepover Secrets. 208p. (0-689-85991-0).
Mates, Dates, and Sole Survivors. 224p. (0-689-85992-9).
Mates, Dates, and Mad Mistakes. 224p. (0-689-86722-0).
Mates, Dates, and Sequin Smiles. 208p. (0-689-8723-9).
Mates, Dates, and Tempting Trouble. 256p. (0-689-87062-0).
Mates, Dates, and Great Escapes. 224p. (0-689-87695-5).

Langan, Paul, ed. Bluford High series. Townsend Press, 2002–2004. $1.00 ea. Grades 8 and up.

Focuses on the lives of a group of high school students and their families. The series draws its name from the school that many of the characters attend: Bluford High, named after Guion "Guy" Bluford, America's first black astronaut.

Lost and Found. 133p. (0-944210-02-3).
A Matter of Trust. 144p. (0-944210-03-1).
Secrets in the Shadows. 126p. (0-944210-05-8).
Someone to Love Me. 162p. (0-944210-06-6).
The Bully. 190p. (0-944210-00-7).
The Gun. 123p. (0-944210-04-X).
Until We Meet Again. 144p. (0-944210-07-4).
Blood Is Thicker. 156p. (1-591940-16-8).
Brothers in Arms. 152p. (1-591940-17-6).
Summer of Secrets. 142p. (1-591940-18-4).

McDaniel, Lurlene. The Girl Death Left Behind series. Skylark, 1999. $4.99 (0-553-57091-9).

While not following the same characters, Lurlene McDaniel's novels are about teenagers who face life-threatening illnesses and sometimes do not survive.

Reach for Tomorrow. Skylark, 1999. 208p. $4.99 (0-553-57109-5).
Angel of Hope. Skylark, 2000. 240p. $4.99 (0-553-57148-6).
To Live Again. Starfire, 2001. 160p. $4.99 (0-553-57151-6).
Angel of Mercy. Starfire, 2001. 224p. $4.99 (0-553-57083-8).
Telling Christina Goodbye. Starfire, 2002. 240p. $4.99 (0-553-357087-0).
A Rose for Melinda. Starfire, 2002. 208p. $4.99 (0-553-57090-0).
How Do I Love Thee: Three Stories. Starfire, 2002. 272p. $5.50 (0-553-57107-9).
Six Months to Live. Darby Creek, 2003. 144p. $4.99 (1-58196-003-4).
I Want to Live. Darby Creek, 2003. 128p. $4.99 (1-58196-004-2).
So Much to Live For. Darby Creek, 2003. 144p. $4.99 (1-58196-005-0).
No Time to Cry. Darby Creek, 2003. 144p. $4.99 (1-58196-006-9).
As Long as We Both Shall Live. Laurel Leaf, 2003. 416p. $6.99 (0-553-57108-7).
My Secret Boyfriend. Darby Creek, 2004. 128p. $4.99 (1-58196-008-5).
If I Should Die Before I Wake. Darby Creek, 2004. 128p. $4.99 (1-58196-009-3).
Always and Forever. Laurel Leaf, 2004. 352p. $6.99 (0-553-49419-8).
A Horse for Mandy. Darby Creek, 2004. 75p. $4.99 (1-58196-011-5).
Journey of Hope: Two Novels. Laurel Leaf, 2004. 448p. $6.99 (0-553-49451-1).
Angels in Pink: Kathleen's Story. Delacorte, 2004. 240p. $12.99 (0-3859-0193-3).
Why Did She Have to Die? Laurel Leaf, 2005. 126p. $4.99 (1-58196-029-8).
Garden of Angels. Laurel Leaf, 2005. 288p. $5.50 (0-55349-432-5).
Angels in Pink: Raina's Story. Delacorte, 2005. 240p. $10.95 (0-385-73157-4).
The Time Capsule. Laurel Leaf, 2005. 224p. $5.50 (0-55349-431-7).
Mother, Please Don't Die. Laurel Leaf, 2005. 128p. $4.99 (1-581-96028-X).

For Lurlene McDaniel read-alikes, try:

Hurwin, Davida Wills. *A Time for Dancing.* Puffin, 1997. 257p. $5.99 (0-1403-8618-1). Grades 6 and up.
Seventeen-year-old best friends Samantha and Juliana narrate their individual stories in alternating chapters as they describe their feelings and the events of their lives after Juliana is diagnosed with terminal cancer. Sequel is *The Farther You Run* (0-1424-0294-X).

Lowry, Lois. *A Summer to Die.* Skylark, 1993. 120p. $5.99. (0-440-21917-5). Grades 6 and up.

Meg, who has always been very conscious of Molly's prettiness, popularity, and happiness, must now face the grim reality of her sister's death.

Minter, J. The Insiders series. Bloomsbury, 2004–2005. $8.95 ea. Grades 9 and up.

In downtown New York City, a sophisticated, stylish high school junior is already having trouble keeping his group of lifelong friends together when his wild cousin Kelli arrives from St. Louis and stirs things up.

The Insiders. 200p. (1-58234-895-2).
Pass It On. 200p. (1-58234-954-1).
Take It Off. 300p. (1-58234-994-0).
Break Every Rule. 300p. (1-58234-667-4).

Parker, Daniel. Watching Alice series. Penguin/Razorbill, 2004–2005. $7.99 ea. Grades 9 and up.

High school senior Tom Sinclair's journal chronicles events leading up to the disappearance of Alice, the only person he has confided in after moving from Vermont to Manhattan in an attempt to run away from his past.

Break the Surface. 208p. (1-59514-001-8).
Walk on the Water. 208p. (1-59514-002-6).
Seek the Prophet. 208p. (1-59514-003-4).
Find the Miracle. 208p. (1-59514-004-2).

Pascal, Francine. Fearless series. Pocket Books, 2000–2004. $5.99 ea. Grades 8 and up.

Teenage Gaia was born without the fear gene—and she is a powerful weapon.

Fearless (#1). 240p. (0-671-03941-5).
Sam (#2). 224p. (0-671-03747-1).
Run (#3). 240p. (0-671-03748-X).
Twisted (#4). 250p. (0-671-03944-X).
Kiss (#5). 224p. (0-671-77344-5).
Payback (#6). 131p. (0-671-77351-8).
Rebel (#7). 224p. (0-671-03748-X).
Heat (#8). 220p. (0-671-03948-2).
Blood (#9). 224p. (0-671-03949-0).
Liar (#10). 240p. (0-671-03951-2).
Trust (#11). 240p. (0-671-03952-0).
Killer (#12). 240p. (0-671-03953-9).

Bad (#13). 224p. (0-7434-1247-8).
Missing (#14). 224p. (0-7434-1248-6).
Tears (#15). 240p. (0-7434-1249-4).
Naked (#16). 240p. (0-7434-1250-8).
Flee (#17). 240p. (0-7434-1251-6).
Love (#18). 240p. (0-7434-1252-4).
Twins (#19). 240p. (0-7434-4397-7).
Sex (#20). 256p. (0-7434-4398-5).
Blind (#21). 224p. (0-7434-4399-3).
Alone (#22). 240p. (0-7434-4400-0).
Before Gaia (special edition). 320p. (0-689-85179-0).
Fear (#23). 195p. (0-7434-4401-9).
Betrayed (#24). 240p. (0-7434-4402-7).
Lost (#25). 224p. (0-689-85551-6).
Shock (#26). 224p. (0-689-85764-0).
Escape (#27). 272p. (0-689-85555-9).
Gaia Abducted (special edition). 384p. (0-689-86019-6).
Chase (#28). 224p. (0-689-85765-9).
Lust (#29). 240p. (0-689-85766-7).
Freak (#30). 240p. (0-689-85767-5).
Normal (#31). 272p. (0-689-86706-9).
Terror (#32). 224p. (0-689-86707-7).
Gaia Reborn (special edition). 384p. (0-689-86284-3).
Wired (#33). 224p. (0-689-86916-9).
Fake (#34). 224p. (0-689-86917-7).
Exposed (#35). 224p. (0-689-86918-5).

Pascal, Francine. Fearless FBI series. Simon Pulse, 2005. $7.99 ea. Grades 7 and up.

Gaia faces new challenges as an FBI trainee and learns the hard way that she will have to adjust to becoming a team player if she plans to have any success as an agent who hunts down serial killers.

Kill Game. 272p. (0-689-87821-4).
Live Bait. 208p. (0-689-87822-2).

Rabb, M. E. Missing Persons series. Penguin/Speak, 2004–2005. $5.99 ea. Grades 7 and up.

Two sisters from Queens escape their evil stepmother by moving to Venice, Indiana, and solving missing-persons cases on their own.

The Rose Queen (#1). 186p. (0-14-250041-0).
The Chocolate Lover (#2). 185p. (0-14-250042-9).

The Venetian Policeman (#3). 176p. (0-14-250043-7).
The Unsuspecting Gourmet (#4). 185p. (0-14-250044-5).

Rennison, Louise. Georgia Nicholson series. HarperCollins, 2000–2004. Grades 7 and up.

Georgia Nicholson and her teenage friends are obsessed with boys in this British series.

Angus, Thongs, and Full-Frontal Snogging: Confessions of Georgia Nicholson. 272p. $6.99 (0-06-447227-2).
On the Bright Side I'm Now the Girlfriend of a Sex God: Further Confessions of Georgia Nicholson. 272p. $6.99 (0-06-447226-4).
Knocked Out by My Nunga Nungas: Further Confessions of Georgia Nicholson. 290p. $6.99 (0-06-447362-7).
Dancing in My Nuddy-Pants: Even Further Confessions of Georgia Nicholson. 240p. $6.99 (0-06-009748-5).
Away Laughing on a Fast Camel: Even More Confessions of Georgia Nicholson. 276p. $6.99 (0-06-058936-1).
Then He Ate My Boy Entrancers: More Mad, Marvy Confessions of Georgia Nicholson. 312p. $15.99 (0-06-058937-X).

Rose, Malcolm. Traces series. Larousse Kingfisher Chambers, 2005. $5.95 ea. Grades 6 and up.

Teen forensic investigator Luke Harding and his robot sidekick Malc investigate murders.

Framed! 232p. (0-7534-5923-X).
Lost Bullet. 232p. (0-7534-5830-6).
Roll Call. 224p. (0-7534-5923-X).

Sciezska, Jon. Time Warp Trio series. Penguin/Viking, 1999–2004. Grades 6 and up.

Boys will be boys in this series written for younger readers.

Oh Say, I Can't See. 72p. $14.99 (0-670-06025-9).
Da Wild, Da Crazy, Da Vinci. $14.99 (0-670-05926-9).
Me Oh Maya! 80p. $4.99 (1-5819-6028-X).
Hey Kid, Want to Buy a Bridge? 96p. $4.99 (0-14-240089-0).
Viking It and Liking It. 96p. $4.99 (0-14-240002-5).
See You Later, Gladiator. 87p. $4.99 (0-14-240117-X).
It's All Greek to Me. 80p. $4.99 (0-14-240116-1).
Summer Reading Is Killing Me. 80p. $4.99 (0-14-240115-3).
Sam Samurai. 80p. $4.99 (0-14-240088-2).

Your Mother Was a Neanderthal. 80p. $4.99 (0-14-240048-3).
Tut, Tut. 74p. $4.99 (0-14-240047-5).
The Good, the Bad and the Goofy. 80p. $4.99 (0-14-240046-7).
The Not-So-Jolly Roger. 64p. $4.99 (0-14-240045-9).
2095. 80p. $4.99 (0-14-240044-0).
Knights of the Kitchen Table. 64p. $4.99 (0-14-240043-1).

Shan, Darren. Cirque du Freak series. Little, Brown, 2002–2004. $6.50 ea. Grades 6 and up.

Darren Shan begins a journey that will take him from average teen boy to vampire prince.

A Living Nightmare (#1). 272p. (0-316-60510-7).
The Vampire's Assistant (#2). 256p. (0-316-60684-7).
Tunnels of Blood (#3). 240p. (0-316-60608-1).
Vampire Mountain (#4). 208p. (0-316-60542-5).
Trials of Death (#5). 224p. (0-316-60395-3).
The Vampire Prince (#6). 208p. (0-316-60274-4).
Hunters of the Dusk (#7). 224p. (0-316-60211-6).
Allies of the Night (#8). 192p. (0-316-15570-5).
Killers of the Dawn (#9). 224p. (0-316-15626-4).
The Lake of Souls (#10). 302p. (0-316-15627-2).

Stephens, J. B. The Big Empty series. Penguin/Razorbill, 2004–2005. $6.99 ea. Grades 8 and up.

After half of the world's population is killed by a plague, seven teenagers seek a better life in a nightmarish future by deciphering coded messages and trying to avoid the Slashers.

The Big Empty (#1). 208p. (1-59514-006-9).
Paradise City (#2). 208p. (1-59514-007-7).
Desolation Angels (#3). 240p. (1-59514-008-5).
No Exit (#4). 240p. (1-59514-009-3).

Stine, R. L. Fear Street series. Simon Pulse, 2005 reprints. $5.99 ea. Grades 7 and up.

All kinds of strange and deadly things happen on a street called Fear.

The Stepsister. 180p. (1-4169-0029-2).
The Perfect Date. 160p. (1-4169-0323-2).
Killer's Kiss. 160p. (1-4169-0320-8).
All-Night Party. 160p. (1-4169-0321-6).
The Rich Girl. 180p. (1-4169-0324-0).

The Confession. 160p. (1-4169-0322-4).
First Date. 160p. (1-4169-0819-6).
Secret Admirer. 160p. (1-4169-0820-X).

Stine, R. L. Fear Street Nights series. Simon Pulse, 2005– . $5.99 ea. Grades 7 and up.
It's a whole new crowd at Shadyside High, but the evil on Fear Street never dies.

Moonlight Secrets. 160p. (0-689-87864-8).
Midnight Games. 160p. (0-689-87865-6).
Darkest Dawn. 192p. (0-689-87866-4).

Stolarz, Laurie F. Llewellyn, 2003–2005. $8.95. Grades 7 and up.
Teenager Stacey is a hereditary witch—are her dreams predicting the future?

Blue Is for Nightmares. 283p. (0-7387-0391-5).
White Is for Magic. 312p. (0-7387-0443-1).
Silver Is for Secrets. 312p. (0-7387-0631-0).
Red Is for Remembrance. 320p. (0-7387-0760-0).

Von Ziegesar, Cecily. Gossip Girl series. Little, Brown, 2002–2005. $8.99 ea. Grades 10 and up.
Presents a world of jealousy and betrayal at an exclusive private school in Manhattan.

Gossip Girl. 208p. (0-316-91033-3).
You Know You Love Me. 225p. (0-316-91148-8).
All I Want Is Everything. 213p. (0-316-91212-3).
Because I'm Worth It. 232p. (0-316-90968-8).
I Like It Like That. 201p. (0-316-73518-3).
You're the One That I Want. 227p. (0-316-73516-7).
Nobody Does It Better. 229p. (0-316-73512-4).
Nothing Can Keep Us Together. 250p. (0-316-73509-4).

Westerfeld, Scott. Midnighters series. HarperCollins/Eos, 2004–2005. Grades 7 and up.
Fifteen-year-old Jessica Day learns that she is one of a group of people who have special abilities that help them fight ancient creatures living in an hour hidden at midnight.

The Secret Hour. 400p. $6.99 (0-06-0519-533-0).
Touching Darkness. 336p. $15.99 (0-06-051-954-1).

> "You don't always have to mug your reader with conflict and action, although those usually work. Another way to create instant interest is with a strong or quirky voice. A character who experiences the mundane in an unexpected way can draw the reader in just as completely as a car chase. One of the coolest things we can get from a book is the feeling that we're seeing the world in a new way."
>
> Scott Westerfeld

Wilson, Jacqueline. Girlfriends series. Random House, 2002–2003. $9.95 ea. Grades 6 and up.

Ellie and the rest of her ninth grade friends deal with boys, beauty, friendships and life.

Girls in Love (#1). 192p. (0-385-90040-6).
Girls under Pressure (#2). 224p. (0-385-72975-8).
Girls Out Late (#3). 224p. (0-385-72976-6).
Girls in Tears (#4). 176p. (0-385-73082-9).

Nonfiction

BOOKS THAT READ LIKE MAGAZINES

Boyer, David. *Kings and Queens: Queers at the Prom*. Soft Skull Press, 2004. 160p. $24.95 (1-9323-6024-7). Grades 7 and up.
A photographic history of gay couples at their high school proms.

CosmoGirl Quiz Book: All about You. Hearst, 2004. 112p. $5.95 (1-58816-381-4). Grades 7 and up.
Multiple-choice answers to questions like "Are you a bore?"

CosmoGirl Quiz Book: All about Guys. Hearst, 2004. 112p. $5.95 (0-58816-382-2). Grades 7 and up.
Multiple-choice answers to questions like "Is it love or lust?"

Fulghum, Hunter. *Don't Try This at Home: How to Win a Sumo Match, Catch a Great White Shark, and Start an Independent Nation and Other Extraordinary Feats (for Ordinary People)*. Broadway Books, 2002. 264p. $14.00 (0-7679-1159-8). Grades 6 and up.
A how-to for everything you shouldn't do.

Gregory, Leland. *Stupid Crook Book*. Andrews McMeel, 2002. 231p. $9.95 (0-7407-2694-3). Grades 8 and up.
Relates anecdotes of criminals who were caught in the act or arrested due to their own ineptitude.

How to Hold a Crocodile. Firefly Books, 2003. 196p. $19.95 (1-55297-805-2). Grades 6 and up.
A colorfully illustrated manual with instructions for many situations. Need to roast an ox? Magnetize a walnut? Tie a bow tie?

Jacobs, Thomas. *They Broke the Law; You Be the Judge: True Cases of Teen Crime.* Free Spirit, 2004. 224p. $15.95 (1-57542-134-8). Grades 7 and up.

Introduction to the juvenile justice system that invites readers to preside over twenty-one real-life cases of teens in trouble with the law, after which they find out what happened and where each offender is today.

Koon, Jeff, and Andy Powell. *Wearing of This Garment Does Not Enable You to Fly: 101 Real Dumb Warning Labels.* Free Press, 2003. 160p. $12.95 (0-7432-4475-3). Grades 7 and up.

Written by teenagers, this is a collection of the most ridiculous warning labels around.

Levy, Joel. *Really Useful: Origins of Everyday Things.* Firefly, 2003. 240p. $39.95 (1-55297-623-8). Grades 8 and up.

Did you know that the ant is the only animal that can survive being cooked in a microwave? Other interesting facts about everyday items.

Masoff, Joy. *Oh, Yuck! The Encyclopedia of Everything Nasty.* Workman, 2000. 212p. $14.95 (0-7611-0771-1). Grades 6 and up.

From ants to bacteria, worms to zits—this book covers everything disgusting.

Packer, Alex J. *How Rude! The Teenager's Guide to Good Manners, Proper Behavior and Not Grossing People Out.* 448p. Free Spirit, 1998. 448p. $19.95 (1-57542-024-4). Grades 6 and up.

A practical but hilarious "how to" for teen civility, written for the skeptical teen who groans at the mere concept of manners.

Piven, Jeremy. *As Luck Would Have It: Incredible Stories, from Lottery Wins to Lightning Strikes.* Random House/Villard, 2004. 150p. $9.95 (0812968670). Grades 8 and up.

True stories about lucky and unlucky people, from someone surviving a plane crash to a bank teller getting struck by lightning—inside the bank.

Rothbart, Davy. *Found: The Best Lost, Tossed and Forgotten Items from around the World.* Simon & Schuster/Fireside, 2004. 256p. $14.00 (0-7432-5114-8). Grades 10 and up. (M)

A collection of items all found by contributors to the foundmagazine.com Web site.

Schiff, Nancy Rica. *Odd Jobs: Portraits of Unusual Occupations.* Ten Speed Press, 2002. 144p. $16.95 (1-58008-457-5). Grades 8 and up.

Text and photographs of people and some of their unusual jobs, including armpit sniffer and coin polisher.

Shaw, Tucker. *"What's That Smell?" (Oh It's Me): 50 Mortifying Situations and How to Deal.* Alloy/17th Street Productions, 2003. 160p. $7.99 (0-14-250011-9). Grades 8 and up.

Mood swings, zits, strange new bodily functions, the prom . . . The teenage years are tough enough, but when something really mortifying happens, they can be unbearable.

Teen People: Real Life Diaries: Inspiring True Stories from Celebrities and Real Teens. Edited by Linda Friedman and Dana White. HarperCollins/Avon, 2001. 144p. $12.95 (0-06-447329-5). Grades 6 and up.

Features true stories from famous adolescents and everyday teens.

This Book Really Sucks: The Science behind Gravity, Flight, Leeches, Black Holes, Tornadoes, Our Friend the Vacuum Cleaner, and Most Everything Else. Planet Dexter, 1999. $12.99 (0-448-44075-X). Grades 6 and up.

A humorous, but factual, discussion of all sorts of things that suck: gravity, leeches, babies, straws, and more.

YM's the Best of Say Anything. Random House/Bantam, 2004. 112p. $6.95 (0-553-37601-2). Grades 7 and up.

Everyone has an embarrassing moment they'd like to forget about. *YM* magazine has compiled some of the silliest, craziest, most embarrassing stories ever heard!

CELEBRITIES AND FAMOUS FOLK

Ashanti. *Foolish/Unfoolish: Reflections on Love.* Hyperion, 2002. Unpaged. $16.95 (1-4013-0030-8). Grades 8 and up.

The popular R & B artist shares her earliest writings from her teenage years.

Christe, Ian. *Sound of the Beast: The Complete Headbanging History of Heavy Metal.* Morrow/Avon, 2004. 416p. $13.95 (0-380-81127-8). Grades 9 and up.

The ultimate headbanger history, revealing tales of concert hysteria, courtroom drama, and musical triumph in the history of heavy metal.

Cobain, Kurt. *Journals: Kurt Cobain.* Riverhead/Penguin Putnam, 2003. 194p. $19.95 (1-57322-359-X). Grades 10 and up. (M)

Lyrics, drawings, poems, and letters directly from late rock star Kurt Cobain's personal papers.

Coker, Cheo Hodari. *Unbelievable: The Life, Death and Afterlife of the Notorious B.I.G.* Three Rivers Press, 2004. 341p. $19.95 (0-609-80835-4). Grades 10 and up. (M)

Portrait of the late rap artist Biggie Smalls, aka Notorious B.I.G.

Destiny's Child: The Complete Story. Busta Books, 2001. 112p. $12.95 (0-97-02224-4-0). Grades 7 and up.
A biography of the popular R & B music trio.

Fontaine, Smokey D. *E.A.R.L.: The Autobiography of DMX.* Harper Entertainment/HarperCollins, 2003. 346p. $14.95 (0-06-09340-3). Grades 10 and up. (M)
Biography of the troubled childhood and current success of this wildly successful rap star and actor.

Fricke, Jim. *Yes Yes Y'all: The Experience Music Project Oral History of Hip-Hop's First Decade.* Da Capo Press. 2002. 340p. $29.95 (0-306-81224-X). Grades 9 and up.
The origins of hip-hop as seen through the eyes of its founders and stars.

Gerard, Jim. *Celebrity Skin: Tattoos, Brands, and Body Adornments of the Stars.* Thunder's Mouth Press, 2001. 159p. $22.95 (1-56025-323-1). Grades 8 and up. (M)
Portraits of the tattoos—and the stories behind them—of today's hottest celebrities.

Hip Hop Divas. Crown/Three Rivers Press, 2001. 211p. $17.95 (0-609-80836-2). Grades 10 and up. (M)
An examination of the female stars of today's hip-hop scene.

Kenner, Rob, and Pitts, George. *VX: 10 Years of Vibe Photography.* Harry Abrams/Vibe Books, 2003. 208p. $40.00 (0-8109-4546-0). Grades 9 and up. (M)
A journey through the first ten years of *Vibe* magazine.

Keys, Alicia. *Tears for Water: Songbook of Poems and Lyrics.* Penguin Putnam, 2004. 179p. $19.95 (0-399-15257-1). Grades 7 and up.
A collection of the famous singer's journals and notebooks.

Knowles, Tina. *Destiny's Style: Bootylicious Fashion, Beauty, and Lifestyle Secrets from Destiny's Child.* Regan Books/HarperCollins, 2002. 204p. $24.95 (0-06-009777-9). Grades 7 and up.
Secrets from the women who created the fashion look of the R & B trio.

Kool Moe Dee. *There's a God on the Mic: The True 50 Greatest MCs.* 224p. $24.95 (1-56025-533-1). Grades 9 and up.
Debatable countdown of the best MCs in hip-hop history.

Krulik, Nancy. *Lisa Lopes: The Life of a Supernova.* Simon & Schuster, 2002. 101p. $4.99 (0-689-85690-3). Grades 6 and up.

Traces the life of performer Lisa "Left Eye" Lopes, from her childhood to her tragic death in 2002.

Malone, Bonz. *Hip Hop Immortals: The Remix.* Avalon Publishing Group, 2003. 272p. $39.95 (1-56025-518-8). Grades 10 and up.
    Portraits and text about the most famous names in the hip-hop world.

Nathan, M. M. *"Cribs": A Guided Tour Inside the Homes of Your Favorite Stars.* MTV/Pocket Books, 2002. 168p. $19.95 (0-7434-5174-0). Grades 6 and up.
    Insider secrets and photographs from the MTV show *Cribs,* which tours the homes of celebrities.

Nickson, Chris. *Hey Ya! The Unauthorized Biography of OutKast.* St. Martins, 2004. 224p. $11.99 (0-312-33735-3). Grades 8 and up.
    A biography of the world renowned music group OutKast, who have been reinventing the rules of hip-hop since 1994.

Paniccioli, Ernie. *Who Shot Ya? Three Decades of Hip Hop Photography.* HarperCollins, 2004. 202p. $18.95 (0-06-093639-8). Grades 10 and up. (M)
    Photographic portrait of hip-hop, from its beginning to today.

Simpson, Jessica. *Jessica Simpson I Do: Achieving Your Dream Wedding.* NVU/Innerworkings, 2003. 174p. $29.95 (0-9724-5753-4). Grades 6 and up.
    The star of MTV's *Newlyweds* describes the planning that went into her 2002 wedding to Nick Lachey.

Stubbs, David. *Cleaning Out My Closet: Eminem: The Stories behind Every Song.* Thunder's Mouth, 2004. 144p. $23.95 (1-56025-553-6). Grades 10 and up. (M)
    Marshall Mathers's story told through his music.

Tattoo Nation: Portraits of Celebrity Body Art. AOL Time Warner Book Group/Bulfinch Press, 2002. 100p. $35.00 (0-8212-2781-5). Grades 10 and up. (M)
    Portraits from *Rolling Stone* magazine celebrate the tattoo as an art form.

Thorley, Joe. *Avril Lavigne: The Unofficial Book.* Virgin Publishing, 2003. 80p. $14.95 (1-85227-0497). Grades 7 and up.
    Up-to-date biography of one of the most popular young musical stars around.

Tupac: Resurrection 1971–1996. Atria Books, 2003. 242p. $29.95 (0-7434-7434-1). Grades 10 and up. (M)
    This companion to the documentary film chronicles the life and death of rapper Tupac Shakur.

SPORTS

Boards: The Art and Design of the Skateboard. MTV/Universe, 2003. 224p. $18.95 (0-7893-0977-7). Grades 6 and up.

Skateboarding is one of the most popular extreme sports today, and as its popularity has grown, so has interest in the actual graphics on the boards themselves, as they serve as one of the most creative vehicles for graphic designers today.

Brisick, Jamie. *Have Board, Will Travel: The Definitive History of Surf, Skate, and Snow.* Harper Entertainment, 2004. 208p. $19.95 (0-06-056359-1). Grades 8 and up.

The history of surfing, skateboarding, and snowboarding is filled with rugged personalities, exotic locales, wild innovation, and the dream of becoming one with the oceans, streets, and mountains.

Brooke, Michael. *The Concrete Wave: The History of Skateboarding.* Warwick, 1999. 200p. $19.95 (1-894020-54-5). Grades 8 and up.

Designed for a dedicated readership of skateboarding fans and aficionados, this book provides a history of skateboarding, hundreds of photographs, and an interview with world champion Tony Hawk.

Clarkson, Mark. *"Battlebots": The Official Guide.* McGraw Hill/Osbourne, 2002. 272p. $24.95 (0-07-222425-8). Grades 8 and up.

View the metal-crunching destruction from the front lines with this fully authorized guide to one of today's hottest TV shows.

Davis, Jamie. *Skateboarding Is Not a Crime: 50 Years of Street Culture.* Firefly, 2004. 110p. $19.95 (1-55407-001-5). Grades 7 and up.

Skateboarding Is Not a Crime is a celebration of the success of both the sport and the subculture. Illustrated with dramatic action photography, the book recounts the history of the sport and explains its unique codes and customs.

Finch, Richard. *Monster Garage: How to Weld Damn Near Everything.* Motorbooks International/MBI Publishing, 2004. 160p. $19.95 (0-7603-1808-5). Grades 6 and up.

This invaluable guide to welding covers techniques used for Indy and NASCAR race cars, experimental aircraft, and other applications requiring high-quality welds, including welding 4130 steel, stainless, and aluminum, as well as plasma cutting.

Genat, Robert. *Funny Cars.* MBI Publishing, 2000. 96p. $14.95 (0-7603-0795-4). Grades 6 and up.

This colorful book examines the evolution of funny cars from the 1960s to the present and features interviews with such legendary drivers as Don Nicholson, Don Prudhomme, and Dale Armstrong.

Genat, Robert. *Lowriders.* MBI Publishing, 2001. 96p. $14.95 (0-7603-0962-0). Grades 6 and up.

Bilingual Spanish-English book examines major types of lowriders—traditional, bombs, trucks, Euros, and new age—and depicts stunning examples of each, emphasizing the painstaking artistic and mechanical ingenuity that goes into the cars.

Gottlieb, Andrew. *In the Paint: Tattoos of the NBA and the Stories behind Them.* Hyperion, 2003. 112p. $16.95 (0-7868-8868-7). Grades 6 and up.

Tattoos of NBA stars and the stories behind them.

Hameister, Eric. *I Am Jesse James.* Penguin/Viking Studio, 2004. 160p. $18.95 (0-14-200503-7). Grades 8 and up.

The owner of West Coast Choppers shows readers an up-close look at the man and his machines.

Hareas, John. *NBA's Greatest.* DK, 2003. 160p. $30.00 (0-7894-9977-0). Grades 6 and up.

An in-depth look at basketball's greatest players, teams, coaches, and moments, including great upsets, virtuoso performances, clutch shots, great duels, and the most exciting games.

Hawk, Tony. *Between Boardslides and Burnout: My Notes from the Road.* Regan Books/HarperCollins, 2002. 176p. $15.95 (0-06-0008631-9). Grades 7 and up.

With this all-access pass, Tony Hawk—one of the most famous professional skateboarders—shares the joys, the exhaustion, the adrenaline, and the pain of life on the road.

Hoffman, Mat, with Mark Lewman. *The Ride of My Life.* Harper Trade, 2003. 320p. $13.95 (0-06-009416-8). Grades 10 and up.

Childhood for Mat Hoffman was a high-flying, hazardous, nonstop search for the next big rush. At age eleven, he experimented with his bike on a plywood ramp and discovered his true calling—BMX freestyle.

Huebner, Mark. *Sports Bloopers: All-Star Flubs and Fumbles.* Firefly Books, 2003. 128p. $19.95 (1-55297-627-0). Grades 6 and up.

Athletes are highly trained individuals whose superior conditioning, reflexes, and talents allow them to run, throw, skate, catch, aim, jump, and perform better than anyone else—except in this book, which shows professional athletes at their worst.

Johnstone, Mike. *NASCAR: The Need for Speed*. Lerner Sports/Lerner Publishing Group, 2003. 32p. $7.95 (0-8225-0392-1). Grades 6 and up.
Describes some of the major races, cars, and key figures connected with stock-car racing sponsored by NASCAR.

Klancher, Lee. *Monster Garage: How to Customize Damn Near Everything*. Motorbooks International/MBI Publishing, 2003. 224p. $19.95 (0-7603-1748-8). Grades 6 and up.
Presents a guide to customizing anything—from one's car or truck to the toaster. Begins with project planning and moves on to constructing bodywork, adding paint, and applying details.

Klancher, Lee. *Monster Garage: How to Custom Paint Damn Near Everything*. Motorbooks International/MBI Publishing, 2004. 159p. $19.95 (0-7603-1809-3). Grades 6 and up.
Contains the tricks and techniques required to transform a battered beater into a show-stopping street beauty.

Kleh, Cindy. *Snowboarding Skills: The Back-to-Basics Essentials for All Levels*. Firefly Books, 2002. 128p. $16.95 (1-55297-626-2). Grades 6 and up.
With its breakneck speed, upstart attitude, and stunning locales, snowboarding is the definitive sport for those who thrive on adrenaline rushes and winter activities.

Lane, Billy. *Billy Lane Chop Fiction*. Motorbooks International/MBI Publishing, 2004. 160p. $24.95 (076-032-011X). Grades 9 and up. (M)
Autobiography of Billy Lane—one of the most famous chopper builders in the world.

Leiker, Ken. *Unscripted*. Simon & Schuster, 2003. 240p. $45.00 (0-7434-7761-8). Grades 8 and up.
In their own words, World Wrestling Entertainment's superstars share their stories—from life on the road, traveling more than two hundred days a year, to performing in front of hundreds of thousands. Illustrated with multiple photographs.

Macdonald, Andy. *Dropping In with Andy Mac: Life of a Pro Skateboarder*. Simon & Schuster/Pulse, 2003. 170p. $9.99 (0-689-85784-5). Grades 8 and up.
How did Andy Macdonald go from death-defying stunts as a child to world champion skateboarder?

Milan, Garth. *Freestyle Motorcross 2: Air Sickness: More Jump Tricks for the Pros*. MBI, 2002. 198p. $19.95 (0-7603-1184-6). Grades 6 and up.

Heart-stopping photographs show each trick step-by-step from several angles.

Miller, Timothy, and Steve Milton. *NASCAR Now*. Firefly, 2004. 160p. $19.95 (1-55297-829-X). Grades 6 and up.

Behind the scenes look at exclusive driver interviews and a candid look at how the racing business works.

Mirra, Dave. *Mirra Images: The Story of My Life*. HarperCollins, 2003. 208p. $15.95 (0-06-098916-5). Grades 9 and up.

Six months after he was injured by a drunk driver and told by his doctors that he would never ride again, he was back on his bike, competing in—and winning—high-profile BMX events.

Morgan, David Lee. *LeBron James: The Rise of a Star*. Gray, 2003. 240p. $14.95 (1-886228-74-4). Grades 8 and up.

The odds were against LeBron from the start; he could have become just another scarred product of a rough childhood in the projects. Instead, he's an NBA superstar.

MX: The Way of the MotoCrosser. Harry N. Abrams, 2003. 160p. $29.95 (0-8109-4272-0). Grades 7 and up.

Combining a history of the sport from its origins in the 1920s with profiles of the top riders in the world and details of the leading events, this volume offers a comprehensive overview of the fast-growing sport of motocross.

Myers, Walter Dean. *The Greatest: Muhammad Ali*. Scholastic, 2002. 192p. $4.99 (0-590-54343-1). Grades 7 and up.

This biography of the African American boxing champ covers Ali's career and his battle with Parkinson's disease.

Palmer, Chris. *Streetball: All the Ballers' Moves, Slams and Shine*. HarperCollins/ Harper Resource, 2004. 217p. $16.95 (0-06-072444-7). Grades 7 and up.

Overview of the sport of streetball (basketball as played on city playgrounds).

Platt, Larry. *Only the Strong Survive: The Odyssey of Allen Iverson*. Harper-Collins/Regan, 2003. 272p. $12.95 (0-06-009774-4). Grades 10 and up. (M)

Part sports star, part antihero, part hip-hop icon, Allen Iverson—the six-foot Philadelphia 76ers point guard—has managed to cross over into the mainstream of American culture without compromise.

Seate, Mike. *Jesse James: The Man and His Machines.* Motorbooks International, 2003. 195p. $24.95 (0-7603-1614-7). Grades 7 and up.

On the surface, with his collection of skulls, pet sharks, pit bulls, and tattoos, Jesse James is the consummate motorcycle outlaw. And a huge guy favorite.

Seate, Mike. *Streetbike Extreme.* MBI, 2002. 128p. $19.95 (0-7603-1299-0). Grades 7 and up.

With the style, dress, and charm of outrageous rock stars, stunt-riding streetbike riders are violating every known law of traffic and physics.

Sports Illustrated Kids Year in Sports 2005. Scholastic, 2004. 320p. $9.95 (0-439-65082-8). Grades 6 and up.

This easy-to-browse sports almanac will tell kids all they need to know about the previous year in sports.

"Thrasher": Insane Terrain. Rizzoli/Universe, 2001. 192p. $27.50 (0-7893-0536-4). Grades 6 and up.

Published in celebration of the magazine's twentieth anniversary in 2001, this book captures the intense mix of graphics, music, gear, style, and riding that is skateboarding today.

"Thrasher" Presents: How to Build Skateboard Ramps. Edited by Kevin Thatcher. High Speed Productions, 2001. 76p. $9.95 (0-9657271-4-9). Grades 6 and up.

How to buy materials and lay out and assemble everything from a small portable street structure to a full-size half pipe with vertical walls.

Tomlinson, Joe, with Ed Leigh. *Extreme Sports: In Search of the Ultimate Thrill.* Firefly, 2004. 192p. $19.95 (1-55297-992-X). Grades 6 and up.

Extreme sports vigorously test the limits of an individual's strength, agility, and courage.

Vose, Ken. *Inside Monster Garage.* Meredith Books, 2003. 176p. $19.95 (0-696-21890-9). Grades 8 and up.

Monster Garage is the Discovery Channel's hit series in which a crew of designers, mechanics, and welders takes standard, everyday vehicles and turns them into extraordinary and fully functional monster machines.

Zimberoff, Tom. *Art of the Chopper.* Motorbooks International/MBI Publishing, 2003. 256p. $39.95 (0-7603-1572-8). Grades 7 and up.

Photographic—and text—review of the exotic custom motorcycles built by today's hottest builders, such as Billy Lane and Dave Perowitz.

POETRY

Abdullah, Omanii. *I Wanna Be the Kinda Father My Mother Was.* New Readers Press, 1993. 64p. $8.00 (0-88336-033-0). Grades 8 and up.
Poems and thoughts about black males, black pride, relationships, and love.

Carlson, Lori, ed. *Cool Salsa: Bilingual Poems on Growing Up Latino in the United States.* Ballantine, 1995. 136p. $6.99 (0-44970-436-X). Grades 8 and up.
A collection of poems in Spanish and English.

Carlson, Lori, ed. *Red Hot Salsa: Bilingual Poems on Growing Up Latino in the United States.* Henry Holt, 2005. 140p. $14.95 (0-8050-7616-6). Grades 8 and up.
This follow-up to the first volume includes words by Latino poets about who they are and their hopes for the future.

Galvez, Jose. *Vatos.* Cinco Puntos Press, 2000. 95p. $19.95 (0-93817-52-0). Grades 7 and up.
Latino men in a variety of situations portray Mexican American culture and heritage.

Grandits, John. *Technically, It's Not My Fault: Concrete Poems.* Clarion, 2004. Unpaged. $5.95 (0-618-80361-7). Grades 6 and up.
Documents the creative, imaginative, and weird thoughts of an eleven-year-old boy through a collection of poetry and fun illustrations.

Janeczko, Paul, ed. *Blushing: Expressions of Love in Poems and Letters.* Scholastic, 2004. 112p. $15.95 (0-436-53056-3). Grades 8 and up.
A collection of love poetry from a variety of authors.

Myers, Walter Dean. *Harlem.* Scholastic, 1997. Unpaged. $16.95 (0-590-54340-7). Grades 6 and up.
Colorful collages are combined with a poem.

Shakur, Tupac. *The Rose That Grew from Concrete.* Simon & Schuster, 1999. 149p. $21.00 (0-671-02844-8). Grades 8 and up.
A collection of verse by the late hip-hop star Tupac Shakur.

Silverstein, Shel. *Falling Up.* Harper, 1996. 171p. $17.99 (0-06-024-802-5). Grades 6 and up.
A collection of humorous poems and drawings.

Silverstein, Shel. *A Light in the Attic.* Harper, 2001. 171p. $22.99 (0-06-623-617-7). Grades 6 and up.
Another classic collection of humorous poems.

Silverstein, Shel. *Where the Sidewalk Ends.* Harper, 2004. 183p. $17.99 (0-06-057-234-5). Grades 6 and up.

A classic collection of poetry, still very popular with middle school students.

The Spoken Word Revolution: Slam, Hip Hop and the Poetry of a New Generation. Sourcebooks Inc./Media Fusion, 2003. 241p. $24.95 (1-4022-0037-4). Grades 10 and up. (M)

Describes how contemporary poetry intended to be spoken out loud has brought about a revitalization of interest in poetry, and presents works by more than forty leading poets.

THEIR OWN VOICES—POETRY AND WRITING BY TEENAGERS

Angst! Teen Verses from the Edge. Edited by Tom, Karen, and Kiki. Workman, 2001. 133p. $8.95 (0-7611-2383-0). Grades 7 and up.

Collects poetry by teen girls about society, crushes, anger, and love, and provides tips for aspiring poets.

Blue Jean: What Young Women Are Thinking, Saying and Doing. Compiled by Sherry S. Handel. Blue Jean Press, 2001. 246p. $14.95 (0-970-66091-X). Grades 7 and up.

Essays and short fiction discussing volunteering, activism, feminism, homelessness, ethnicity, body image, gender bias, zines, and filmmaking.

Irwin, Cait. *Conquering the Beast Within: How I Fought Depression and Won—and How You Can, Too.* Random House, 1999. $14.00 (0-8129-3247-1). Grades 7 and up.

A teenager offers an account of her battle against depression.

My Sisters' Voices: Teenage Girls of Color Speak Out. Compiled by Iris Jacob. Owl Books, 2002. 246p. $13.00 (0-8050-6821-X). Grades 7 and up.

Powerful collection of thought-provoking essays by teenage girls of African American, Hispanic, Asian American, Native American, and biracial backgrounds.

The Pain Tree and Other Teenage Angst-Ridden Poetry. Edited by Watson, Esther Pearl, and Mark Todd. Houghton Mifflin, 2000. 62p. $16.00 (0-618-01558-2). Grades 7 and up.

Poetry about angst of all kinds.

Paint Me Like I Am: Teen Poems from Writerscorps. HarperCollins, 2003. 128p. $6.99 (0-06-447264-7). Grades 6 and up.

The diverse voices of teens from San Francisco; Washington, D.C.; and the Bronx are brought together in this collection of poems.

Patnaik, Gayatri, and Michelle T. Shinseki. *The Secret Life of Teens: Young People Speak Out about Their Lives.* Harper San Francisco, 2000. 173p. $12.95 (0-688-17176-5). Grades 6 and up.

In more than two hundred candid letters, American teenagers share their thoughts on current issues and experiences.

Quiet Storm: Voices of Young Black Poets. Edited by Lydia Omolola Okutoro. Hyperion/Jump at the Sun, 2002. 102p. $4.99 (0-7868-1320-2). Grades 8 and up.

A collection of poems celebrating the African Diaspora through the eyes of youths of African descent from the United States and around the world.

Shandler, Sara. *Ophelia Speaks: Adolescent Girls Write about Their Search for Self.* HarperPerennial, 1999. 285p. $12.95 (0-06-095297-0). Grades 6 and up.

A collection of the writings of teenage girls from all backgrounds and all parts of the country.

Sugar in the Raw: Voices of Young Black Girls in America. Edited by Rebecca Carroll. Crown, 1997. 144p. $14.00 (0-517-88-497-6). Grades 8 and up.

In a collection of interviews, fifteen African American girls share their thoughts on their lives, self-esteem, personal identity, values, race, and dreams for the future.

Things I Have to Tell You: Poems and Writings by Teenage Girls. Edited by Betsy Franco. Candlewick Press, 2001. 63p. $8.99 (0-7636-1035-6). Grades 6 and up.

A collection of poems, stories, and essays written by girls twelve to eighteen years of age revealing the secrets that enabled them to overcome the challenges they faced.

Yell-Oh Girls: Emerging Voices Explore Culture, Identity, and Growing Up Asian-American. Edited by Vickie Nam. HarperCollins, 2001. 297p. $13.95 (0-06-095944-4). Grades 8 and up.

A collection of illuminating, poignant, and incisive essays and observations capture the complex realities of life for young Asian American women.

You Hear Me? Poems and Writing by Teenage Boys. Edited by Betsy Franco. Candlewick, 2001. 107p. $6.99 (0-7636-1159-X). Grades 6 and up.

An anthology of stories, poems, and essays by adolescent boys on issues that concern them, including identity, girls, death, anger, appearance, and family.

CHANGING BODIES

Drill, Esther, Heather McDonald, and Rebecca Odes. *Deal with It! A Whole New Approach to Your Body, Brain, and Life as a Gurl.* Pocket, 1999. 304p. $15.00 (0-671-04157-6). Grades 7 and up.

This intelligent, funny guide to the female body, sexuality, and a host of other important topics by the creators of gurl.com shows young women how to navigate the tricky waters of "gurlhood."

Girlsource: A Book by and for Young Women. Ten Speed Press, 2003. 96p. $12.95 (1-58008-555-5). Grades 8 and up.

Offers advice for teenage girls and young women about relationships, stress, dating, sex, pregnancy, drugs and alcohol, school, work, and discrimination.

Jukes, Mavis. *The Guy Book: An Owner's Manual.* Crown/Random House, 2002. 159p. $12.95 (0-67-989028-9). Grades 8 and up.

From purchasing birth control to getting rid of acne, this is a helpful and informative guide for young men dealing with puberty and the common challenges of the teen years.

Madaras, Lynda, and Area Madaras. *The What's Happening to My Body Book for Boys: A Growing Up Guide for Parents and Sons.* Newmarket Press, 2000. 238p. $12.95 (1-55704-443-0). Grades 6 and up.

Provides information and advice concerning the physical, psychological, and behavioral changes associated with puberty.

Madaras, Lynda, and Area Madaras. *The What's Happening to My Body Book for Girls: A Growing Up Guide for Parents and Daughters.* Newmarket Press, 2000. 262p. $12.95 (1-55704-444-9). Grades 6 and up.

Provides information and advice concerning the physical, psychological, and behavioral changes associated with puberty.

Pavanel, Jane. *The Sex Book: The Alphabet of Smarter Love.* Lobster Press, 2001. 200p. $14.95 (1-894222-30-X). Grades 9 and up.

Alphabetical entries discuss reproductive anatomy, sexual behavior, birth control, sexually transmitted diseases, psychological implications of sexual activity, and related topics, and answer common teen questions.

Shaw, Tucker, and Fiona Gibb. *This Book Is about Sex.* Penguin Putnam/ Alloy, 2000. 167p. $5.99 (0-14-131019-7). Grades 10 and up.

The authors—sex experts on the alloy.com Web site—answer questions teenagers have asked about sexual terminology, health and social issues, sexual identity, and relationship concerns.

The Teenage Guy's Survival Guide: The Real Deal on Girls, Growing Up, and Other Guy Stuff. Little, Brown, 1999. 136p. $8.95 (0-316-17824-1). Grades 8 and up.

A humorous guide for boys ages ten to fourteen offers advice on all those things a growing guy wants to know but doesn't want to ask, such as questions about dating, sex, body changes, and social life.

TRUE STORIES

Abdul-Jabbar, Kareem, ed. *Black Profiles in Courage: A Legacy of African-American Achievement.* HarperCollins/Avon, 2000. 261p. $13.00 (0-380-81341-6). Grades 7 and up.

Inspirational stories of influential African Americans, including Crispus Attucks, Frederick Douglass, and Rosa Parks.

Alexander, Caroline. *The Endurance: Shackleton's Legendary Antarctic Expedition.* Knopf, 1998. 224p. $29.95 (0-375-40403-1). Grades 6 and up.

This companion volume to an exhibition at the American Museum of Natural History chronicles the perilous 1914–1915 expedition of Sir Ernest Shackleton in Antarctica, when he and his crew became stranded in the frozen Weddell Sea and faced a twenty-month struggle for survival.

Armstrong, Jennifer, and Todd Brewster. *The Century for Young People.* Random House, 1999. 256p. $19.95 (0-385-32708-0). Grades 6 and up.

Documents how the twentieth century has been a time of tremendous change—the most eventful hundred years in human history.

Ash, Russell. *Top Ten of Everything 2005.* DK, 2004. 256p. $19.00 (0-7566-0518-0). Grades 6 and up.

The essential illustrated reference guide for trivia fans of all ages and walks of life.

Bachrach, Susan. *Tell Them We Remember: The Story of the Holocaust.* Little, Brown, 1994. 128p. $15.99 (0-316-07484-5). Grades 6 and up.

This book is full of pictures and personal stories of those who survived persecution by the Nazis and of many family members who did not.

Beals, Melba Pattillo. *Warriors Don't Cry: A Searing Memoir of the Battle to Integrate Little Rock's Central High.* Simon & Schuster/Simon Pulse, 1995. 226p. $6.99 (0-6718-9900-7). Grades 8 and up.

One of the first nine students to integrate Central High School in Little Rock, Arkansas, shares the journal she kept of that fateful school year in 1957.

Benchley, Peter. *Shark Life: True Stories about Sharks and the Sea*. Delacorte, 2005. 193p. $15.95 (0-385-73109-4). Grades 6 and up.

The author of *Jaws* offers a comprehensive and informative guide to these incredible creatures through a review of the different types of sharks that exist, their swimming patterns in relation to the tides, and the common behaviors and traits they share.

Bridges, Ruby, and Margo Lundell. *Through My Eyes*. Scholastic, 1999. 63p. $16.95 (0-590-18923-9). Grades 6 and up.

Ruby Bridges recounts the story of her involvement, as a six-year-old, in the integration of her school in New Orleans in 1960.

Burch, Jennings. *They Cage the Animals at Night*. New American Library/Signet, 1988 reprint. 293p. $5.99 (045-115-9411). Grades 8 and up.

Left by his incapacitated mother at a Catholic orphanage in Brooklyn, Burch describes his unhappy life as a foster child, his experiences as a runaway, his struggle for survival, his growth of self-reliance, and his triumph over loneliness. Good for *A Child Called It* fans.

Calabro, Marian. *The Perilous Journey of the Donner Party*. Clarion, 1999. 192p. $19.99 (0-395-86610-3). Grades 7 and up.

The story of the ill-fated Donner Party and their horrifying end on their way to California, as seen through the eyes of twelve-year-old Virginia Reed.

Caught in the Crossfire: Growing Up in a War Zone. Walker, 1995. 128p. $19.95 (0-8027-8363-5). Grades 7 and up.

Uses incidents from Lebanon, El Salvador, Mozambique, Bosnia-Herzegovina, and Washington, D.C., to examine the effect on children of growing up in a war zone.

Coe, Michael D. *The Titanic: Disaster at Sea*. Enslow Publishers, 2001. 48p. $18.95 (0-7660-1557-2). Grades 6 and up.

Describes the ill-fated steamship, recounts its tragic sinking, and touches on the discovery of the wreckage in 1985.

Colman, Penny. *Corpses, Coffins and Crypts*. Holt, 1997. 224p. $19.95 (0-8050-5066-3). Grades 6 and up.

Documents the burial process throughout the centuries and in different cultures.

Colman, Penny. *Toilets, Bathtubs, Sinks and Sewers: A History of the Bathroom*. Atheneum, 1994. 96p. $16.00 (0-689-31894-4). Grades 6 and up.

An interesting, well-written introduction to the history of technology and inventions related to personal cleanliness and hygiene.

Conniff, Richard. *Rats! The Good, the Bad, and the Ugly.* Crown, 2002. 35p. $15.95 (0-375-81207-5). Grades 6 and up.

Discusses the physical characteristics, behavior, origins, and various types of rats as well as their interaction with humans.

Crime Scene: The Ultimate Guide to Forensic Science. Edited by Richard Platt. Dorling Kindersley, 2003. 144p. $25.00 (0-7894-8891-4). Grades 7 and up.

This richly illustrated introduction to the high-tech world of forensic science shows how the latest methods of scientific detection are used to uncover the truth about a crime scene.

Crowe, Chris. *Getting Away with Murder: The True Story of the Emmett Till Case.* Penguin, 2003. 128p. $18.99 (0-803-72804-2). Grades 7 and up.

When fourteen-year-old Emmett Till left Chicago to visit family in a small town in Mississippi and was soon murdered for whistling at a white woman, a series of events took place that changed the ways of the South and the nation forever.

Davis, Sampson, George Jenkins, Rameck Hunt, and Sharon Draper. *We Beat the Street: How a Friendship Pact Led to Success.* Penguin, 2005. 194p. $16.99 (0-5254-7407-2). Grades 8 and up.

Three boys, who made a pact to stick together through the rough times in their impoverished Newark neighborhood, found the strength to work through their difficulties and complete high school, college, and medical school together.

Duncan, Lois. *Who Killed My Daughter?* Dell/Bantam, 1994. 354p. $7.99 (0-440-21342-8). Grades 9 and up.

The best-selling young-adult novelist recounts her daughter's mysterious shooting death and her own investigation into the crime, describing her use of a psychic to contact her dead child and expose the truth.

Fisher, Antwone. *Finding Fish.* HarperCollins, 2002. 369p. $7.50 (0-060-53986-0). Grades 8 and up.

Born in prison to a single mom and raised in the foster-care system, Antwone Fisher resisted drugs and crime and built a successful life for himself. Made into a motion picture.

Fleischman, John. *Phineas Gage: A Gruesome but True Story about Brain Science.* Houghton Mifflin, 2004. 86p. $8.95 (0-618-49478-2). Grades 6 and up.

A railroad construction foreman, Phineas was blasting rock near Cavendish, Vermont, in 1848 when a thirteen-pound iron rod was shot through his brain.

Jackson, Donna M. *The Bone Detectives: How Forensic Science Helps Solve Crimes and Uncover Mysteries of the Dead.* Little, Brown, 1996. 48p. $17.95 (0-316-82935-8). Grades 6 and up.

Explores the world of forensic anthropology and its applications in solving crimes.

Jacobs, Thomas A. *What Are My Rights? 95 Questions and Answers about Teens and the Law.* Free Spirit, 1997. 208p. $14.95 (1-57542-028-7). Grades 8 and up.

A guide to teenagers' legal rights.

Janeczko, Paul. *Top Secret: A Handbook of Codes, Ciphers and Secret Writing.* Candlewick, 2004. 136p. $16.99 (0-7636-0971-4). Grades 6 and up.

Presents history, trivia, and code-breaking tales in a guide to the world of secret writing that includes examples of a variety of codes and ciphers.

Katz, Jon. *Geeks: How Two Lost Boys Rode the Internet Out of Idaho.* Broadway Books, 2001. 256p. $12.95 (0-7679-0699-3). Grades 10 and up.

Jesse Dailey and his friend Eric Twilegar fixed computers for a living but were social outcasts in their high school.

Lavender, Don. *Snowbound: The Tragic Story of the Donner Party.* Holiday House, 1996. 96p. $22.95 (0-8234-1231-8). Grades 6 and up.

With extensive use of primary documents and excellent illustrations, this account vividly reconstructs the hardships and horrors of the Donner party's attempt to cross the Rockies.

LeBlanc, Adrian Nicole. *Random Family: Love, Drugs, Trouble and Coming of Age in the Bronx.* Simon & Schuster/Scribner, 2004. 409p. $14.95 (0743254430). Grades 10 and up. (M)

Nineteen-year-old Jessica, fourteen-year-old Coco, and their friends and family experience challenges with sex, teen parenthood, and gangs while living in the Bronx.

MacAuley, David. *The New the Way Things Work.* Houghton Mifflin, 1998. 400p. $35.00 (0395938473). Grades 6 and up.

Demystifies the machinery of the computer age with the help of a charming woolly mammoth in a completely updated version of an earlier work, which details the latest innovations from cars and microchips to watches and lasers.

McCall, Nathan. *Makes Me Wanna Holler: A Young Black Man in America.* Knopf, 1995. 432p. $14.00 (0-679-74070-8). Grades 10 and up. (M)

McCall describes his early years in Portsmouth, Virginia, as a young black male—the recipient of a twelve-year prison sentence for armed robbery— whose life was dangerously out of control.

McManners, Hugh. *Ultimate Special Forces.* DK, 2003. 192p. $30.00 (0-7894-9973-8). Grades 6 and up.
A riveting exploration of the world's most highly trained military units, from the ancient Spartans to modern-day U.S. Navy SEALs.

Morse, Jennifer Corr. *Scholastic Book of World Records 2005.* Scholastic, 2004. 320p. $9.95 (0-439-64935-8). Grades 6 and up.
Whether kids want to know which movie had the biggest box-office open- ing weekend, who is the world's top-earning tennis player, or which state har- vests the most catfish, the answers are here.

Murphy, Jim. *The Great Fire.* Scholastic, 1995. 144p. $17.95 (0-590-47267-4). Grades 6 and up.
A dramatic re-creation of the catastrophic Chicago fire of 1871 that left 100,000 people homeless.

Myers, Walter Dean. *Bad Boy: A Memoir.* HarperTempest, 2002. 224p. $6.99 (0-06-447288-4). Grades 7 and up.
As a boy, Walter Dean Myers was quick-tempered and physically strong, always ready for a fight.

Owen, David. *Hidden Evidence: 40 True Crimes and How Forensic Science Helped Solve Them.* Firefly Books, 2000. 240p. $24.95 (1-55209-483-9). Grades 9 and up. (M)
This thought-provoking look at the role of forensic science in criminal in- vestigations examines forty high-profile cases and the diverse technologies used to solve them, including fingerprinting, handwriting analyses, DNA testing, and toxicology.

Pelzer, Dave. *A Child Called It: One Child's Courage to Survive.* HCI, 1995. 195p. $9.95 (1-55874-366-9). Grades 9 and up.
The author shares his unforgettable story of the many abuses he suffered at the hands of his alcoholic mother and the averted eyes of his neglectful father.

Pelzer, Dave. *The Lost Boy: A Foster Child's Search for the Love of a Family.* HCI, 1997. 250p. $10.95 (1-55874-515-7). Grades 9 and up.
Imagine a young boy who has never had a loving home. His only posses- sions are the old, torn clothes he carries in a paper bag; the only world he knows is one of isolation and fear.

Pfetzer, Mark. *Within Reach: My Everest Story.* Penguin Puffin, 2000. 208p. $7.99 (0-14-130497-9). Grades 9 and up.

In May 1996 at age sixteen, Mark Pfetzer was the youngest climber on Mount Everest to reach 26,000 feet, and his gripping autobiography focuses exclusively on his mountain-climbing achievements.

Ralston, Aron. *Between a Rock and a Hard Place.* Simon & Schuster, 2004. 368p. $26.00 (0-7434-9281-1). Grades 9 and up.

Ralston was forced to self-amputate his right arm after it was caught between a boulder and a canyon wall during what began as a routine day hike in the Utah canyons.

Roach, Mary. *Stiff: The Curious Lives of Human Cadavers.* Norton, 2004. 303p. $13.95 (039-3324-826). Grades 9 and up. (M)

A look inside the world of forensics examines the use of human cadavers in a wide range of endeavors, including research into new surgical procedures, space exploration, and a Tennessee human decay research facility.

Rodriguez, Luis. *Always Running: La Vida Loca: Gang Days in L.A.* Simon & Schuster, 1994. 272p. $13.00 (0-671-88231-7). Grades 10 and up. (M)

By age twelve, Luis Rodriguez was a veteran of East L.A. gang warfare.

Shales, Tom. *Live from New York: An Uncensored History of "Saturday Night Live."* Little, Brown, 2003. 638p. $15.95 (0316735655). Grades 10 and up. (M)

A history of the long-running television series draws on backstage anecdotes and uncensored reminiscences to create an oral history of *Saturday Night Live.*

Sullivan, Robert. *Rats: Observations on the History and Habitat of the City's Most Unwanted Inhabitants.* Bloomsbury USA, 2005. 256p. $14.95 (1-5823-4477-9). Grades 9 and up.

Rat facts and entertaining rat stories, the history of rats, and descriptions of how the author, with the aid of a notebook and night-vision gear, sat nightly in a garbage-filled alley getting to know the wild city rat.

Wilcox, Charlotte. *Mummies, Bones and Body Parts.* Lerner, 2000. 64p. $7.95 (1-57505-486-8). Grades 6 and up.

Describes the wide variety of human remains, the use and abuse of them, what they reveal about life in the past, and contemporary attitudes toward the dead.

Williams, Stanley "Tookie." *Life in Prison*. Seastar, 2001. 80p. $5.95 (0-688-15589-8). Grades 6 and up.

This shocking testimony by a death-row inmate and cofounder of the Crips gang debunks current myths about prison life and offers straightforward, honest prose that challenges young people to choose the right path.

ART AND DRAWING

Agee, Jon. *Elvis Lives! and Other Anagrams*. Farrar, Straus and Giroux, 2004. 80p. $8.95 (0-374-42095-5). Grades 6 and up.

Another installment of witty wordplay, this book contains over sixty anagrams (words or phrases rearranged to form new words or phrases), each hilariously illustrated by the author. Other titles from this author include *Palindromania; Sit on a Potato Pan, Otis; So Many Dynamos;* and *Go Hang a Salami, I'm a Lasagna Hog.*

Caldwell, Ben. *Action! Cartooning*. Sterling, 2004. 95p. $9.95 (0-8069-8739-4). Grades 6 and up.

Offers step-by-step instructions for drawing faces and anatomy, creating emotion, and drawing figures in action settings.

Ganz, Nicholas. *Graffiti World: Street Art from Five Continents*. Abrams, 2004. 376p. $35.00 (08-1094979-2). Grades 9 and up.

This book is packed with full-color photographs representative of graffiti styles and artists from around the world.

Hart, Christopher. *Anime Mania: How to Draw Characters for Japanese Animation*. Watson-Guptill, 2002. 144p. $19.95 (0-8230-0158-X). Grades 6 and up.

Step-by-step instructions for drawing anime (Japanese animation) and manga (Japanese comics). Each volume focuses on a specific aspect and characters.

Hart, Christopher. *Manga Mania Fantasy Worlds: How to Draw the Enchanted Worlds of Japanese Comics*. Watson-Guptill, 2003. 144p. $19.95 (0823-02972-7). Grades 6 and up.

Hart, Christopher. *Manga Mania: How to Draw Japanese Comics*. Watson-Guptill, 2001. 144p. $19.95 (0-8230-3035-0). Grades 6 and up.

Hart, Christopher. *Manga Mania Shoujo: How to Draw the Charming and Romantic Characters of Japanese Comics*. Watson-Guptill, 2004. 144p. $19.95 (0-8230-2973-5). Grades 6 and up.

Hart, Christopher. *Manga Mania Video Games: How to Draw the Characters, Fighting Poses, and Environments of Manga Style Video Games.* Watson-Guptill, 2004. $19.95 (0-8230-2974-3). Grades 6 and up.

Hart, Christopher. *Manga Mania Villains: How to Draw the Super Villains of Manga and Anime.* Watson-Guptill, 2003. 144p. $19.95 (0-823-02971-9). Grades 6 and up.

Hart, Christopher. *Manhwa Mania: How to Draw Korean Comics.* Watson-Guptill, 2004. 144p. $19.95 (0-8230-2976-X). Grades 6 and up.

Hart, Christopher. *Mecha Mania: How to Draw the Battling Robots, Cool Spaceships, and Military Vehicles of Japanese Comics.* Watson-Guptill, 2002. 144p. $19.95 (0-8230-3056-3). Grades 6 and up.

Lamm, Spencer, ed. *The Art of the* Matrix. Newmarket Press, 2001. 488p. $50.00 (1-55704-405-8). Grades 6 and up.
　　Details the computer animation and artwork that went into the movie.

Mignola, Mike. Hellboy: *The Art of the Movie.* Dark Horse. 2004. 199p. $24.95 (1-59307-188-4). Grades 8 and up.
　　Behind-the-scenes trip into the making of the *Hellboy* movie.

Miller, Steve, and Bryan Baugh. *Scared! How to Draw Fantastic Horror Comic Characters.* Watson-Guptill, 2004. 144p. $19.95 (0-8230-1664-1). Grades 6 and up.
　　This in-depth guide to drawing horror comics provides a brief history of the genre, from EC Comics to Vertigo, and offers detailed, step-by-step instructions for drawing werewolves, vampires, swamp creatures, and other popular monsters.

Nagatomo, Haruno. *Draw Your Own Manga: All the Basics.* Kodansha America, 2004. 1105p. $19.95 (4-7700-2951-9). Grades 6 and up.
　　A step-by-step guide to drawing in the popular Japanese style of manga.

Polhemus, Ted. *Hot Bodies, Cool Styles: New Techniques in Self Adornment.* Thames and Hudson, 2004. 176p. $24.95 (0-500-28500-4). Grades 8 and up.
　　This photographic tour of the art of body decoration covers tattoos, piercings, henna design, ultraviolet paint, non-gem jewelry, extreme hair fashion, and more.

Seckel, Al. *Great Book of Optical Illusions.* Firefly Books, 2002. 270p. $24.95 (1-55297-650-5). Grades 6 and up.
　　Presents over 270 examples and works of art designed to trick the eye.

Wick, Walter. *Optical Tricks.* Scholastic, 1998. 41p. $13.95 (0-590-22227-9). Grades 6 and up.

More tricks for your eyes.

ASTROLOGY

Collier-Thompson, Kristi. *The Girls' Guide to Dreams.* Sterling, 2003. 128p. $12.95 (1-4027-0032-6). Grades 6 and up.

What did that dream mean?

Edut, Tali, and Ophira. *Astrostyle: Star-Studded Advice for Love, Life, and Looking Good.* Simon & Schuster, 2003. 245p. $12.00 (0-7432-4985-2). Grades 6 and up.

This hip astrological guide for young people provides readers with insights and advice based on the signs of the zodiac.

Gravelle, Karen. *Five Ways to Know about You.* Walker, 2002. 176p. $16.95 (0-8027-8749-5). Grades 7 and up.

Explains astrology, palm reading, numerology, Chinese horoscopes, and handwriting analysis. Worksheets help readers learn more about themselves.

Manoy, Lauren. *Where to Park Your Broomstick: A Teen's Guide to Witchcraft.* Fireside, 2002. 311p. $13.00 (0-684-85500-3). Grades 6 and up.

The latest guide to all things Wicca for teens.

Olmstead, Kathleen. *Girls' Guide to Tarot.* Sterling, 2002. 128p. $12.95 (0-8069-8072-9). Grades 6 and up.

Full instructions on how to use tarot cards.

Rain, Gwinevere. *Spellcraft for Teens: A Magical Guide to Writing and Casting Spells.* Llewellyn, 2002. 139p. $12.95 (0-7387-0225-0). Grades 7 and up.

Presents instructions on a variety of spells and chants.

Reid, Lori. *The Art of Hand Reading.* Dorling Kindersley, 1999. 120p. $15.00 (0-78-944837-8). Grades 6 and up.

Describes the various lines that are found on the hand and how they are interpreted.

Shaw, Maria. *Maria Shaw's Star Gazer: Your Soul Searching, Dream Seeking, Make Something Happen Guide to the Future.* Llewellyn, 2003. 308p. $17.95 (0-7387-0422-9). Grades 6 and up.

Describes the basic techniques of astrology, tarot, aura readings, crystals, numerology, palmistry, and dream interpretation.

Shaw, Tucker. *Dreams: Explore the You That You Can't Control.* Penguin/Alloy, 2000. 160p. $5.99 (0-14-130920-2). Grades 6 and up.

The Alloy.com dream guru helps teens unravel the mysteries of dreams while offering insightful dream analysis, history, and practical tactics for understanding the dream world.

CRAFTS AND DIY PROJECTS

Bonnell, Jennifer. *D.I.Y. Girl: The Real Girl's Guide to Making Everything from Lip Gloss to Lamps.* Penguin, 2003. 85p. $12.99 (0-14-250048-8). Grades 6 and up.

A step-by-step guide to making clothes, beauty products, fashion accessories, and decorative items for the home using commonly available materials.

Jaynes, Ella. *Planet Yumthing's DIY: Create, Design, Reinvent and Make It Yours.* Bantam Doubleday Dell, 2003. 88p. $12.95 (0-553-37595-4). Grades 6 and up.

Provides easy-to-follow instructions for creating cool and hip accessories and home decor projects.

Montano, Mark. *Super Suite: The Ultimate Bedroom Makeover Guide for Girls.* Universe Publishing, 2002. 127p. $17.95 (0-7893-0811-8). Grades 6 and up.

Easy decorating on the cheap.

Murillo, Kathy, et al. *The Crafty Diva's DIY Stylebook: A Grrl's Guide to Cool Creations You Can Make, Show Off and Share.* Watson-Guptill, 2004. 144p. $12.95 (0-8230-6993-1). Grades 6 and up.

Make clothing that doesn't look like you actually made it!

Traig, Wendy. *Crafty Girl Accessories: Things to Make and Do.* Chronicle, 2002. 120p. $12.95 (0-8118-3151-5). Grades 6 and up.

Presents forty ways to create accessories that range from bags and hats to hair-wear and shoes, all of it kooky, cute and completely wearable.

Traig, Wendy. *Crafty Girl Hair: Things to Make and Do.* Chronicle, 2004. 120p. $12.95 (0-8118-4033-6). Grades 6 and up.

Outlines how to maintain healthy hair, provides instructions for making hair products and accessories, and demonstrates how to achieve certain looks, from Veronica Lake to Punk Princess.

Traig, Jennifer. *Crafty Girl Makeup: Things to Make and Do.* Chronicle, 2003. 120p. $12.95 (0-8118-3679-7).Grades 6 and up.

Outlines how to apply makeup and maintain healthy skin, provides recipes for making cosmetics, and demonstrates how to achieve certain looks, from Indian Princess to Geisha Girl, and from Peachy Keen to Goth Girl.

Traig, Jennifer. *Crafty Girl Slumber Parties: Things to Make and Do.* Chronicle Books, 2002. 120p. $12.95 (0-8118-3571-5). Grades 6 and up.

Suggests fifteen to twenty slumber party themes and ideas, including activities, decor, and menus, from Fright Night to Spa Spectacular to Gypsy Jubilee.

BEAUTY

Brous, Elizabeth. *How to Be Gorgeous: The Ultimate Beauty Guide to Hair, Makeup and More.* HarperCollins, 2000. 160p. $14.95 (0-06-440871-X). Grades 6 and up.

Offers hundreds of tips, tricks, and secrets for hair, makeup, skin, and nails, and includes quizzes, charts, and shopping lists.

Brown, Bobbi, and Annemarie Iverson. *Bobbi Brown Teenage Beauty: Everything You Need to Know to Look Pretty, Natural, Sexy and Awesome.* HarperCollins, 2000. 200p. $25.00 (0-06-019636-X). Grades 6 and up.

Addresses the aspects of a young woman's beauty, from skin care and diet to exercise and hair care, providing coverage specifically for the teenage years and for all races, skin types, and lifestyles.

Fornay, Alfred. *Born Beautiful: The African American Teenager's Complete Beauty Guide.* Amber Books/Wiley and Sons, 2002. 166p. $14.95 (0-471-40275-3). Grades 6 and up.

Provides advice for young African American women on skin care, makeup, hairstyling, diet, and exercise, as well as other beauty secrets.

Irons, Diane. *Teen Beauty Secrets: Fresh, Simple and Sassy Tips for Your Perfect Look.* Sourcebooks, 2002. 263p. $14.95 (1-57071-959-4). Grades 6 and up.

Presents fashion and grooming tips for teenage girls, covering such topics as skin care, makeup, hair care, exercise, nutrition, and wardrobe.

Marron, Maggie. *Stylin': Great Looks for Teens.* Friedman, 2001. 96p. $12.95 (1-58663-079-2). Grades 6 and up.

Offers tips on hairstyles, makeup, skin care, fitness, and fashion from such celebrities as Britney Spears, Jennifer Lopez, and Halle Berry.

Mason, Linda. *Teen Makeup: Looks to Match Your Every Mood.* Watson-Guptill, 2004. 144p. $16.95 (0-8230-2980-8). Grades 6 and up.

This makeup artist to the stars has created a glossy, how-to guide for teens.

Odes, Rebecca, Esther Drill, and Heather McDonald. *The Looks Book: A Whole New Approach to Beauty, Body Image, and Style*. Penguin Putnam, 2002. 151p. $17.00 (0-14-200211-9). Grades 7 and up.

Offers a study of the history, science, culture, and business of beauty, with insights into body-image issues, including imagination, self-expression, self-invention, and irreverence toward traditional ideals of beauty.

Roppatte, Vincent. *Cool Hair: A Teenager's Guide to the Best Beauty Secrets on Hair, Make-Up, and Style*. St. Martin's, 2003. 158p. $24.95 (0-3123-1251-2). Grades 6 and up.

This illustrated guide by a Saks Fifth Avenue stylist invites teen girls to develop a personal style.

Teen People Celebrity Beauty Guide: Star Secrets for Gorgeous Hair, Makeup, Skin, and More! Edited by *Teen People* editors, with Lauren McCann and Maria Neuman. Little, Brown, 2005. 157p. $15.95 (1-932273-39-5). Grades 6 and up.

Helpful advice from celebrities and their stylists and how-to illustrations offer tips on everything from makeup and skin care to hair conditioning, style, and fashion.

Worthington, Charles. *The Complete Book of Hairstyling*. Firefly Books, 2002. 304p. $19.95 (1-55297-576-2). Grades 6 and up.

Filled with creative hairstyles, easy-to-follow instructions, valuable tips, and salon secrets, this is the indispensable hair bible for teen girls.

SELECTED NONFICTION SERIES

Epidemics: Deadly Diseases throughout History series. Rosen, 2002–2004. $19.95 ea. Grades 6 and up.

AIDS (0-8239-3344-X).
Amebic Dysentery (0-8239-4196-5).
Botulism (0-8239-4197-3).
Cholera (0-8239-3345-8).
Chronic Wasting Disease (0-8239-4198-1).
Creutzfeldt-Jakob Disease (0-8239-4199-X).
Dengue Fever (0-8239-4200-7).
E. coli (0-8239-4201-5).
Ebola (0-8239-3496-9).

Influenza (0-8239-3347-4).
Legionnaire's Disease (0-8239-3497-7).
Leprosy (Hansen's Disease) (0-8239-3498-5).
Listeriosis (0-8239-4202-3).
Mad Cow Disease: Bovine Spongiform Encephalopathy (0-8239-3487-X).
Malaria (0-8239-3342-3).
The Plague (0-8239-3343-1).
Polio (0-8239-3348-2).
Sleeping Sickness and Other Parasitic Tropical Diseases (0-8239-3499-3).
Smallpox (0-8239-3346-6).
Syphilis and Other Sexually Transmitted Diseases (0-8239-3488-8).
Tuberculosis (0-8239-3349-0).
Typhoid Fever (0-8239-3572-8).
West Nile Virus (0-8239-4203-1).
Yellow Fever (0-8239-3489-6).

Extreme Sports series. National Geographic, 2002. $8.95 ea. Grades 6 and up. Guide to extreme sports for kids and teenagers.

Ski! (0-7922-6738-9).
Snowboard! (0-7922-6740-0).
Bike! (0-7922-6742-7).
Dive! (0-7922-6743-5).
Climb! (0-7922-6744-3).
Skateboard! (0-7922-8229-9).
Surf! (0-7922-5108-3).
Skate! (0-7922-5107-5).

The Incredibly Disgusting Story series. Rosen Publishing, 2001–2002. 48p. $18.95 ea. Grades 6 and up.

The dangers of a variety of drugs, presented in an interesting though disgusting manner.

Inhalants and Your Nasal Passages (0-8239-3392-X).
Speed and Your Brain (0-8239-4091-8).
Barbiturates and Your Central Nervous System (0-8239-3388-1).
Ecstasy and Your Heart (0-8239-3390-3).
Crack and Your Circulatory System (0-8239-3389-X).
Steroids and Your Muscles (0-8239-3393-8).
Hallucinogens and Your Neurons (0-8239-3391-1).
Alcohol and Your Liver (0-8239-3254-0).
Cocaine and Your Nose (0-8239-3251-6).

Heroin and Your Veins (0-8239-3249-4).
Tobacco and Your Mouth (0-8239-3250-8).
Marijuana and Your Lungs (0-8239-3252-4).

Inside Special Operations series. Rosen Publishing Group, 2003. $26.50 ea. Grades 6 and up.
Inside the world's military special-operations forces.

Navy SEALs: Special Operations for the U.S. Navy (0-8239-3809-3).
Army Rangers: Surveillance and Reconnaissance for the U.S. Army (0-8239-3805-0).
Inside Israel's Mossad: The Institute for Intelligence and Special Tasks (0-8239-3815-8).
SAS: British Special Air Service (0-8239-3810-7).
British Royal Marines: Amphibious Division of the United Kingdom's Royal Navy (0-8239-3806-9).
Delta Force: Counterterrorism Unit of the U.S. Army (0-8239-3807-7).
Green Berets: The U.S. Army Special Forces (0-8239-3808-5).

Military Hardware in Action series. Lerner, 2004. $25.00 ea. Grades 6 and up.

Aircraft Carriers (0-8225-4702-3).
Battlefield Support (0-8225-4708-2).
Bombers (0-8225-4705-8).
Fighter Planes (0-8225-4706-6).
Helicopters (0-8225-4707-4).
Missiles and Rockets (0-8225-4709-0).
Submarines (0-8225-4704-X).
Tanks (0-8225-4701-5).
Warships (0-8225-4703-1).

New Wave Sports biographies. Millbrook Press, 1999–2003. $15.95 ea. Grades 6 and up.
Athletes' lives, from childhood to their current famous status.

Alex Rodriguez (0-7613-1515-2).
Chamique Holdsclaw (0-7613-1801-1).
Daunte Culpepper (0-7613-2613-8).
Derek Jeter (0-7613-1516-0).
Ichiro Suzuki (0-7613-2616-2).
Jackie Stiles (0-7613-2614-6).
Jeff Gordon (0-7613-1871-2).
Jevon Kearse (0-7613-2269-8).

Kevin Garnett (0-7613-2615-4).
Kobe Bryant (0-7613-1800-3).
Kurt Warner (0-7613-1953-0).
Marion Jones (0-7613-1870-4).
Mia Hamm (0-7613-1802-X).
Nomar Garciaparra (0-7613-1520-9).
Peyton Manning (0-7613-1517-9).
Randy Moss (0-7613-1518-7).
Scott Gomez (0-7613-2268-X).
Se Ri Pak (0-7613-1519-5).
Steve McNair (0-7613-1954-9).
Terrell Davis (0-7613-1514-4).
Tim Duncan (0-7613-1513-6).
Todd Helton (0-7613-2271-X).
Tom Brady (0-7613-2907-2).
Venus and Serena Williams (0-7613-1803-8).
Vince Carter (0-7613-2270-1).

Rad Sports series. Rosen, 2003–2004. $26.50 ea. Grades 6 and up.
Extreme sports' techniques and tips.

Rock Sport Climbing (0-8239-3847-6).
Mountain Biking (0-8239-3845-X).
BMX Bicycle Racing (0-8239-3843-3).
Wakeboarding (0-8239-3850-6).
Skateboarding (0-8239-3848-4).
In-Line Skating (0-8239-3844-1).
Snowboarding (0-8239-3849-2).
Kick Scooters (0-8239-3846-8).

Sports Illustrated for Kids series. Rosen, 2003–2004. $18.95–$22.95 ea. Grades 7 and up.
Biographies of some of the most famous sports stars in the game today.

Baseball All-Stars: Today's Greatest Players (0-8239-3688-0).
Basketball All-Stars (0-8239-3689-9).
Dare to Be Different: Athletes Who Changed Sports (0-8239-3696-1).
Football All-Stars (0-8239-3690-2).
Grant Hill: Superstar Forward (0-8239-3578-7).
Gridiron Greats: 8 of Today's Hottest NFL Stars (0-8239-3691-0).
HoopMania: The Book of Basketball History and Trivia (0-8239-3697-X).
Ken Griffey, Jr. (0-8239-3687-2).
Rising Stars: The 10 Best Young Players in Baseball (0-8239-3576-0).

Rising Stars: The 10 Best Young Players in the NBA (0-8239-3574-4).
Rising Stars: The 10 Best Young Players in the NFL (0-8239-3573-6).
Rising Stars: The 10 Best Young Players in the NHL (0-8239-3575-2).
Shaquille O Neal: Superhero at Center (0-8239-3577-9).
Sports Superstars: 8 of Today's Hottest Athletes (0-8239-3692-9).
The Top Teams Ever: Football, Baseball, Basketball, and Hockey Winners (0-8239-3693-7).
The 20 Greatest Athletes of the 20th Century (0-8239-3694-5).
Women Winners: Then and Now (0-8239-3695-3).
World of Soccer: A Complete Guide to the World's Most Popular Sport (0-8239-3698-8).

Terrorist Attacks series. Rosen, 2004. $19.95 ea. Grades 6 and up.
High-interest attacks by terrorists from around the world.

Anthrax Attacks around the World (0-8239-3859-X).
Murder at the 1972 Olympics in Munich (0-8239-3654-6).
The Attack Against the U.S. Embassies in Kenya and Tanzania (0-8239-3652-X).
The Attack on the Pentagon on September 11, 2001 (0-8239-3858-1).
The Attack on the USS Cole in Yemen on October 12, 2000 (0-8239-3860-3).
The Attack on U.S. Marines in Lebanon on October 23, 1983 (0-8239-3862-X).
The Attack on U.S. Servicemen in Saudi Arabia on June 25, 1996 (0-8239-3861-1).
The Attacks on the World Trade Center: February 26, 1993, and September 11, 2001 (0-8239-3657-0).
The Bombing of Pan Am Flight 103 (0-8239-3656-2).
The Crash of United Flight 93 on September 11, 2001 (0-8239-3857-3).
The Nerve Gas Attack on the Tokyo Subway (0-8239-3653-8).
The Oklahoma City Bombing (0-8239-3655-4).

The Unexplained series. Lerner, 2004–2005. $26.60 ea. Grades 6 and up.
Investigates mysterious incidents throughout history.

Aliens (0-8225-0960-1).
Hoaxes (0-8225-1629-2).
ESP (0-8225-1628-4).
UFOs (0-8225-0961-X).
Vanished (0-8225-1631-4).
Monsters (0-8225-1626-8).
Beyond the Grave (0-8225-2403-1).
Lands of Mystery (0-8225-1630-6).

When Disaster Strikes! series. Rosen, 2003–2004. 48p. $19.95 ea. Grades 6 and up.

Chronicles disasters throughout history.

The Crash of the Concorde (0-8239-3673-2).
The Exxon Valdez *Oil Spill* (0-8239-3675-9).
The Meltdown at Three Mile Island (0-8239-3678-3).
The Tragedy of the Titanic (0-8239-3679-1).
The USS Greeneville *Submarine Disaster* (0-8239-3676-7).
The Wreck of the Andrea Gail: *Three Days of a Perfect Storm* (0-8239-3677-5).

Graphic Novels and Comics

See earlier in this book for a caveat about using graphic novels and comics with reluctant readers. Graphic novels can be an exciting way for anti-readers to discover a new format they may enjoy. The titles listed here are a selection of graphic novels from a variety of genres because after all, graphic novels are just a format, not a genre.

SUPERHEROES

Bendis, Brian Michael. *Ultimate Spider-Man*. Marvel Comics. $12.99 ea. Grades 6 and up.
   The web-slinging superhero is still around!

> *Power and Responsibility* (0-785-10786-X).
> *Learning Curve* (0-785-10820-3).
> *Double Trouble* (0-785-10879-3).
> *Legacy* (0-785-10879-3).
> *Public Scrutiny* (0-78-511087-9).
> *Venom* (0-785-11094-1).
> *Irresponsible* (0-785-11092-5).
> *Cats and Kings* (0-785-11250-2).
> *Ultimate Six* (0-785-11312-6).
> *Hollywood* (0-785-11402-5).
> *Script Book* (0-785-11402-5).
> *Carnage* (0-785-11403-3).

Brubaker, Ed, and Mike Allred. *Catwoman: The Dark End of the Street*. DC Comics, 2002. $12.95 (1-563-89908-6). Grades 7 and up.

Catwoman (Selina Kyle) defends Gotham City's citizens.

David, Peter. *Spyboy*. Dark Horse Comics, 2001–2003. $8.95 ea. Grades 8 and up.
   One day Alex Fleming is getting beat up by bullies in his school bathroom; the next day he's fighting international evil!

The Deadly Gourmet Affair (1-56971-463-0).
Trial and Terror (1-56971-501-7).
Bet Your Life (1-56971-617-X).
Undercover Underwear (1-56971-664-1).
Spy-School Confidential (1-56971-834-2).
The M*A*N*G*A Affair (1-56971-984-5).

Dini, Paul, and Alex Ross. *Wonder Woman: The Spirit of Truth*. DC Comics, 2001. $9.95 (1-563-89861-6). Grades 6 and up.
   Wonder Woman explores heroism, power, and politics.

Dixon, Charles, and Scott Beatty. *Robin: Year One*. DC Comics, 2002. $14.95 (1-563-89805-5). Grades 6 and up.
   Robin, just beginning his crime fighting, solves a series of strange crimes.

Jemas, Bill. *Origin: The True Story of Wolverine*. Marvel Comics, 2002. $34.95 (0-7851-0866-1). Grades 7 and up.
   Logan's past—and what transformed him into Wolverine—are revealed in this story.

Johns, Geoff. *Teen Titans: A Kid's Game*. DC Comics, 2004. $9.99 (1-4012-0308-6). Grades 6 and up.
   The second generation of Teen Titans is sick and tired of adults telling them what they can and cannot do.

"Mad" about Super Heroes. Edited by Nick Meglin and John Ficarra. DC Comics. $9.95 (1-56389-886-1). Grades 7 and up.
   Mad magazine's take on the world of superheroes.

Mignola, Mike. *Hellboy: Seed of Destruction*. Dark Horse Comics, 2004. $17.95 (1593070942). Grades 9 and up.
   In 1945, the Nazis use occult means to summon forth a demon, intended to be used to beat back the Allied armies. Rescued from their clutches, the demon child grows up into a force for good and becomes the world's greatest paranormal detective. His name is Hellboy.

Miller, Mark. *Ultimate X-Men: The Tomorrow People*. Marvel Comics, 2001. $14.95 (0-785-10788-6). Grades 6 and up.

The X-men are a team of mutants—each with a different ability that has made the rest of society cast them out.

Moore, Alan. *League of Extraordinary Gentlemen*. DC Comics, 2002. $14.95 (1-563-89858-6). Grades 8 and up.

Superheroes and history combine in this series starring Captain Nemo, Allan Quartermain, the Invisible Man, Wilhelmina "Mina" Murray, and Dr. Jekyll and Mr. Hyde.

Smith, Kevin. *Green Arrow: Quiver*. DC Comics, 2002. $17.95 (1-563-89965-5). Grades 9 and up.

The origin of Oliver Queen—otherwise known as Green Arrow.

HISTORY

Anderson, Ho Che. *King: A Comic Book Biography*. Fantagraphics, 2005 reprint. $22.95 (1560976225). Grades 9 and up.

This groundbreaking graphic novel about Martin Luther King records all of the key events of the civil rights leader's life in a unique and compelling format, from the violence of the southern police to the internal struggles that marked the birth of the civil rights movement in America.

Gaiman, Neil, et al. *9–11: September 11th, 2001*. DC Comics. $9.95 (1-56389-878-0). Grades 8 and up.

A variety of writers' and artists' responses to 9–11.

Gonick, Larry. *Cartoon History of the Universe*. Norton, 1997, 2001, 2002. $21.95 ea. Grades 7 and up.

An entertaining yet informative history of the world.

Volume I: *From the Big Bang to Alexander the Great* (0-385-26520-4).
Volume II: *From the Springtime of China to the Fall of Rome* (0-385-42093-5).
Volume III: *From the Rise of Arabia to the Renaissance* (0-393-32403-6).

Hartman, Rachel. *Unbounded: Belondweg Blossoming*. Pug House Press, 2002. $16.95 (0-9717-9000-0). Grades 6 and up.

Set during the Middle Ages, this is a coming-of-age story about the life of fourteen-year-old Amy.

Kubert, Joe. *Fax from Sarajevo: A Story of Survival*. Dark Horse Comics, 1998. $24.95 (1-569-71346-4). Grades 8 and up.

Ervin tries to escape wartorn Sarajevo.

A condensed summary of the history of African Americans in the United States, from Jamestown to the present.

Sacco, Joe. *Palestine*. Fantagraphics, 2001. $24.95 (1-560-97432-X). Grades 8 and up.
The author, a reporter in Palestine, pursues all sides of the crisis in the Middle East.

Satrapi, Marijane. *Persepolis: The Story of a Childhood*. Pantheon Books, 2003. $11.95 (0-375-71457-X). Grades 10 and up.
The author describes growing up in Tehran, Iran, in the seventies and early eighties.

Shanower, Eric. *Age of Bronze: A Thousand Ships*. Image Comics, 2001. $19.94 (1-58240-200-0). Grades 6 and up.
Draws on ancient myths, medieval romances, and modern scholarship to offer a graphic novel portraying the Trojan War.

Spiegelman, Art. *Maus*. Random House, 1986. $14.95 (0-394-74-723-2). Grades 8 and up.
Possibly the most well-known graphic novel ever, the author retells his father's life during the Holocaust.

HUMOR

Boyd, Andrew. *Scurvy Dogs*. AIT-Planet Lar (Distributed by Diamond Comics), 2005. $12.95 (1-932-05127-9). Grades 9 and up. (M)

Groening, Matt. Simpsons Comics. Perennial/HarperCollins, 1996–2004. $14.95 ea. Grades 6 and up.
Ongoing humorous adventures of TV's favorite dysfunctional family.

Simpsons Comics *Extravaganza* (0-06-095086-2).
Simpsons Comics *Spectacular* (0-06-095148-6).
Simpsons Comics *Strikes Back* (0-06-095212-1).
Simpsons Comics *Simps-o-rama* (0-06-095199-0).
Simpsons Comics *Wingding* (0-06-095245-8).
Simpsons Comics *On Parade* (0-06-095280-6).
Simpsons Comics *Big Bonanza* (0-06-095280-6).
Simpsons Comics *A-Go-Go* (0-06-095566-X).
Simpsons Comics *Unchained* (0-06-000797-4).
Simpsons Comics *Royale* (0-06-093378-X).
Simpsons Comics *Madness* (0-06-053061-8).

Simpsons Comics *Belly Buster* (0-06-058750-4).
Simpsons Comics *Barn Burne* (0-06-074818-4).

Smith, Jeff. *Bone*. Vol. 1, *Out from Boneville*. Cartoon Books, 1995. $14.95 (0-963-66099-3). Grades 6 and up.

Bone and his cousins—and their strange and humorous adventures.

Takahashi, Rumiko. *Ranma 1/2*. Vol. 1. Viz Communications, 1993. $16.95 (0-92-927993-X). Grades 8 and up.

Ranma is a normal young man—until he comes in contact with cold water. Then he's a normal young woman instead.

MYSTERY

Naifeh, Ted. *Courtney Crumrin and the Night Things*. Oni Press, 2002. $11.95 (1-929-99860-0). Grades 6 and up.

Courtney's parents have dragged her out to a high-to-do suburb to live with her creepy great-uncle Aloysius in his spooky old house.

Robinson, James, and Paul Smith. *Leave It to Chance: Volume 1: Shaman's Rain*. Image Comics, 2003. $14.95 (1-582-40253-1). Grades 6 and up.

Chance Falconer, the fourteen-year-old daughter of an investigator, pursues strange happenings on her own.

SCIENCE FICTION AND FANTASY

Brennan, Michael. *Electric Girl*. Mighty Gremlin, 2000. $9.95 (0-970-35550-5) (0-970-35551-3). Grades 6 and up.

Electric Girl is a normal teenager in most ways, except for her ability to conduct electricity.

Lahaye, Tim, and Jerry Jenkins. *Left Behind: A Graphic Novel of Earth's Last Days*. Tyndale, $14.00 (0-8423-7395-0) (0-8423-5503-0) (0-8423-5504-9) (0-8423-5505-7) (0-8423-5506-5). Grades 6 and up.

An illustrated depiction of the chaos that remains after much of the world's population is removed from the earth.

Marvitt, Lawrence. *Sparks: An Urban Fairytale*. $35.95 (0-943151-62-7). Grades 7 and up.

Jo, a young woman with a bad job and an unhappy family, builds the perfect man out of spare auto parts.

Medley, Linda. *Castle Waiting: The Lucky Road*. Olio Press, 2002. $17.95 (1-965-18523-0). Grades 6 and up.

Jain tries to escape her past and start again at a castle full of human and animal characters. Note: Free curriculum for this graphic novel is available at: http://bookshelf.diamondcomics.com/lessonplans/

Roman, Dave, and John Green. *Jax Epoch and the Quicken Forbidden: Borrowed Magic*. AIT/Planet Lar (Distributed by Diamond Comics), 2003. $14.95 (1-932051-11-2). Grades 7 and up.

Teenager Jax finds an interdimensional portal, and upon returning home, she finds her life slightly altered.

Tolkien, J.R.R. *The Hobbit: An Illustrated Edition of the Fantasy Classic*. Abridged. Illustrated by David Wenzel. Drawn and Quarterly, 2001. $15.95 (0-3454-4560-0). Grades 7 and up.

A graphic retelling of Tolkien's classic, of special interest in recent years.

Whedon, Joss. *Fray*. Dark Horse, 2003. $19.95 (1-56971-751-6). Grades 8 and up.

A futuristic story about another tough vampire killer, from the creator of *Buffy the Vampire Slayer*.

SCIENCE

Hosler, Jay. *Active Snapse*. Clan Apis, 2000. $15.00 (0-96-772550-X). Grades 6 and up.

All about Nyuki, a honeybee, and his honeybee world.

Ottaviani, Jim. *Dignifying Science*. G.T. Labs, 2000. $16.95 (0-9660-1061-2). Grades 8 and up.

True stories of famous women in science.

SPORTS

Nishiyama, Yuriko. *Harlem Beat*. Tokyopop, 1999. $9.95 (1-892213-04-4). Grades 6 and up.

The Johnan High School varsity basketball team has won a spot in the National Basketball Championships, but they still face serious competition from another school.

Sturm, James. *The Golem's Mighty Swing*. Drawn and Quarterly, 2003. $16.95 (1-8965-9771-8). Grades 8 and up.

Set in the 1920s, this title follows the Stars of David, one of many barnstorming baseball teams touring the country—the team's distinction being that all the team members are Jewish.

ROMANCE

Soryo, Fuyumi. *Mars*. Vol. 1. Tokyopop, 2002. $9.99 (1-93151-458-5). Grades 10 and up.

Rei's rebellious attitude and good looks make him very attractive to most girls, but it is the shy Kira that he pursues.

Ueda, Miwa. *Peach Girl*. Vol. 1. Tokyopop, 2000. $9.99 (1-89221-362-1). Grades 8 and up.

Momo is unhappy with her looks and is frequently teased, which makes it difficult for her to attract the attention of Toji.

TEEN SOCIAL ISSUES

Arnoldi, Katherine. *The Amazing "True" Story of a Teenage Single Mom*. Hyperion, 1998. $16.00 (0-7868-6420-6). Grades 9 and up.

Dreams can come true, even for a single teenage mother.

Clowes, Daniel. *Ghost World*. Fantagraphics Books, 1998. $9.95 (1-56-097-427-3). Grades 10 and up. (M)

Enid and Rebecca have graduated from high school, and their relationship is beginning to change.

Fisher, Jane Smith. *WJHC: On the Air*. Wilson Place Comics, 2003. $11.95 (0974423505). Grades 6 and up.

Jane tries to get a high school radio station up and running.

Gownley, Jimmy. Amelia Rules! series. Simon & Schuster, 2003–2004. $14.95. Grades 6 and up.

Amelia moves from Manhattan to a small town after her parents' divorce.

The Whole World's Crazy (0-74-347503-8).
What Makes You Happy (0-74-347909-2).

McKeever, Sean. *The Waiting Place*. Slave Labor Graphics (Distributed by Diamond Comics), 2001. $15.95 (0943151368). Grades 10 and up. (M)

Talbot, Bryan. *The Tale of One Bad Rat*. Dark Horse, 1995. $14.95 (1-565971-077-5). Grades 8 and up.

Teenage Helen Potter, abused as a child, travels through England.

Van Meter, Jan. *Hopeless Savages*. Oni Press, 2003. $13.95 (1-929-99875-9). Grades 8 and up.

If you ever dreamed of having a hip family with cool siblings who still cared deeply for each other, you'll love these adventures with attitude.

Winick, Judd. *Pedro and Me.* Henry Holt, 2000. $15.00 (0-8050-6403-6). Grades 9 and up.

True story of an MTV *Real World* cast member who became an AIDS activist.

MANGA

In some areas, Japanese culture is very different from American culture. What is an acceptable level of nudity and sexuality for teenagers in Japan may be very different from what is acceptable in your community or at your school. The following is a statement from Tokyopop, the leading manga publisher in the United States:

"There are notable cultural differences in many titles. These may include but are not limited to crude humor, nudity, ambiguous sexuality and gender roles, and fashion that may be considered unusual. These issues are deemed acceptable to Japanese readers and are a part of what makes Tokyopop manga authentic, popular, and cool with young people in the U.S.A."

Most American publishers use a ratings system to help guide you toward titles that are appropriate for your audience. The following is from the Tokyopop Web site:

> A (All Ages)—Appropriate for all ages. No offensive material.
> Y (Youth, ages 10+)—Appropriate for ages 10 and up. May contain violence.
> T (Teen, ages 13+)—Appropriate for ages 13 and up. May contain violence, profanity, and semi-nudity.
> OT (Older Teen, ages 16+)—Appropriate for ages 16 and up. May contain violence, profanity, semi-nudity, and some sexual themes.
> M (Mature, ages 18+)—Appropriate for ages 18 and up. May contain graphic violence, nudity, profanity, sex, and intense sexual themes.

Please be aware that these are only guidelines, and that the best way to determine the appropriateness of a manga title for your collection and your community is to review it first yourself. There are also an increasing number of manga reviews available to assist you, and most of the titles have manga preview pages on the Tokyopop Web site for your convenience.

Selecting Manga

- Ask your students—they're the experts.
- Read reviews to get ideas.

- Look at best-seller lists.
- Talk to staff at bookstores and comic-book stores.
- Stay up-to-date.
- Select a variety of genres and topics.
- Once you find a series that works, put it on standing order.

According to Tokyopop and Ingram Library Services, the following were the most frequently purchased manga titles for libraries. It should be noted, however, that this list is from 2004.

Top-15 Library Series for 2004:

1. Peach Girl
2. Fruits Basket
3. Mars
4. Kare Kano
5. Rave Master
6. Cardcaptor Sakura
7. SpongeBob SquarePants
8. Dragon Knights
9. Digimon
10. Tokyo Mew Mew
11. Love Hina
12. Jing: King of Bandits
13. Sailor Moon
14. Chobits
15. Rebound

Other Terms to Know:

- Manhwa—Korean manga
- Shojo—character-driven stories that primarily appeal to girls
- Shonon—action-driven stories that primarily appeal to men
- Bi-shonon—literally, "pretty boys"; stories have male characters but appeal to girls

A tip that will make you seem like you know what you're talking about: The manga series (and cartoon network TV show) "FLCL" is pronounced "Foolie Coolie."

Other Lists

BEST BOOKS AND BEST QUICK PICKS FROM YALSA

Every year, YALSA's Best Books and Quick Picks committees compile lists of the "best" titles, there is usually little overlap. For titles to make both lists, they must serve the masters of popularity and quality; they must be titles that reluctant readers will find not only accessible but also so well written they'll want to keep on reading. Here is a list of fiction titles from the past ten years that appeared on both lists.

Anderson, Laurie Halse. *Speak*
Appelt, Kathi. *Kissing Tennessee and Other Stories from the Stardust Dance*
Atkins, Catherine. *When Jeff Comes Home*
Bauer, Cat. *Harley Like a Person*
Bauer, Joan. *Rules of the Road*
Bechard, Margaret. *Hanging On to Max*
Cabot, Meg. *Princess Diaries*
Cart, Michael (Editor). *Love and Sex: Ten Stories of Truth*
Cart, Michael (Editor). *Tomorrowland: Ten Stories about the Future*
Carter, Alden R. *Bull Catcher*
Chbosky, Stephen. *Perks of Being a Wallflower*
Cohn, Rachel. *Gingerbread*
Cormier, Robert. *Heroes: A Novel*
Cormier, Robert. *In the Middle of the Night*
Dessen, Sarah. *Keeping the Moon*
Dessen, Sarah. *Someone Like You*
Drake, Ernest. *Dr. Ernest Drake's Dragonology*
Draper, Sharon. *Forged by Fire*

Ferris, Jean. *Bad*

Flake, Sharon. *The Skin I'm In*

Flake, Sharon. *Who Am I without Him? A Short Story Collection about Girls and the Boys in Their Lives*

Fleischman, Paul. *Seedfolks*

Flinn, Alex. *Breathing Underwater*

Flinn, Alex. *Nothing to Lose*

Frank, E. R. *America*

Gallo, Donald (Editor). *No Easy Answers: Short Stories about Teenagers Making Tough Choices*

Galloway, Priscilla. *Truly Grim Tales*

Giles, Gail. *Shattering Glass*

Gilmore, Kate. *Exchange Student*

Griffin, Adele. *Amandine*

Grimes, Nikki. *Bronx Masquerade*

Haddix, Margaret Peterson. *Among the Hidden*

Haddix, Margaret Peterson. *Don't You Dare Read This, Mrs. Dunphrey*

Haddix, Margaret Peterson. *Just Ella*

Haddix, Margaret Peterson. *Running Out of Time*

Hesser, Terry Spencer. *Kissing Doorknobs*

Hobbs, Will. *Far North*

Hobbs, Will. *Jason's Gold*

Hobbs, Will. *The Maze*

Hogan, James. *Bug Park*

Horowitz, Anthony. *Eagle Strike*

Johnson, Scott. *Safe at Second*

Klause, Annette Curtis. *Blood and Chocolate*

Koertge, Ronald. *Stoner and Spaz*

Korman, Gordon. *Son of the Mob*

Koss, Amy Goldman. *The Girls*

"Often the battle is fought and won before the reader even opens the novel to page one. I find that many of the reluctant readers who enjoyed *Son of the Mob* were sold on premise alone. Mobster's son dates FBI agent's daughter. It was just something they wanted to find out more about. That's not to say that the novel itself is irrelevant—it has to hold teens, reluctant readers even more so."

Gordon Korman

Larson, Gary. *There's a Hair in My Dirt! A Worm's Story*
Lawrence, Iain. *Smugglers*
Lawrence, Iain. *Wreckers*
Lester, Julius. *Othello: A Novel*
Levine, Gail Carson. *Ella Enchanted*
Logue, Mary. *Dancing with an Alien*
Lubar, David. *Hidden Talents*
Lynch, Chris. *Slot Machine*
Matas, Carol. *After the War*
McCants, William. *Much Ado about Prom Night*
McNamee, Graham. *Hate You*
Myers, Walter Dean. *Monster*
Myers, Walter Dean. *145th Street Short Stories*
Myers, Walter Dean. *Slam!*
Nelson Blake. *Rock Star, Superstar*
Oppell, Kenneth. *Airborn*
Ortiz Cofer, Judith. *An Island Like You: Stories of the Barrio*
Paulsen, Gary. *Schernoff Discoveries*
Paulsen, Gary. *Soldier's Heart*
Peck, Richard. *Last Safe Place on Earth*
Peters, Julie Anne. *Define "Normal": A Novel*
Powell, Randy. *Dean Duffy*
Qualey, Marsha. *Close to a Killer*
Randle, Kristen D. *Only Alien on the Planet*
Rennison, Louise. *Angus, Thongs, and Full-Frontal Snogging: Confessions of Georgia Nicholson*
Rochman, Hazel, and Darlene Z. McCampbell (Editors). *Leaving Home*
Sachar, Louis. *Holes*
Shusterman, Neal. *Dark Side of Nowhere*
Shusterman, Neal. *Downsiders*
Skurzynski, Gloria. *Virtual War*
Sones, Sonya. *What My Mother Doesn't Know*
Soto, Gary. *Buried Onions*
Strasser, Todd. *Can't Get There from Here*
Stratton, Allan. *Leslie's Journal*
Testa, Maria. *Dancing Pink Flamingos and Other Stories*
Thomas, Rob. *Doing Time: Notes from the Undergrad*
Thomas, Rob. *Rats Saw God*
Tomey, Ingrid. *Nobody Else Has to Know*
Trueman, Terry. *Stuck in Neutral*
Vande Velde, Vivian. *Companions of the Night*

Vande Velde, Vivian. *Never Trust a Dead Man*
Vries, Anke De. *Bruises*
Wallace, Rich. *Playing without the Ball: A Novel in Four Quarters*
Wallace, Rich. *Wrestling Sturbridge*
Werlin, Nancy. *Killer's Cousin*
Wersba, Barbara. *Whistle Me Home*
Whedon, Joss. *Fray*
Williams, Carol Lynch. *True Colors of Caitlynne Jackson*
Williams-Garcia, Rita. *Like Sisters on the Homefront*
Wittlinger, Ellen. *Hard Love*
Woodson, Jacqueline. *Behind You*
Yolen, Jane. *Armageddon Summer*

THE PERFECT TENS LIST

The professional journal *Voice of Youth Advocates (VOYA)* uses a unique re-view code. Each book is given a 1 to 5 rating (1 lowest/5 highest) on its Qual-ity (Q) and Popularity (P). Now, while many a 5Q book might put off a reluctant reader, not every 5P book is going to give even a reluctant reader a satisfactory reading experience, so wouldn't the "best" books for nonreaders be those that score a 5 in each category? Thus, we created the *VOYA* "Perfect Tens" (originally published in the June 2001 issue of *VOYA*)—a listing of books that earned both a 5Q (the highest literacy quality) and a 5P ("every YA was dying to read it yesterday"). We've added most of the Perfect Tens for the years 2001–2004 as well and, unlike other lists, include some books that are sadly no longer in print, so this is more of a book talk or display than an actual order list. Finally, we left off a few titles that may have seemed to be of high quality and high accessibility at the time, but that have not proven themselves successful at reaching reluctant readers. The annotations are adapted from the *VOYA* articles.

Barlowe, Wayne. *Barlowe's Guide to Fantasy*. HarperCollins, 1996. 136p.
   Fifty fantasy creatures are brought to life in vivid drawings.

Bauer, Joan. *Stand Tall*. Putnam's, 2003. 192p.
   Strong, memorable characters in realistic, special relationships as always highlight Bauer's novels.

Bujold, Lois McMaster. *The Curse of Chalion*. Eos/HarperCollins, 2001.
   Subtle yet powerful language, crashing swords, and dark magical powers combine in a page-turning fantasy.

Card, Orson Scott. *Enchantment.* Del Rey, 1999. 390p.

This retelling of "Sleeping Beauty" is coupled with a time-travel twist.

Card, Orson Scott. *Shadow of the Hegemon.* Tor, 2000. 363p.

Brilliant young characters face deadly peril while engaging in fast-paced action and heroic deeds.

Cooney, Caroline. *Voice on the Radio.* Delacorte Press, 1996. 180p.

The third book in the Face on the Milk Carton trilogy finds Janie once again betrayed by someone she loves.

Cormier, Robert. *Tenderness.* Delacorte Press, 1997. 240p.

A runaway teen falls in love with a young man recently released from prison for murdering his mother and stepfather.

Creech, Stacy. *Absolutely Normal Chaos.* HarperCollins Juvenile Books, 1995. 230p.

Mary Lou Finney's journal of the summer she was thirteen is filled with suspense, romance, and lots of humor.

Crist-Evans, Craig. *Amaryllis.* Candlewick, 2003. 184p.

Set in the Vietnam War era, this novel is filled with metaphor and portrayals of a family dealing with unbearable loss.

Dessen, Sarah. *Keeping the Moon.* Viking Children's Books, 1999. 224p.

Colie is shipped off for the summer by her mother, only to find in her aunt and new friends more than she—or her mother—bargained for.

Dessen, Sarah. *This Lullaby.* Viking, 2002. 352p.

Through a deceptively simple summer romance plot, unique and fully realized characters portray adolescent life brilliantly.

Earls, Nick. *48 Shades of Brown.* Graphia/Houghton Mifflin, 2004. 288p.

Older teens will not be able to put down this enchanting, too-true, coming-of-age novel as their smiles become belly laughs.

Fredericks, Mariah. *The True Meaning of Cleavage.* Atheneum/S & S, 2003. 224p.

A provocative love story about what happens when young lovers mature at different paces.

Frost, Helen. *Keesha's House.* Frances Foster Books/Farrar, Straus and Giroux, 2003. 128p.

Joe's house offers shelter, safety, and healing to bewildered youth, including Keesha, who is escaping her abusive father after her mother's death.

Gantos, Jack. *Joey Pigza Loses Control.* Farrar, Straus and Giroux, 2000. 196p.

Joey struggles to maintain control in his ADHD world in this brilliant portrayal touched with humor.

Gantos, Jack. *What Would Joey Do?* Farrar, Straus and Giroux, 2002. 240p.

This novel follows up on the acclaimed earlier adventures of Joey, the remarkable hyperactive hero.

Grimes, Nikki. *Bronx Masquerade.* Dial, 2002. 176p.

Eighteen disjointed people unite in compassion against a backdrop of broken homes, tumult, and peer pressure, speaking to the poet in every teen.

Hamilton, Jake. *Special Effects in Film and Television.* DK Publishing, 1998. 32p.

An oversized book jammed with color photos describing special effects and illustrating each effect from a famous movie or television show.

Harder, Jens. *Leviathan.* Comics Lit/NBM, 2004. 144p.

Harder's art and wordless story leave this graphic novel's depiction of the whale wide open for interpretation, a virtual visual buffet from which the reader never wants to turn away.

Horowitz, Anthony. *Devil and His Boy.* Philomel Books, 2000. 192p.

The adventures of a thirteen-year-old orphan boy growing up in the sixteenth century comprise a fast-paced tale of humor, intrigue, magic, and memorable characters.

Koller, Jackie French. *The Falcon.* Atheneum, 1998. 192p.

The diary of seventeen-year-old Luke Carver reveals the drama of his present and the trauma of his past.

Koontz, Dean. *Fear Nothing.* Bantam Books, 1998. 391p.

It is the end of the world as we know it, and monkeys are to blame, in this nonstop thrill ride of good versus evil.

Korman, Gordon. *Son of the Mob Hollywood Hustle.* Hyperion, 2004. 272p.

Mixing deft touches of reality with a clever comedy of errors, Korman's second book about Vincent Luca is filled with brilliant characterizations, sneaky plot twists, and humor that will make teens fall off their chairs with laughter.

Lisle, Janet Taylor. *The Crying Rocks.* Atheneum/S & S, 2003. 208p.

Sure to attract readers of all ages, historical intrigue, adolescent exploration, and mystery combine as thirteen-year-old Joelle finds surprising answers to the questions raised by the secrets of her past.

Love and Sex: Ten Stories of Truth for Teens. Edited by Michael Cart. Simon & Schuster, 2001. 256p.

An intriguing collection of subtle, finely tuned stories sheds light on several sexual topics with which teens struggle.

Lynch, Chris. *Blood Relations.* HarperTrophy, 1996. 192p.

Lynch, Chris. *Dog Eat Dog.* HarperTrophy, 1996. 144p.

Lynch, Chris. *Mick.* HarperTrophy, 1996. 128p.
Three books about Mick, a fifteen-year-old boy living in a changing Boston neighborhood during the 1960s. The action-packing trilogy tells powerful stories of friendship, courage, humor, love, brutality, violence, hate, and understanding, all in a crisp, rough, realistic language.

Marin, Albert. *Commander in Chief: Abraham Lincoln.* Dutton Books, 1997. 218p.
Looking behind the myth of Lincoln, this biography paints a portrait of Lincoln as a human being, flawed like any man, who does his best based on strong convictions, moral courage, and sensitivity.

McNamee, Graham. *Acceleration.* Random House, 2003. 176p.
A fast-paced thrill ride, as seventeen-year-old Duncan pursues a psychopathic killer.

Muharrar, Aisha. *More Than a Label: Why What You Wear or Who You're with Doesn't Define Who You Are.* Free Spirit, 2002. 144p.
A seventeen-year-old speaks out on the realities and cruelties of labeling, interweaving other teens' thoughts with her own commentary.

Myers, Walter Dean. *The Dream Bearer.* HarperCollins, 2003. 240p.
Myers's easy, natural language beautifully orchestrates dreams realized and dreams imagined.

Myers, Walter Dean. *Slam!* Scholastic, 1996. 266p.
Greg Harris is a natural basketball talent, but his time spent off the court—avoiding the temptations and dead ends of his Harlem neighborhood—is his toughest opponent.

Paulsen, Gary. *Brian's Winter.* Delacorte Press, 1996. 133p.
An alternative ending to the award-winning Hatchet: What if Brian had not been rescued and therefore forced to spend more time stranded in the wilderness?

Paulsen, Gary. *Schernoff Discoveries.* Bantam Books, 1997. 128p.
Slapstick humor abounds in the story of two boys trying to use scientific formulas to attract girls, which continuously leads to hilarious results.

Platt, Richard. *Stephen Biesty's Incredible Everything.* DK Publishing, 1997. 32p.

A look into the technology lurking underneath everyday life, from doughnuts to rockets, illustrated with fantastic drawing filled with intricate details.

Pullman, Philip. *Amber Spyclass* (His Dark Materials #3). Knopf, 2000. 518p.
The final volume of the trilogy follows Will and Lyra on a perilous and agonizing journey to the dark world of the dead.

Pullman, Philip. *Golden Compass (His Dark Materials #1).* Knopf, 1996. 416p.
When Lyra foils an attempt to assassinate her father, events are set in motion that destroy her innocent childhood, sending her into a dangerous alternative world.

Pullman, Philip. *Subtle Knife (His Dark Materials #2).* Knopf, 1997. 384p.
Lyra is joined by Will, who is on a quest to find his father, but both are plunged into a strange world of soul-eating Spectries.

Reynolds, David West. *"Star Wars Episode One": Incredible Cross Sections.* DK Publishing, 1999. 32p.
The force is with you as fascinating diagrams and detailed illustrations are used explain the "Star Wars" universe.

Reynolds, David West. *"Star Wars Episode One": A Visual Dictionary.* DK Publishing, 1999. 64p.
A visual feast with double-page articles and a profusion of detailed information on creatures and characters from the world's most popular movie series.

Rogasky, Barbara. *Smoke and Ashes: The Story of the Holocaust.* Revised and expanded ed. Holiday House, 2002. 256p.
Rogasky admonishes readers to never forget the lessons of the Holocaust.

Rowling, J. K. *Harry Potter and the Chamber of Secrets.* Scholastic, 1999. 341p.
Harry and his friend Ron arrive for their second year at Hogwarts School of Witchcraft and Wizardry to face new challenges, including a monster released from the legendary Chamber of Secrets.

Rowling, J. K. *Harry Potter and the Order of the Phoenix.* Scholastic, 2003. 896p.
In the fifth installment of Harry's battles with the evil Voldemort, the Hogwarts students struggle to reveal themselves as adolescents.

Rowling, J. K. *Harry Potter and the Prisoner of Azkaban.* Scholastic, 1999. 435p.

Harry faces great danger when the man accused of betraying his parents escapes from prison.

Rowling, J. K. *Harry Potter and the Sorcerer's Stone.* Scholastic, 1998. 309p.
Harry Potter learns a few things the year that he turns eleven—that his parents were not killed in an accident but murdered, and that he is not just a boy but a wizard.

Scieszka, Jon. *Math Curse.* Viking Children's Books, 1995. unpaged.
More whacked-out humor when everything—everything—becomes a math problem.

Spinelli, Jerry. *Library Card.* Scholastic, 1997. 148p.
Interconnected stories about how a library card changes the lives, if only for a short time, of four young people.

Stravinsky, John. *Muhammad Ali.* Random House, 1997. 208p.
From the makers of the television show Biography comes the life story of "the Great One" told in photos and text, and filled with sidelights including samples of Ali's poetry.

Whelan, Gloria. *Homeless Bird.* HarperCollins, 2000. 192p.
Thirteen-year-old Koly must marry the boy her parents choose for her in India, only to face a horrific mother-in-law.

Williams-Garcia, Rita. *Like Sisters on the Home Front.* Lodestar Books, 1995.
Pregnant with her second child, fourteen-year-old Gayle Ann is sent by her mother to live with relatives in the South in an attempt to get her to change her life.

Zeises, Lara M. *Contents under Pressure.* Delacorte, 2004. 256p.
Strong female role models carry readers through an entire range of emotions in Zeises's engrossing, fast-paced, and funny novel about Lucy seeking to make sense of her complicated world.

BOOK/MOVIE CONNECTIONS

Adams, Douglas. *A Hitchhiker's Guide to the Galaxy.*
Adams, Richard. *Watership Down.*
Alcott, Louisa May. *Little Women.*
Alexie, Sherman. *The Lone Ranger and Tonto Fistfight in Heaven. (Smoke Signals)*
Anderson, Laurie Halse. *Speak.*
Asimov, Issac. *I, Robot.*

Austen, Jane. *Emma*. (Related, *Clueless*)

Austen, Jane. *Sense and Sensibility*.

Babbit, Natalie. *Tuck Everlasting*.

Barrett, William E. *Lilies of the Field*.

Bissinger, H. G. *Friday Night Lights*.

Bradbury, Ray. *Fahrenheit 451*.

Brashares, Ann. *The Sisterhood of the Traveling Pants*.

Brin, David. *The Postman*.

Brontë, Charlotte. *Jane Eyre*.

Cabot, Meg. *The Princess Diaries*.

Cather, Willa. *My Antonia*.

Chevalier, Tracy. *Girl with a Pearl Earring*.

Christie, Agatha. *Murder on the Orient Express*.

Conroy, Pat. *The Great Santini*.

Cooper, James Fenimore. *The Last of the Mohicans*.

Cormier, Robert. *I Am the Cheese*.

Crichton, Michael. *Jurassic Park*.

Dahl, Roald. *Charlie and the Chocolate Factory*. (*Willy Wonka and the Chocolate Factory*)

Dessen, Sarah. *Someone Like You/That Summer*. (*How to Deal*)

DiCamillo, Kate. *Because of Winn-Dixie*.

Du Maurier, Daphne. *Rebecca*.

Duncan, Lois. *I Know What You Did Last Summer*.

Frank, Anne. *Diary of a Young Girl*. (*Diary of Anne Frank*)

Frazier, Charles. *Cold Mountain*.

Gilbreth, Frank B. *Cheaper by the Dozen*.

Golding, William. *Lord of the Flies*.

Goldman, William. *The Princess Bride*.

Grisham, John. *The Firm*.

Grisham, John. *The Runaway Jury*.

Grisham, John. *Skipping Christmas*. (*Christmas with the Kranks*)

Guest, Judith. *Ordinary People*.

Hickam, Homer. *Rocket Boys: A Memoir*. (*October Sky*)

Hinton, S. E. *The Outsiders*.

Hornby, Nick. *About a Boy*.

Hornby, Nick. *High Fidelity*.

Hugo, Victor. *The Hunchback of Notre Dame*.

Junger, Sebastian. *The Perfect Storm*.

Kaufman, Bel. *Up the Down Staircase*.

Kaysen, Susanna. *Girl, Interrupted*.

King, Stephen. *Carrie*.

King, Stephen. *Different Seasons*. (*Stand by Me*)

Kinsella, W. P. *Shoeless Joe. (Field of Dreams)*

Kleinbaum, N. H. *Dead Poet's Society.*

Lee, Harper. *To Kill a Mockingbird.*

Letts, Billie. *Where the Heart Is.*

Levine, Gail Carson. *Ella Enchanted.*

Levithan, David. *The Perfect Score.*

London, Jack. *White Fang.*

Mitchell, Margaret. *Gone with the Wind.*

O'Brian, Patrick. *Master and Commander: The Far Side of the World.*

Orwell, George. *Animal Farm.*

Paulsen, Gary. *Hatchet. (Cry of the Wild)*

Perrotta, Tom. *Election.*

Philbrick, Rodman. *Freak the Mighty. (The Mighty)*

Potok, Chaim. *The Chosen.*

Powell, Anthony. *The Fisher King.*

Rowling, J. K. *Harry Potter and the Sorcerer's Stone.*

Sachar, Louis. *Holes.*

Shakespeare, William. *Taming of the Shrew. (Ten Things I Hate about You)*

Sheldon, Dyan. *Confessions of a Teenage Drama Queen.*

Shelley, Mary Wollstonecraft. *Frankenstein. (Mary Shelley's Frankenstein)*

Smith, Betty. *A Tree Grows in Brooklyn.*

Snicket, Lemony. *A Series of Unfortunate Events.*

Sparks, Nicholas. *The Notebook.*

Sparks, Nicholas. *A Walk to Remember.*

Steinbeck, John. *Of Mice and Men.*

Strasser, Todd. *How I Created My Perfect Prom Date. (Drive Me Crazy)*

Tolkien, J.R.R. *The Lord of the Rings* trilogy.

Verne, Jules. *Around the World in 80 Days.*

Walker, Alice. *The Color Purple.*

Wallace, Daniel. *Big Fish: A Novel of Mythic Proportions.*

Wolff, Tobias. *This Boy's Life: A Memoir. (This Boy's Life: A True Story)*

Wright, Richard. *Native Son.*

X, Malcolm. *The Autobiography of Malcolm X. (Malcolm X)*

BEST NEW ADULT FICTION BOOKS FOR RELUCTANT TEEN READERS (SELECTED BY PATRICIA TAYLOR)

1. *The Lovely Bones.* Alice Sebold. Little Brown & Company. ISBN: 0316666343. 1st edition, June 2002. 288 pages.
2. *The Last Time They Met.* Anita Shreve. Little Brown & Company. ISBN: 0316781142. April 2001. 313 pages.

3. *The Eyre Affair: A Novel.* Jasper Fforde. Viking Press. ISBN: 0670030643. January 28, 2002. 374 pages.
4. *The Blue Nowhere.* Jeffrey Deaver. Simon & Schuster. ISBN: 068487127. May 1, 2001. 426 pages.
5. *The Last Report on the Miracles at Little No Horse.* Louise Erdich. Harper-Perennial. ISBN: 0060931221. 1st edition, April 2, 2002. 384 pages.
6. *The Bestseller.* Olivia Goldsmith. Harper Mass Market Paperbacks. ISBN: 0061096083. Reprint edition, August 1997. 720 pages.
7. *Life of Pi.* Yann Martel. Canada's 2001 Hugh MacLennan Prize for Fiction. Harcourt. ISBN: 0151008116. June 4, 2002. 336 pages.
8. *Empire Falls.* Richard Russo. Vintage Books. ISBN: 0375726403. April 12, 2002. 483 pages.
9. *Little Altars Everywhere.* Rebecca Wells. HarperCollins (paper). ISBN: 0060976845. Reprint edition, May 1996. 240 pages.
10. *Fall on Your Knees.* Ann-Marie McDonald. Scribner. ISBN: 0743237188. Oprah edition, January 24, 2002. 508 pages.
11. *The Perks of Being a Wallflower.* Stephen Chobosky. Pocket Books. ISBN: 0671027344. February 1999. 213 pages.
12. *The Way to Somewhere.* Angie Day. Simon & Schuster. ISBN: 0743223322. March 2002. 302 pages.
13. *Never Change.* Elizabeth Berg. Washington Square Press. ISBN: 0743411331. May 2002. 214 pages.
14. *Isaac's Storm: A Man, a Time, and the Deadliest Hurricane in History.* Erik Larson, Isaac Monroe Cline. Vintage Books. ISBN: 0375708278. July 11, 2000. 323 pages.
15. *Welcome to Temptation.* Jennifer Crusie. St. Martin's Mass Market Paper. ISBN: 0312974256. April 2001. 416 pages.
16. *Double Deuce.* Robert B. Parker. Berkley Pub Group. ISBN: 042513793. Reprint edition, April 1993.
17. *Crimson Joy.* Robert B. Parker. Dell Pub Co. ISBN: 0440203430. Reissue edition, January 1997.
18. *The Sweet Potato Queens' Book of Love.* Jill Connor Browne. Three Rivers Press. ISBN: 0609804138. March 1999. 213 pages.
19. *Prayers for Rain.* Dennis Lehane. Three Rivers Press. ISBN: 0609804138. March 1999. 416 pages.
20. *Dark Debts.* Karen Lynne Hall. Ivy Books. ISBN: 0804116555. Reprint edition, June 1997. 507 pages.
21. *The Silence of the Lambs.* Thomas Harris. St. Martin's Mass Market Paper. ISBN: 0312924585. Reissue edition, February 1991. 367 pages.
22. *Red Dragon.* Thomas Harris. Dell Pub Co. ISBN: 0440206154. Reissue edition, May 9, 2000. 454 pages.

23. *Eyes of Prey.* John Sandford. Berkley Pub Group. ISBN: 0425132048. Reprint edition, April 2, 2002. 368 pages.
24. *Outlander.* Diana Gabaldon. Dell Books. ISBN: 0440212561. Reissue edition, July 1, 1992. 850 pages.
25. *Dragonfly in Amber.* Diana Gabaldon. Dell Books. ISBN: 0440215625. Reprint edition, December 1993. 947 pages.
26. *The Brothers K.* David James Duncan. Bantam Books. ISBN: 055337849X. July 1996.
27. *Daughter of My People: A Novel.* James Kilgo. University of Georgia Press. ISBN: 0820320021. May 1998. 312 pages.
28. *Deux-X.* Joseph Citro. Twilight Pub. ISBN: 0963858513. May 1994.
29. *The Fall of Rome.* Martha Southgate. Scribner. ISBN: 0684865009. January 1, 2002. 223 pages.
30. *Gone for Good.* Harlan Coben. Delacorte Press. ISBN: 038533558X. April 30, 2002. 352 pages.
31. *Confessions of an Ugly Stepsister.* Gregory Maguire, Bill Sanderson (illustrator). Regan Books. ISBN: 0060392827. November 1999. 384 pages.
32. *Any Way the Wind Blows.* E. Lynn Harris. Doubleday. ISBN: 0385495056. July 10, 2001. 342 pages.
33. *The Basic Eight.* Daniel Handler. Griffin Trade Paperback. ISBN: 0312253737. March 2000. 352 pages.
34. *The Boy Next Door.* Meg Cabot. Avon Books. ISBN: 0060096195. October 8, 2002. 374 pages.

BEST LITERATURE BOOKS FOR RELUCTANT READERS (SELECTED BY PATRICIA TAYLOR)

1. *Flowers for Algernon.* Daniel Keyes. Skylark. ISBN: 0553274503. Reissue edition, April 1, 1984. 216 pages.
2. *Rebecca.* Daphne Du Maurier. Avon. ISBN: 0380778556. Reissue edition, August 1996. 384 pages.
3. *She's Come Undone.* Wally Lamb. Pocket Books. ISBN: 0671021001. June 1998. 465 pages.
4. *The Rapture of Canaan.* Sheri Reynolds. Berkley Pub Group. ISBN: 0425155439. November 1996. 317 pages.
5. *The Bluest Eye.* Toni Morrison. Penguin USA (Paper). ISBN: 0452282195. April 27, 2000. 216 pages.
6. *The Joy Luck Club.* Amy Tan. Prentice Hall (K–12). ISBN: 0804106304. October 1994. 337 pages.
7. *East of Eden.* John Steinbeck. Penguin USA (Paper). ISBN: 0142000655. January 31, 2002. 608 pages.

8. *Gone with the Wind.* Margaret Mitchell. Warner Books. ISBN: 0446365386. Reprint edition, November 1994. 1,024 pages.

9. *The Stand.* Stephen King. Signet. ISBN: 0451169530. Reprint edition, May 1991. 1,168 pages.

10. *I Know This Much Is True.* Wally Lamb. Regan Books. ISBN: 0060987561. Reprint edition, April 6, 1999. 912 pages.

11. *The Great Divorce.* Valerie Martin. Vintage Books. ISBN: 0375727183. February 4, 2003. 352 pages.

12. *The Poisonwood Bible.* Barbara Kingsolver. HarperPerennial. ISBN: 0060930535. October 1999. 506 pages.

13. *Barbara Kingsolver's "The Poisonwood Bible": A Reader's Guide.* Linda Wagner-Martin. Continuum Pub Group. ISBN: 0826452345. September 2001. 96 pages.

14. *Midnight in the Garden of Good and Evil.* John Berendt. Vintage Books. ISBN: 0679751521. July 6, 1999. 386 pages. (Nonfiction)

15. *Alias Grace.* Margaret Atwood. Doubleday. ISBN: 0385490445. Reprint edition, November 1997. 468 pages.

16. *The Robber Bride.* Margaret Atwood. Anchor Books. ISBN: 0385491034. February 1998. 432 pages.

17. *Sense and Sensibility.* Jane Austen. Oxford University Press. ISBN: 0192833588. July 1998.

18. *The Exorcist.* William Peter Blatty. HarperCollins. ISBN: 0061007226. Reissue edition, March 2000.

19. *Rosemary's Baby.* Ira Levin. Signet. ISBN: 0451194004. September 1997. 320 pages.

20. *Wuthering Heights.* Emily Brontë. Bantam Classics. ISBN: 0553212583. Reissue edition, November 1, 1983. 315 pages.

21. *A Tale of Two Cities.* Charles Dickens. Signet Classic. ISBN: 0451526562. Reissue edition, August 1997. 371 pages.

22. *Invisible Man.* Ralph Ellison. Vintage Books. ISBN: 0679732764. 2nd edition, March 1995. 581 pages.

23. *The Princess Bride: S Morgenstern's Classic Tale of True Love and High Adventure (The Good Parts Version).* William Goldman. Ballantine Books. ISBN: 0345348036. Reissue edition, December 1990. 283 pages.

24. *Ordinary People.* Judith Guest. Penguin USA (Paper). ISBN: 0140065172. Reprint edition, January 1993. 263 pages.

25. *Catch-22.* Joseph Heller. Scribner Paperback Fiction. ISBN: 068483339. Reprint edition, September 1996. 463 pages.

26. *The World According to Garp*. John Irving. Ballantine Books. ISBN: 034536676X. Reissue edition, August 1994. 609 pages.
27. *We Have Always Lived in the Castle*. Shirley Jackson. Viking Press. ISBN: 0140071075. Reprint edition, June 1984. 214 pages.
28. *Different Seasons*. Stephen King. Dutton. ISBN: 0451167538. 1982. 527 pages.
29. *It*. Stephen King. Dutton. ISBN: 0451169514. September 1986. 1,139 pages.
30. *Salem's Lot*. Stephen King. Simon & Schuster. ISBN: 0671039741. November 1, 1999.
31. *A Separate Peace*. John Knowles. Bantam. ISBN: 0553280414. January 1, 1985. 186 pages.
32. *To Kill a Mockingbird*. Harper Lee. HarperPerennial. ISBN: 0060933275. November 1, 1999. 323 pages.
33. *A Wrinkle in Time*. Madeleine L'Engle. Dell. ISBN: 0440998050. March 1, 1976. 212 pages.
34. *Mary Reilly*. Valerie Martin. Vintage Anchor. ISBN: 0375725997. March 1, 2001. 263 pages.
35. *The Forever King*. Molly Cochran and Warren Murphy. Tor Books. ISBN: 0812517164. Reprint edition, March 1993.
36. *Alas, Babylon!* Pat Frank. HarperCollins (paper). ISBN: 0060931396. April 1999. 323 pages.
37. *Cat's Cradle*. Kurt Vonnegut Jr. Delta. ISBN: 038533348X. October 1998. 287 pages.
38. *Welcome to the Monkey House*. Kurt Vonnegut Jr. Delta. ISBN: 0385333501. October 1998. 331 pages.
39. *The Bell Jar*. Sylvia Plath. HarperPerennial. ISBN: 0060930187. January 2000. 288 pages.
40. *The Godfather*. Mario Puzo. Signet. ISBN: 0451167716. Reissue edition, December 1995. 444 pages.
41. *The Fountainhead*. Ayn Rand. Signet. ISBN: 0451191153. 50th anniversary edition, September 1996. 704 pages.
42. *All Quiet on the Western Front*. Erich Maria Remarque. Fawcett Books. ISBN: 0449213943. Reissue edition, June 1995. 295 pages.
43. *Interview with the Vampire*. Anne Rice. Ballantine Books. ISBN: 0345337662. Reissue edition, October 1993. 342 pages.
44. *The Vampire Lestat*. Anne Rice. Ballantine Books. ISBN: 0345313860. Reprint edition, October 1993. 550 pages.
45. *The Catcher in the Rye*. J. D. Salinger. Lb Books. ISBN: 0316769487. Reissue edition, May 1991. 214 pages.

46. *Letters from the Earth*. Mark Twain. HarperPerennial. ISBN: 0060921056. Reprint edition, November 1991. 320 pages.

47. *I Know Why the Caged Bird Sings*. Maya Angelou. Bantam Books. ISBN: 0553279378. Reissue edition, May 1, 1983. 289 pages.

48. *Zen and the Art of Motorcycle Maintenance*. Robert Pirsig. Bantam Books. ISBN: 0553277472. Reissue edition, April 1, 1984. 380 pages.

49. *The House of Mirth*. Edith Wharton. Scribner Paperback Fiction. ISBN: 068480123X. Reprint edition, August 1995.

50. *The Accidental Tourist*. Anne Tyler. Ballantine Books. ISBN: 034545200. April 9, 2002.

51. *One Flew over the Cuckoo's Nest*. Ken Kesey. New American Library. ISBN: 0451163966. Reissue edition, July 1989. 272 pages.

52. *Ragtime*. Plume. ISBN: 0452279070. May 1997. 270 pages.

53. *The Lottery and Other Stories*. Shirley Jackson. Noonday Press. ISBN: 0374516812. Reissue edition, June 1992.

54. *The Old Ace in the Hole*. Annie Proulx. Scribner. ISBN: 0684813076. December 10, 2002. 384 pages.

55. *The Diary of a Young Girl*. Anne Frank. Bantam Books. ISBN: 0553577123. Reissue edition, March 1997. 335 pages.

56. *The Prince of Tides*. Pat Conroy. Houghton Mifflin Co. ISBN: 0395353009. October 21, 1986. 576 pages.

57. *Needful Things*. Stephen King. Signet. ISBN: 0451172817. Reissue edition, June 1997. 752 pages.

BEST YOUNG ADULT LITERATURE FOR RELUCTANT READERS (SELECTED BY PATRICIA TAYLOR)

1. *Speak*. Laurie Halse Anderson. Speak. ISBN: 014131088X. Reprint edition, April 1, 2001. 208 pages.

2. *Staying Fat for Sarah Byrnes*. Chris Crutcher. Laurel Leaf. ISBN: 044021906X. Reprint edition, March 1995. 216 pages.

3. *The Outsiders*. S. E. Hinton. Speak. ISBN: 014038572X. Reprint edition, November 1997. 180 pages.

4. *Ender's Game*. Orson Scott Card. Tor Books. ISBN: 0812532538. January 1986.

5. *Rats Saw God*. Rob Thomas. Pocket Books. ISBN: 0689807775. June 1996.

6. *Holes*. Louis Sachar. Yearling Books. ISBN: 0440414806. Reprint edition, May 9, 2000. 233 pages.

7. *Weetzie Bat*. Francesca Block. HarperTrophy. ISBN: 0064408183. 10th anniversary edition, April 1999. 128 pages.

8. *The Chocolate War*. Robert Cormier. Laurel Leaf. ISBN: 0440944597. Reissue edition, May 1999. 191 pages.
9. *The Giver*. Lois Lowry. Laurel Leaf. ISBN: 0440237688. September 10, 2002.
10. *Annie on My Mind*. Nancy Garden. Bt Bound. ISBN: 0808587560. October 1999.
11. *House of Stairs*. William Sleator. Puffin. ISBN: 0140345809. Reissue edition, April 1991. 166 pages.
12. *Hitchhiker's Guide to the Galaxy*. Douglas Adams. Ballantine Books. ISBN: 0345391802. Reissue edition, November 1995. 216 pages.
13. *Blood and Chocolate*. Annette Curtis Klause. Laurel Leaf. ISBN: 0440226686. Reprint edition, September 7, 1999. 264 pages.
14. *Memoirs of a Bookbat*. Kathryn Lasky. Harcourt Paperbacks. ISBN: 0152012591. April 1, 1996. 224 pages.
15. *Up the Down Staircase*. Bel Kaufman and Elizabeth Speare. Harper-Perennial. ISBN: 0060973617. Reprint edition, July 1991. 368 pages.
16. *The Witch of Blackbird Pond*. Laurel Leaf. ISBN: 0440995779. Reissue edition, June 1, 1978. 223 pages.
17. *Freak the Mighty*. Rodman Philbrick. Bt Bound. ISBN: 0613360613. April 2002.
18. *Fallen Angels*. Walter Dean Myers. Scholastic Paperbacks. ISBN: 0590409433. Reprint edition, September 1991. 309 pages.
19. *Rules of the Road*. Joan Bauer. Speak. ISBN: 0698118286. Reprint edition, January 2000. 201 pages.
20. *The Sisterhood of the Traveling Pants*. Ann Brashares. Delacorte Press. ISBN: 0385729332. September 11, 2001. 304 pages.
21. *You Don't Know Me*. David Klass. HarperTempest. ISBN: 0064473783. Reprint edition, August 6, 2002. 352 pages.
22. *Beauty*. Robin McKinley. Scott Foresman (Pearson K–12). ISBN: 0064404773. Reissue edition, June 1993. 247 pages.
23. *The Man Who Was Poe*. Avi. Camelot. ISBN: 0380730227. Reissue edition, July 1997. 208 pages.
24. *Losing Joe's Place*. Gordon Korman. Point. ISBN: 0590427695. Reprint edition, June 1993.

BEST FORTY MAGAZINES FOR RELUCTANT READERS

1. *Alternative Press*   music
2. *Blender*   music (mature)
3. *BMX Plus*   sports
4. *Box*   sports—skateboarding

 5. *Computer Gaming World*   computer games
 6. *Cosmo Girl*   general interest
 7. *Dirt Bike*   sports
 8. *Dragon*   science fiction and fantasy
 9. *Dub*   cars
10. *Electronic Gaming Monthly* computer games
11. *Entertainment Weekly*   entertainment
12. *ESPN*   sports
13. *GamePro*   computer games
14. *Hit Parader*   music
15. *Hot Rod*   cars
16. *Inside NASCAR*   sports
17. *Jet*   African American interest
18. *Low Rider*   sports
19. *Mad*   humor
20. *National Enquirer*   tabloid
21. *NBA Inside Stuff*   sports
22. *Nickelodeon*   humor
23. *Nintendo Power*   computer games
24. *PC Gamer*   computer games
25. *Right On*   music
26. *Rolling Stone*   music
27. *Slam*   sports
28. *Snap BMX*   sports
29. *Soccer Jr.*   sports
30. *Source*   music
31. *Spin*   music
32. *Super Street*   cars
33. *Teen People*   entertainment
34. *Transworld Skateboard*   sports
35. *Vibe*   music
36. *Weekly World News*   tabloid
37. *Wizard*   entertainment
38. *Word Up*   music
39. *WWE Raw*   sports
40. *WWE Smackdown*   sports

BEST TWENTY-FIVE COMIC BOOKS FOR RELUCTANT READERS

Title	Released
1. *Adventures of Superman*	Monthly
2. *Amazing Spider-Man*	Monthly
3. *Angel* (Dark Horse)	Monthly
4. *Avengers*	Monthly
5. *Batman*	Monthly
6. *Blade of the Immortal*	Monthly
7. *Buffy the Vampire Slayer* (Dark Horse)	Monthly
8. *Catwoman*	Monthly
9. *Darkness (PG-13)*	Monthly
10. *Dragonball Z* (Viz)	Monthly
11. *Fantastic Four*	Monthly
12. *Fathom (PG-13)*	Bi-monthly
13. *Justice League of America*	Monthly
14. *Simpsons*	Monthly
15. *Spawn (PG-13)*	Monthly
16. *Star Wars* (Dark Horse)	Monthly
17. *Super Manga Blast*	Monthly
18. *Tick*	Monthly
19. *Tomb Raider (PG-13)*	Monthly
20. *Ultimate Marvel*	Monthly
21. *Ultimate X-Men*	Monthly
22. *Uncanny X-Men*	Monthly
23. *Usagi Yojimbo*	Monthly
24. *Wolverine*	Monthly
25. *X-Men*	Monthly

BEST TWENTY-FIVE BOOKS FOR STRUGGLING MIDDLE SCHOOL READERS

Many of these books appeared on the Quick Picks list produced by the Young Adult Library Services Association (http://www.ala.org/yalsa).

1. *145th Street: Short Stories,* by Walter Dean Myers
2. *Bad Beginning (A Series of Unfortunate Events, Book 1),* by Lemony Snicket
3. *Captain Underpants and the Wrath of the Wicked Wedgie Woman,* by Dav Pilky

4. *Define Normal,* by Julie Ann Peters
5. *Dreams: Explore the You That You Can't Control,* by Tucker Shaw
6. *Ella Enchanted,* by Gail Carson Levine
7. *Encyclopedia of Professional Wrestling: 100 Years of the Good, the Bad and the Unforgettable*
8. *Flight #116 Is Down,* by Caroline Cooney
9. *Ghost Train,* by Jess Mowry
10. *Got Issues Much? Celebrities Share Their Traumas and Triumphs,* by Randi Reisfeld
11. *Holes,* by Louis Sachar
12. *I Have a Dream,* by Martin Luther King
13. *In the Forests of the Night,* by Amelia Atwater-Rhodes
14. *Miracle's Boys,* by Jacqueline Woodson
15. *Oh, Yuck! The Encyclopedia of Everything Nasty*
16. *Party Girl,* by Lynne Ewing
17. *Rats,* by Paul Zindel
18. *See You Later, Gladiator* (Time Warp Trio), by Jon Scieszka
19. *The Simpsons: A Complete Guide to Our Favorite Family,* by Matt Groening
20. *Special Effects in Film and Television,* by Jake Hamilton
21. *Spiders in the Hairdo: Modern Urban Legends*
22. *Stuck in Neutral,* by Terry Trueman
23. *Things I Have to Tell You: Poems and Writings by Teenage Girls,* by Betsy Franco
24. *Words with Wings: A Treasury of African-American Poetry and Art,* by Belinda Rochelle
25. *You Hear Me? Poems and Writing by Teenage Boys,* by Betsy Franco

BEST 100 BOOKS FOR BOYS OF ALL AGES

**E = Elementary or Preschool   M = Middle School   J = Junior High
S = Senior High**

Author	Title	Grade
1. Allard	*The Stupids Die*	E
2. Ballard	*Exploring the Titanic*	M
3. Barron	*The Lost Years of Merlin*	M
4. Bloor	*Tangerine*	J
5. Brandenberg	*To the Top of the World*	M
6. Brown	*The Da Vinci Code*	S
7. Burgess	*Doing It*	S

8. Burton	*Mike Mulligan and His Steam Shovel*	E
9. Card	*Ender's Game*	S
10. Carrick	*Patrick's Dinosaurs*	E
11. Choldenko	*Al Capone Does My Shirts*	J
12. Clancy	Net Force series	J
13. Cleary	*The Mouse and the Motorcycle*	E
14. Colfer	*Eternity Code*	J
15. Crichton	*Jurassic Park*	S
16. Crutcher	*Ironman*	S
17. Dahl	*Charlie and the Chocolate Factory*	E
18. Davis	*Vision Quest*	S
19. Eastman	*Go, Dog, Go!*	E
20. Emberley	*Ed Emberley's Drawing Books*	E
21. Erickson	Hank the Cowdog series	E
22. Fitzgerald	The Great Brain series	E
23. Fleishman	*Phineas Gage*	M
24. Flinn	*Breathing Underwater*	S
25. Franco	*You Hear Me? Poems and Writing by Teenage Boys*	S
26. Gantos	*Hole in My Life*	S
27. Gantos	*Joey Pigza Swallowed the Key*	J
28. Groening	*Simpsons Comics Royale* (and others)	J
29. Harris	*The Silence of the Lambs*	S
30. Hawk	*Hawk: Occupation Skateboarder*	S
31. Heinlein	*Starship Troopers*	S
32. Hinton	*The Outsiders*	J
33. Hobbs	*Downriver*	J
34. Horowitz	*Point Blank* (and other Alex Rider books)	J
35. Howe	*Bunnicula*	E
36. Jacques	Redwall series	M
37. Jordan	*Wheel of Time*	S
38. King	*Christine*	S
39. Korman	*No More Dead Dogs*	J
40. Korman	*Son of the Mob*	J
41. Kotzwinkle	*Walter, the Farting Dog*	E
42. Krakauer	*Into Thin Air*	S
43. LaHaye	Left Behind series	S
44. Lawrence	*Smugglers*	J
45. Levy	*KISS Guide to the Unexplained*	S
46. Lobel	Frog and Toad series	E
47. London	*Call of the Wild* (and others)	S
48. London	*Froggy Gets Dressed*	E

49. Lubar	*Hidden Talents*	J
50. Malone	*Hip Hop Immortals: The Remix*	S
51. Marzollo	I Spy series	E
52. Masoff	*Oh, Yuck! The Encyclopedia of Everything Nasty*	M
53. Meglin	*The Mad Gross Book*	M
54. Myers	*Fallen Angels*	S
55. Myers	*Monster*	S
56. Myers	*Slam!*	S
57. Nelson	*Left for Dead*	S
58. Northcutt	*Darwin Awards*	S
59. Onion staff	*Our Dumb Century: 100 Years of Headlines*	S
60. Owen	*Hidden Evidence*	J
61. Palahniuk	*Fight Club*	S
62. Paolini	*Eragon*	J
63. Patterson	*Kiss the Girls*	S
64. Paulsen	*Hatchet* (and sequels)	J
65. Paulsen	*How Angel Peterson Got His Name*	J
66. Paulsen	*Soldier's Heart: A Novel of the Civil War*	J
67. Pilkey	Captain Underpants series	E
68. Pilkey	*Dogzilla*	E
69. Pilkey	*Kat Kong*	E
70. Preston	*Hot Zone*	S
71. Prior	*Encyclopedia of Preserved People*	J
72. Puzo	*Godfather*	S
73. Rawls	*Where the Red Fern Grows*	J
74. Rockwell	*How to Eat Fried Worms*	E
75. Rowling	Harry Potter books	M
76. Sachar	*Sideways Stories from Wayside School*	M
77. Salinger	*The Catcher in the Rye*	S
78. Sandford	Prey books	S
79. Schwartz	*Scary Stories to Tell in the Dark*	M
80. Scieszka	*Stinky Cheese Man and Other Fairly Stupid Tales*	E
81. Scieszka	Time Warp Trio series	E
82. Scieszka	*The True Story of the Three Little Pigs*	E
83. Seckel	*Great Book of Optical Illusions*	M
84. Selznik	*Houdini Box*	E
85. Sendak	*Where the Wild Things Are*	E
86. Seuss	*Cat in the Hat*	E
87. Shakur	*Rose That Grew from Concrete*	S
88. Shakur	*Tupac: Resurrection 1971–1996*	S
89. Shan	Cirque du Freak series	M

90. Silverstein	*Where the Sidewalk Ends*	E
91. Snicket	*Carnivorous Carnival* (and others)	M
92. Sobol	*Encyclopedia Brown, Boy Detective*	E
93. Souljah	*Coldest Winter Ever*	S
94. Spinelli	*Maniac Magee*	J
95. Tolkien	*Lord of the Rings*	S
96. Van Allsburg	*Jumanji*	M
97. *Vibe* magazine	*Tupac*	S
98. Waber	*Ira Sleeps Over*	E
99. White	*Deathwatch*	J
100. Willems	*Don't Let the Pigeon Drive the Bus*	E

TWENTY CHILDREN'S BOOKS FOR RELUCTANT READERS

1. Angelou, Maya. *Life Doesn't Frighten Me*. Stewart, Tabori & Chang, 1996. $17.95 (1-55670-288-4).

Presents Maya Angelou's poem, illustrated with paintings and drawings by Jean-Michel Basquiat.

2. Bunting, Eve. *Smoky Night*. Harcourt Children's Books, 1999. $6.00 (0-15-201884-0).

The Caldecott winning picture books about the L.A. riots.

3. Cronin, Doreen, et al. *Click, Clack, Moo: Cows That Type*. Simon & Schuster Children's Publishing, 2000. $15.95 (0-689-83213-3).

When Farmer Brown's cows learn to type, they send him a note demanding electric blankets.

4. Falconer, Ian. *Olivia*. Simon & Schuster Children's Publishing, 2000. $16.95 (0-689-82953-1).

Whether at home getting ready for the day, enjoying the beach, or at bedtime, Olivia is a feisty pig who has too much energy for her own good.

5. Gaiman, Neil. *The Wolves in the Walls*. HarperCollins, 2005. $6.99 (0-380-81095-6).

Lucy is sure there are wolves living in the walls of her house, although others in her family disagree; when the wolves come out, the adventure begins.

6. Gomi, Taro. *Everyone Poops*. Kane Miller Book Publishers, 2004. $6.95 (1-929132-14-X).

Sometimes the title really does tell us all we need to know.

7. Kotzwinkle, William. *Walter the Farting Dog*. Frog, Limited, 2001. $15.95 (1-58394-053-7).

Walter the dog creates problems with his farts but becomes a hero when burglars enter the house.

8. Myers, Walter Dean. *Harlem: A Poem*. Scholastic, 1997. $16.95 (0-590-54340-7).

Poems and collages celebrate the people, sights, and sounds of Harlem.

9. Pilkey, Dav. *Dogzilla*. Harcourt Children's Books, 2003. $4.95 (0-15-204949-5).

You'll relish this read with all the strength you can muster.

10. Pilkey, Dav. *Kat Kong*. Harcourt Children's Books, 2003. $4.95 (0-15-204950-9).

Starring Flash, Rabies, and Dwayne and introducing Blueberry as the Monster.

11. Raschka, Chris. *Charlie Parker Played Be Bop*. Scholastic, 2004. $6.99 (0-439-57823-X).

The roots of rap and the rhythm of jazz in picture-book form.

12. Rosen, Michael. *Michael Rosen's Sad Book*. Candlewick Press, 2005. $16.99 (0-7636-2597-3).

A man tells about all the emotions that accompany his sadness over the death of his son, and how he tries to cope.

13. Scieszka, Jon. *True Story of the Three Little Pigs*. Penguin, 1996. $6.99 (0-14-054451-8).

The funniest picture book/fractured fairy tale ever.

14. Sendak, Maurice. *Where the Wild Things Are*. HarperCollins Children's Book Group, 1998. $16.95 (0-06-028223-1).

The most famous picture book ever, and with good reason: it's still that good.

15. Silverstein, Shel. *The Giving Tree*. HarperCollins Children's Book Group, 2004. $15.99 (0-06-025665-6).

A young boy grows to manhood and old age experiencing the love and generosity of a tree, which gives to him without thought of return.

16. Taylor, Clark. *The House That Crack Built*. Chronicle Books, 1992. $6.95 (0-8118-0123-3).

Cumulative verses describe the creation, distribution, and destructive effects of crack cocaine. Includes list of sources for information and help.

17. Van Allsburg, Chris. *Jumanji*. Scholastic, 1995. $4.95 (0-590-54551-5).

Two bored and restless children find more excitement than they bargained for in a mysterious and mystical jungle-adventure board game.

18. Willems, Mo. *Don't Let the Pigeon Drive the Bus!* Hyperion Books for Children. 2003. $18.99 (0-7868-1988-X).

An ode to frustration and imagination as pigeon tries to scheme his way behind the wheel.

19. Woodson, Jacqueline. *The Other Side.* Penguin, 2001. $16.99 (0-399-23116-1).

Two girls, one white and one black, gradually get to know each other as they sit on the fence that divides their town.

20. Woodson, Jacqueline. *Show Way.* Penguin, 2005. $16.99 (0-399-23749-6).

The making of "Show ways," or quilts that once served as secret maps for freedom-seeking slaves, is a tradition passed from mother to daughter in the author's family.

READ-ALIKES (FICTION AND NONFICTION)

Child Called . . . (realistic biography)

1. Burch, Jennings Michael. *They Cage the Animals at Night.*
2. Crutcher, Chris. *Chinese Handcuffs.*
3. Fisher, Antwone Quenton. *Finding Fish.*
4. Hayden, Torey L. *Beautiful Child.*
5. Louise, Regina. *Somebody's Someone: A Memoir.*
6. Michener, Anna J. *Becoming Anna: The Autobiography of a Sixteen-Year-Old.*
7. Rapp, Adam. *Little Chicago.*
8. Rapp, Adam. *33 Snowfish.*
9. Shaw, Susan. *Boy from the Basement.*
10. Silverman, Sue William. *Because I Remember Terror, Father, I Remember You.*
11. Talbot, Bryan. *The Tale of One Bad Rat.*
12. Williams, Lori Aurelia. *When Kambia Elaine Flew in from Neptune.*

Cirque Du Freak (horror)

1. Anderson, M. T. *Thirsty.*
2. Atwater-Rhodes, Amelia. *Shattered Mirror.*
3. Bodine, Echo L. *Relax, It's Only a Ghost! My Adventures with Spirits, Hauntings and Things That Go Bump in the Night.*

4. Brunvand, Jan Harold. *Be Afraid, Be Very Afraid: The Book of Scary Urban Legends.*
5. Buller, Laura. *Myths and Monsters: From Dragons to Werewolves.*
6. Gaiman, Neil. *Coraline.*
7. Klause, Annette Curtis. *Alive on the Inside. Freaks!*
8. Rees, Celia. *Soul Taker.*
9. Shusterman, Neal. *Full Tilt.*
10. Stevenson. Jay. *The Complete Idiot's Guide to Vampires.*
11. Stine, R. L. *Beware! R. L. Stine Picks His Favorite Scary Stories.*
12. Vande Velde, Vivian. *Being Dead.*

Coldest Winter Ever (urban stories)

1. Apollo. *Concrete Candy.*
2. Draper, Sharon. *We Beat the Street.*
3. Flake, Sharon. *Begging for Change.*
4. Grimes, Nikki. *Bronx Masquerade.*
5. LeBlanc, Adrian Nicole. *Random Family: Love, Drugs, Trouble, and Coming of Age in the Bronx.*
6. McCall, Nathan. *Makes Me Wanna Hollar.*
7. McDonald, Janet. *Brotherhood.*
8. Morris, Monique. *Too Beautiful for Words.*
9. Mowry, Jess. *Way Past Cool.*
10. Tyree, Omar. *Flyy Girl.*
11. Williams-Garcia, Rita. *Like Sisters on the Homefront.*
12. Woodson, Jacqueline. *Miracle's Boys.*

Hatchet (adventure)

1. Bowden, Mark. *Black Hawk Down: A Story of Modern War.*
2. Hobbs, Will. *Downriver.*
3. Horowitz, Anthony. *Stormbreaker.*
4. Krakauer, Jon. *Into Thin Air: A Personal Account of the Mount Everest Disaster.*
5. McNab, Chris. *Survive in the Jungle with the Special Forces "Green Berets."*
6. Mikaelsen, Ben. *Touching Spirit Bear.*
7. Paulsen, Gary. *Guts: The True Stories Behind "Hatchet" and the Brian Books.*
8. Piven, Joshua. *The Worst-Case Scenario Survival Handbook.*
9. Ralston, Aron. *Between a Rock and a Hard Place.*
10. Sachar, Louis. *Stanley Yelnats' Survival Guide to Camp Green Lake.*

11. Sweeney, Joyce. *Free Fall.*
12. Weaver, Will. *Memory Boy.*

Monster (gang stories)

1. Coburn, Jake. *Prep.*
2. Ewing, Lynne. *Drive By.*
3. Holmes, Shannon. *B-more Careful.*
4. Moore, Y. Blak. *Triple Take.*
5. Myers, Walter Dean. *Autobiography of My Dead Brother.*
6. Rodriguez, Luis. *Always Running.*
7. Sanchez, Reymundo. *My Bloody Life: The Making of a Latin King.*
8. Shakur, Sanyika. *Monster: The Autobiography of an L.A. Gang Member.*
9. Soto, Gary. *Buried Onions.*
10. Williams, Stanley Tookie. *Blue Rage, Black Redemption: A Memoir.*
11. Woods, Brenda. *Emako Blue.*
12. Woods, Teri. *True to the Game.*

Fat Kid Rules the World (music)

1. Anonymous. *Confessions of a Backup Dancer as Told to Tucker Shaw.*
2. Bliesener, Mark. *The Complete Idiot's Guide to Starting a Band.*
3. Brackett, Nathan. *The New "Rolling Stone" Album Guide.*
4. Cohn, Rachel. *Pop Princess.*
5. 50 Cent. *From Pieces to Weight: Once Upon a Time in Southside, Queens.*
6. King, Sahpreem. *A Gotta Get Signed: How to Become a Hip-Hop Producer.*
7. Klosterman, Chuck. *Sex, Drugs, and Cocoa Puffs: A Low Culture Manifesto.*
8. Kool Moe Dee. *There's a God on the Mic: The True 50 Greatest MCs.*
9. Manning, Sarra. *Guitar Girl.*
10. Minchin Adele. *The Beat Goes On.*
11. Nelson, Blake. *Rock Star Superstar.*
12. Zephaniah, Benjamin. *Gangsta Rap.*

Go Ask Alice (drugs)

1. Brooks, Kevin. *Candy.*
2. Chbosky, Stephen. *Perks of Being a Wallflower.*
3. Grant, Cynthia. *White Horse.*

4. Hopkins, Ellen. *Crank.*
5. Hyde, Margaret O. *Drugs 101: An Overview for Teens.*
6. James, Brian. *Pure Sunshine.*
7. Kuhn, Cynthia. *Buzzed: The Straight Facts about the Most Used and Abused Drugs from Alcohol to Ecstasy.*
8. McDonell, Nick. *Twelve: A Novel.*
9. Murray, Jaye. *Bottled Up: A Novel.*
10. Strasser, Todd. *Can't Get There from Here.*
11. Thomas, Rob. *Rats Saw God.*
12. Viswanathan, Neeraja. *Street Law Handbook: Surviving Sex, Drugs, and Petty Crime.*

Doing It (sex)

1. Beckerman, Marty. *Generation S.L.U.T. (Sexually Liberated Urban Teens): A Brutal Feel-Up Session with Today's Sex-Crazed Adolescent Populace.*
2. Bradley, Alex. *24 Girls in 7 Days.*
3. Cann, Kate. *Shacked Up.*
4. Cart, Michael. *Love and Sex: Ten stories of Truth.*
5. Dean, Zoey. *The A-list: A novel.*
6. Lockhart, E. *The Boyfriend List.*
7. Malkin, Nina. *6X: The Uncensored Confessions.*
8. Minter, J. *The Insiders.*
9. Nelson, R. A. *Teach Me.*
10. *One Hot Second: Stories about Desire.*
11. Perez, Marlene. *Unexpected Development.*
12. Ruditis, Paul. *Rainbow Party.*

Part III.   Tools That Work

Booktalking 101 (prepared by Maureen Hartman)

A good booktalk is like:

- A movie trailer
- The blurb on the back cover of a book
- A TV commercial
- A CD cover
- A poster

Some rules of booktalking:

- Don't booktalk a book you haven't read!
- Don't booktalk a book you don't like!
- Never tell the ending!
- Don't make it too long (2–5 minutes).
- It's okay to use notes—Post-its on the back of books are good.
- Make eye contact with your audience—keep looking around.
- Give the author and title and show the cover.
- Instead of bringing the actual books, consider using PowerPoint to scan covers.

FOUR BASIC BOOKTALK STYLES (INVENTED AND POPULARIZED BY JONI BODART)

Plot Summary/Cliffhanger—When **WHAT HAPPENS is** more **important than anything else.**
Don't give away the ending!
Don't tell too much!

Character Description
When WHO is more important than anything else
Describe one of the characters or become a character

Select One Story or Theme
Tells one story or episode from the book
Works well with a short-story collection

Mood-Based Booktalk
Good for mystery or suspense
Could read a short part of the book
Use your voice to make it scary, exciting, etc.

Writing the Booktalk

Think about:
   Who is your audience?
   What makes your book interesting?
   What did you like about the book?
   How would you recommend it to a friend?
   Is it similar to another book you've read?
   Start right away with something that will get your audience's attention—
      something weird or funny or gross or scary.
   Your last sentence must get your audience to read the book. Make it
      catchy!
   Practice!

Especially for Reluctant Readers

- Consider interactive talks—ask questions and listen to answers.
- Use props appropriate to the plot.
- Choice—let students select the books you'll talk from the ones you've brought.
- Bring catchy titles—scary, funny, sad, etc. Play on emotions.
- Make it engaging and exciting.
- Read aloud, but only for short periods.

- Let them guess the ending.
- Ask them what they would do in a similar situation.

SAMPLE BOOKTALKS—OUR FIFTY GREATEST HITS

Abdul-Jabbar, Kareem. **Black Profiles in Courage**

The former basketball great profiles great African Americans throughout history, including such well-known names as Crispus Attucks, Harriet Tubman, and Rosa Parks. But Jabbar also finds other less well-known profiles in courage, such as Joseph Cinque.

Picture the scene: Joseph is twenty-five-year old, tending to his farm in West Africa, when he is attacked, beaten, and chained by the leg. He knows he will never see his wife, his children, or his farm again. He is marched to a sailing vessel, where for two weeks he lives in the crowded hold, with little food to eat or water to drink. He is off-loaded like cargo and taken to a holding pen under the hot Cuban sun, where again he lives in crowded, inhuman conditions for another two weeks. Yet he knows the worst is yet to come.

He is taken to the barracoons, a long roofless building that is nothing more than a slave supermarket. He, along with forty-nine other African men who have shared the same hardships, is purchased by a Spanish farmer. They are marched once again to another ship, another hold, another journey; this time they are chained together. They are released only for short amounts of time. During one of these times, he inquires what is to happen to him. The cook of the ship, perhaps as a joke or perhaps to terrify him, points to a barrel full of beef, implying that he, and the others, will be killed, cooked, and eaten. He is terrified, yet he is not afraid as he reaches down and picks up a discarded nail without the knowledge of his captors.

And it is only right, for Joseph Cinque is a man, not an animal. He knows how to use tools, and use it he does to free himself and the other captured slaves. By nightfall they are ready to strike, and so begins the real story of Joseph Cinque and the takeover of the slave ship Amistad. While thousands of slaves were stolen from Africa, it took the strength and courage of one man to stand up and make a difference. Years later it was Rosa Parks on the bus, Martin Luther King on the bridge at Selma, at Jackie Robinson at second base, but all in some way trace back to Joseph Cinque and his act of rebellion that launched a revolution.

Avi. **Wolf Rider**

You've heard the story about the boy who cried wolf, right? It is a pretty scary little moral tale about telling the truth. Well, that is nothing compared to this dark ride.

Andy's a normal kid, as normal as can be. He's home on a Friday night, getting ready to head out to a party.

> The kitchen phone rings and Andy picks it up. Telemarketer, right?
> And a voice says: "I just killed someone."
> Andy says: "What?"
> The voice says: "I just killed someone."
> Andy says: "I don't understand."
> The voice says: "I have to tell—"
> Andy interrupts him and asks: "Who is this?"
> And the voice says . . . nothing at all.

Andy just heard someone confess to a murder. Who is he going to tell? Who is going to believe him? Is it a lie? Is it the truth? Is it a crank call? Or by picking up the phone, did Andy just become the Wolf Rider?

Cabot, Meg. All-American Girl

Samantha Madison didn't want to skip her drawing class; it was just that the teacher didn't really understand what Sam was trying to do. Sam was already a great artist; she made extra money by drawing pictures of her classmates with movie stars—Heath Ledger was the best-seller—but Susan Boone kept telling her to draw what she sees, not what she knows. Anyway, she was just stifling her creativity.

So Sam skips class—nobody will see her slip into the record store next door. Too bad she won't see that cute David in class, but he probably didn't like her anyway. Everybody likes Sam's sister better—she has neater hair and better clothes.

Sam spends the next couple of hours just hanging out—sampling lots of CDs, but not buying any of them. Come to think of it, there's another guy not buying anything, and he's been listening to Billy Joel's "Uptown Girl" over and over again.

Overall, it was kind of an uneventful day—at least until the president's motorcade pulled up to Capitol Cookies next door and the guy listening to "Uptown Girl" opened his duffel bag and pulled out a machine gun!

Now Samantha Madison is just your average American girl, but what happens next makes her a national hero and an all-American girl.

Cart, Michael. Rush Hour: Sin

Sin. A powerful word, but what does it mean? If you read the Bible, the first sin was Adam and Eve eating the apple, the forbidden fruit. Eating fruit, a sin?

Well, it depends.

In *Rush Hour,* authors and artists and poets use words and pictures to tell you their versions of sin.

Sometimes the sin is small and personal: a lie you tell somebody else, or a lie you tell yourself.

Sometimes the sin is huge in scope and takes place far away. The sin of the Holocaust claiming innocents, or the sins of the jungles of Cambodia claiming the innocent, the guilty, and all of those unlucky enough to be caught in-between.

Sometimes the sin is national in scope and the shame shared by all; even if the burden of slavery and racist lynching are in the past, the shadows of those sins linger today.

And sometimes the sin is how we treat each other, like the girl in the story "Intrinsic Value," who decides to ruin a teacher's life just because she can.

Sin means different things to different people. The stories, poems, and pictures here are fresh, juicy, and ready for the picking. Want a bite?

Chandler, Elizabeth. The Deep End of Fear

Kate has a new job; she's going to live at the huge, fancy Westbrook estate as a nanny to seven-year-old Patrick. She tells her new boss that's she's never been to Westbrook before, but that's not quite true.

Kate remembers Westbrook from years ago when she and her parents had to flee the estate in the middle of the night. She remembers her little friend Ashley, who drowned years ago in the estate's pond.

But all that is in the past. Or so Kate thinks.

Patrick—the little boy she's taking care of—says he talks to Ashley by the pond and does dangerous things, all because Ashley tells him to.

Can Kate discover the mystery of the estate and the unhappy people living there before the evil there takes another life?

Cooney, Caroline. Burning Up

It's such an odd thing: this burnt-out old barn that stands across the street from Macey's old house. Macey has to do a project for school, something about local history. But when she starts asking questions about the barn and the fire, no one seems willing to talk about it—not even her grandparents. But that is not all Macey has to do for school; she's also required to do a community-service project. She leaves her nice suburban home and heads into the inner city to volunteer at a church. It is unlike any world she's every known.

But then there is a fire. Remember, a while back, the rash of church burnings that took place in the South? Black churches were the targets of a series of mysterious fires, and the author here uses that fact in her fiction. Macey escapes safely, as do some of the new friends she's made at the church, including an African American girl about the same age named Venita.

But then there is a death. Venita, dead on the street, right near the church. Macey's upset, but she's about the only one in her family who is. Her parents won't even let her go the funeral. A death that strikes too close to home and a burned-out barn that sits across the street from her grandparent's house— two acts of racial violence that seem apart, unless Macey can figure out how they are connected. She is burning up with curiosity; little does she know, however, that there are people in her town—people in her family—who are burning up with hatred.

Cooney, Caroline. **Flight #116 Down**

It was a day like any other day, except.

Heidi is sixteen and lives out in the country on a huge estate. She's got everything a teenage girl could want inside of her parent's beautiful mansion. She doesn't even have to see her parents much: they are almost always out of town on business. She hasn't earned any of these things; she was just lucky enough to be born into a rich family. Her parents have rich and exciting lives; Heidi has everything you could imagine except a rich and exciting life of her own.

It was a day like any other day, except.

Patrick is eighteen and is living almost a double life. He's still in high school, but he's just completed his EMT training. It's a small town, so all the EMTs, like Patrick, are volunteers. Like anyone who has been trained to do a job, Patrick is eager to get started and prove himself, but there's not much exciting happening.

It was a day like any other day, except.

On the airplane, on flight #116, teenagers read magazines, little kids played with their dolls, and all around people were sleeping safe and sound.

It was a day like any other day, except.

On this day, the lives of Patrick and Heidi and the passengers of flight #116 would come together with a plane dropping out of the sky. On this day, Patrick would test his training and Heidi, for the first time in her life, would need to prove herself. On this day, the passengers of flight #116 wouldn't make it to their final destination. It was a day like any other day except Flight #116 is down.

Crutcher, Chris. **Whale Talk**

Here's the question: When is enough, enough?

For TJ, it is a question he thinks about every day of his life. He's not like everyone else. In his small town in the northwestern part of the United States, most folks are white. TJ isn't white and he isn't black and he isn't Asian; he's all of the above. He's been adopted by a loving family, but he's known abuse in others.

Here's the question: When is enough, enough?

For TJ, the question comes to a head during his senior year at Cutter High. Although a natural athlete, TJ won't participate in school sports, and he resents the dominating force of jocks.

One day TJ witnesses a group of jocks hassling a kid in special education. The kid's name is Chris and he's wearing his dead brother's letter jacket. The jocks are angry since Chris didn't "earn" his jacket. For TJ, watching these so-called student athletes pick on someone smaller and slower than them is too much. Enough is enough.

TJ decides to help Chris earn a letter jacket by forming a swim team. He gathers up an unruly group of misfits: a muscle man, a giant, a chameleon, and a psychopath. Swimming is hard, and forming a team is made even harder by opposition from the other athletes and even some of the faculty.

Here's the question: When is enough, enough?

Here's the answer for TJ. When the odds are against you, when everyone tells you to stop, when people throw obstacles in your way, then enough isn't too much; instead, it is just want you need to fight the good fight, to stand up for right. TJ is no superhero and he doesn't wear a cape. He doesn't fly: he just swims and listens to the whale talk.

Curtis, Christopher Paul. Bucking the Sarge

"Flint is nothing but the *Titanic*," says fifteen-year-old Sparky, Luther Farrell's best friend, and when Luther looks around, he can see that Sparky is right. It's going down, and his friends and family are not helping. His pal Sparky is looking for a big score in the form of a lawsuit, and he'll do just about whatever it takes—from getting hit in the head to having a rat bite him—to seal the deal. Maybe other people in Flint are starving, scraping to get by, but not Luther or his mother, whom he calls the Sarge. Luther's about the only kid in his school that can drive his own car, has his own credit cards, and doesn't have to live at home. Looking in, you might say Luther has it all. You'd be wrong. The money comes from stealing from the poor and giving to the rich. He's got to watch as his mother evicts a buddy out of his house, feel his buddy's anger, see his younger sister's tears, and watch a family humiliated, all for a few bucks for the Sarge. Luther's mom—the Sarge—is one of Flint's biggest slumlords, whose buildings have a habit of burning down for insurance money. She's also a loan shark, whose clients have a habit of paying back or else. The Sarge also runs group homes, whose residents have a habit of getting their money swindled. The Sarge knows every angle, plays every scam, and never looks back, because if she did, she just might see that she's got a problem in her own house. Little does she know this is true: keep your friends close, your enemies closer, and your family the closest. Flint may be the *Titanic,* the Sarge may be the captain, but Luther is one guy who is not going down with the ship.

David, Peter. Spyboy in the Deadly Gourmet Affair

Alex Fleming is just a regular kid. A regular kid who gets beat up at school for talking to the bully's girlfriend. A regular kid who knows the bullies aren't just beating up kids for lunch money; they're into some serious stuff—selling drugs around school. Alex wishes he could find a way to track them down and turn them into the police, but everybody says he should mind his own business and not get involved. But there's something that everyone's not telling Alex. Something that everybody knows except him. That he has a secret identity. That he has a special talent. That he has an amazing ability. And that ability will mean he's not just regular high school student Alex Fleming. He's Spyboy . . .

Fontaine, Smokey D. E.A.R.L.: The Autobiography of DMX

Let's face it—you probably know a lot more about DMX than I do. You probably already know that he had to live on the street when he was younger, with only his dog Boomer for company. That he was abandoned by his dad and grew to distrust the world around him. How he lived with his grandmother for a while, ran away a lot, and was in and out of detention centers and later, prison. In fact, as he says it, his life was full of running, robbing, and rapping.

And that's where his lyrics come from—from pain, from suffering. But they also come from happiness and spirituality, too—his wife Tashera, his kids, and the fame and success that he now enjoys as one of the most famous rappers around.

Draper, Sharon. Darkness before Dawn

This is the third book in a series about African American teenagers attending Hazelwood High School. The novel continues the story of the characters from previous titles in the trilogy: *Tears for a Tiger* and *Forged by Fire.* Although this book has an urban setting, it is as much a story of survival as those set in the wilderness.

This title focuses on high school senior Keisha, whose senior year is loaded with loss. Her ex-boyfriend has killed himself, and a good friend has died in an auto accident. She finds comfort in her friends and her family, but a sadness still hangs over her life. It is not just that she misses her boyfriend, but she misses having that one person who cares about her. Enter Jonathon Hathaway.

At first, she's embarrassed by the attention. She and her friends are laughing about it. But then she notices how kind he is to her. She thinks he's funny, and while she wouldn't admit it out loud to her friends, she thinks he's a little bit sexy. She starts noticing how nicely he dresses, how he talks to her, but mostly how he doesn't treat her like some stupid kid, because she's not stupid and, as a senior in high school, she's not a kid anymore either. And neither is he. Jonathon Hathaway is her track coach. He is twenty-three years old. He is the son of the school principal. Keisha's had some hard times in her life, and she's looking for someone to help her feel better. But Jonathon is looking for something else. He is the flame and Keisha is the moth. He is the darkness before dawn.

Drill, Esther. Deal with It

I remember very clearly the book *Boys and Sex*. It was this crappy little paperback that we passed around in junior high. Despite the fact that it was boring, had no pictures, and used lots of scientific terms, hey, at least it was something.

That was then, this is now.

Esther Drill's *Deal with It* is a whole new approach to your body, your brain, and life as a girl and is everything that book wasn't. It's fun, it's funny, and it's frank. It's colorful, and the layout is just amazing. It's loaded with lots of facts, but also lots of voices of teenage girls asking questions and getting answers. From the first chapter, "Boobs," to the final one on "Being Yourself," the book consistently looks at issues faced by every teenage girl, such as body image, nutrition, and birth control. And then there are the things that teenage girls shouldn't have to deal with but do: sexual harassment, rape, and molestation. A book can't make the bad stuff go away, but it can tell you that you're not alone and give you a way to think. Also, this book is loaded with information about other resources, such as books on specific topics.

There's a big section on mood swings, risk-taking behavior, eating disorders, cutting, as well as lots of information about substance abuse. The book isn't like some DARE scare-the-hell-out-of-you approach, but instead says, "here is the truth; here are the consequences." Want more? It's here: ideas on dealing with family, friends, and people at school. Figuring out what you believe and then putting it all together and figuring out who you are and where you fit in. This isn't really about how to deal with it but how to rise above it; how to live and how to thrive as a g-u-r-l.

Dumas, Amy. Lita

Amy moved around a lot when she was growing up. When she got to be a teenager, she stayed restless. Always looking for something exciting, especially after her parents got divorced when she was seventeen, she doubled up her credits in high school, graduated early, got an apartment, and got a job. But it was just a job, because music was her life: listening and following punk rock bands on the East Coast. Somewhere around this time she got her first tattoo and a nose ring. Wanting to travel but short on cash, Amy takes a job as a stripper. The money was good, but the life wasn't. Amy was still restless, still looking for herself, and then she found herself on television—found something that would ease the restlessness.

Found something that would let her travel and see the world.

Found something with the energy of punk.

Found something that would make her a star.

She found her life on television one Monday night in the apartment of a friend who was watching wrestling. Amy was bored by the show until a wrestler wearing a mask appeared on the screen. His name was Rey Mysterio, a Mexican wrestler—also known as a luchador. Amy watched in amazement as Mysterio flew around the ring like an acrobat. With no connections, nothing but a few years of high school Spanish, and less than $100 in her pocket, Amy flew to Mexico to ease her restlessness. When she went down to Mexico, she was restless Amy Dumas. When she returned, she was Lita, one of the top stars in the World Wrestling Federation. You don't even need to like wrestling to love Lita's story of turning from restless teen to television star.

Fisher, Antwone. Finding Fish

Baby Boy Fish—as he was documented in the child-welfare case records— was raised in institutions from the moment of his birth in prison to a single mother. Father: unknown. After his birth, he is placed in an orphanage, but soon finds life in a foster home. Until age two. Then he dies again—a daily death, as he is placed in a second foster home, where he enters a world of emotional assaults and unspeakable physical abuse. Every day he dies a little; every day he wants to be dead—that is how bad it is. At age sixteen, he is re- moved from the home and placed in a boy's reform school. But that doesn't last, and before he's even eighteen years old, Baby Boy Fisher was living on the streets: eating garbage, sleeping in boxes; dying a little every day.

Yet, along the way, Antwone was not entirely alone. Through the system, as busy and broken and as bad as it can be at times, he found adults who cared. Instead of fighting against them, he started to listen, to learn, and to live. But it took hitting rock bottom, then bouncing back up to find a place he could belong: the U.S. Navy.

It is in the navy where all of this past, which he has tried so hard to keep to himself, is revealed. Pushed down deep inside, all the anger he is holding in is killing Antwone a little bit every day. Only when he can talk it out, release the anger, and find his voice, is he finally free. He may have been born in prison, he may have spent his life entrapped by poverty and pain, but he is free at last. He was lost; now he his found. This is a story of discovery, not of another place or time, but of a busted self that becomes healed by keeping hope alive.

If you've seen the movie, read the book. If you've read books like *A Child Called It,* then you'll like this one. And if you want to learn how to survive the worst of times, then start reading *Finding Fish.*

Flinn, Alex. Nothing to Lose

Michael's on the football field, but his mind is elsewhere. He's on the field, but his eyes are up in the stands. Looking. Searching. Asking. Where is she?

And he knows.

He drops a pass, in part because his mind isn't on the game but on his Mom. Michael's wondering why she isn't in the stands to watch him play.

And he knows.

Walker. His new stepdad. Mister I'm a Successful Lawyer Master of the Universe Don't Talk Back to Me Unless You Want to Get Hurt. Walker.

He gets home from the game, but now he's running. Running through the house, kicking open doors like they were opposing blockers, following not a pass, but a sound. A scream. His mother's scream.

Michael races through the house and it's the same scene as before. His stepdad Walker, Master of the Universe, his hands wrapped around his mom's throat. Her face is bruised, her nose is bleeding, and Walker's hand is around her throat. Michael pries his hands away, and Walker doesn't fight back, this time. This time.

But Michael knows they'll be a next time and a time after that, since his mother won't leave and Walker won't go away. Walker sits smiling the next morning at the table, a huge grin on his face, and he says the words to Michael, to his mother, to the universe: "I always win." When you are up against someone who always wins, you have nothing to lose—but your life, or his.

Friel, John. The 7 Best Things (Smart) Teens Do

And they are?

1. Become competent: What are you good at? What can you do as well as anybody else? What can you do even better?
2. Master your feelings: Turn your mind around first—it is smaller than the rest of your body. The only thing stupid is thinking you are stupid.
3. Break the silence: Cancer isn't the only thing that eats you up from the inside. Bad stuff happens—that is a given. So the question is what to do about it. Talk it out: with a teacher, a friend, your social worker, but especially someone in your life who you trust. I just read a book about a guy who went into one of these rehab hospitals. He had been an alcoholic for ten years; he was twenty-three years old. For a decade, since the age of thirteen, he'd been drinking and doing drugs. Why? He didn't know until he got into therapy and broke his silence.
4. Get healthy: You guys know all about this one. It is a simple math equation: for every action, there is a consequence. Healthy action gets you the lollipop; unhealthy action gets you the fuzzy end, a day in the secure unit, and another trip back here.
5. Face the big stuff: Life hurts; get used to it. It is not fair. Get over it. Now what? Depression can be treated; abuse can be treated; life can be made better, not perfect.
6. Find an identity: Choose how you dress, wear you hair; how you talk and what you write. What you read defines who you are: choose a dictionary, not a thesaurus.
7. Balance: Avoid the extremes and the extremes will avoid you.

Oh, there's also an eighth best thing smart teen do: read this book about the seven best things smart teens do.

Gallo, Don. No Easy Answers

Wouldn't it be nice if there were easy answers to everything? But life is too complicated for that, and this collection of stories shows people trying to make tough choices in hard times. There's the story "X-15," about a young man joining a gang, and the story "Confession," about a group of young people who decide to fight back against a gang, with terrible results. Some of the stories are funny, and some are tragic—like "Wishing It Away," by Rita Williams Garcia.

It started simply enough: a couple of teenagers flirting. Soon, words turned to action, and Belinda was cutting school to spend time with her boyfriend, Teddy. Sometimes they shop, but mostly they go back to Belinda's mother house. Sometimes they fight, like the time Belinda asked him to wear a condom she took from her mother's bedroom dresser drawer, but mostly they don't fight, although they're still making plenty of noise. Only once is there the noise of her mother yelling: "I know what you are doing up there," but she doesn't stop them or say a thing.

One morning, Belinda gets up and feels sick, and she knows. She knows, but she thinks she'll just go about wishing it away. She tries for a while stuff she reads about, but she can't do a million sit-ups, she can't stand on her head, and she's not swallowing Ajax bleach a second time. She's always been big, so she's used to hiding her body—ain't that much different, ain't much to do other than keep on wishing it away. Then it happens, in her bedroom. She fights away the pain, delivers the baby, then goes to sleep on the side of the bed without any blood.

When your choices are few, sometimes it is easier just to wish it away, but as Belinda learns, that is no easy answer.

Grimes, Nikki. Jazmin's Notebook

Jazmin has been passed around. Do you know that expression? Passed around. With her father dead and her mother unable to care for her, Jazmin has lived with relatives and foster families most of her young life. Now, she thinks she's found a home: living in Harlem with her sister. But her real home, which is where the heart is, is her notebooks. Jazmin fills page after page in her notebooks with her poems, some of them long epics of anger, others just reflecting on paper what she sees in her neighborhood.

She writes: "The homes / are just fine. / It's the people / who are broken."
She writes: "Nightly bullet ricochets / remind me / that Death plays / hide-and-seek / around here."

She writes: "My mom's away / not just her body / but her mind / Where does she go? / How should I know?"

Words, though, aren't enough sometimes. Words don't always work when you spend your days dodging bullets, both real and imagined. The bullets of hate, poverty, and heartache are the real killers, not of the body but of the soul.

Just like Tupac would write of himself as a rose that grew from concrete, there are plenty of flowers and lots of life, light, and laughter here in *Jazmin's Notebook*.

Hartinger, Brent. Last Chance Texaco

Fifteen years old and parentless, Lucy Pitt has spent the last eight years being shifted from one foster home to another. Now she's ended up at Kindle

Home, a place for foster kids who aren't wanted anywhere else. Among the residents, Kindle Home is known as the Last Chance Texaco, because it's the last stop before being shipped off to the high-security juvenile detention center on nearby Rabbit Island—better known as Eat-Their-Young Island to anyone who knows what it's really like. The kids at Kindle are all hard cases and tough on new kids, even those who know the system like Lucy. And Kindle House is full of systems: social workers to get into your head, housemates who betray you, and rules, always rules, which need to be followed. But what she notices most about Kindle House is how everything, even the people like herself, is broken somehow.

But if things are tough proving herself at Kindle House, they are worse when she starts school.

"You the new groupie, huh?"

"Yeah," I said. "So?"

"So no one wants you here. Why don't you go back where you came from?"

Lucy's used to no one wanting her and she would love a real home to go back to, but for now, she's living on the edge with the other hard cases at the Last Chance Texaco.

Hautman, Pete. Sweetblood

Lucy is sitting alone in the school cafeteria. This is fairly new: she used to be one of those kids who people sat and joked with, who did well in school—the kind of person that most everyone liked. But no more.

Lucy is sitting alone in the school cafeteria sipping red liquid from a box when the new kid at school—Dylan—comes up to the table. He sits down with her, then asks, "So how come you are sitting all by yourself?"

Lucy says: "I have an incurable highly contagious disease."

Dylan says: "Really? What is it? Bubonic Plague?

Lucy says: "Worse."

"AIDS?"

"Much worse."

"I know. Leprosy."

Lucy tells him: "You don't want to know what I have."

Dylan says: "Really?"

But then she tells him anyway. She sucks the box with the red liquid dry and says: "Fact is, I'm a vampire."

Lucy is a sixteen-year-old diabetic. She's convinced the insulin that keeps her alive is merely a substitute for blood. She believes she's a vampire and in fact that all diabetics are vampires. She believes, and gets caught up in the online world of the Goth subculture. Her parents call her Lucy, but at night, she is what she thirsts for: sweetblood.

Hinds, Selwyn. Gunshots in my Cook-Up

Hinds is the former editor of the *Source* magazine. This book is a collection of short essays and profiles about the rap artists Hinds interviewed, partied, and fought with. More than essays, these are short looks at the behind-the-scene world of hip-hop. And Hinds loves the music. He hates the record labels, hates the hype, hates the posers, but mostly hates how the music has been commercialized: used for selling soap, used to make the wrong people rich and keep other people poor. Hinds loves hip-hop and hates those who've ripped it off. Hinds knew everybody: read his reporting here about the murder of Tupac, the start of the East vs. West feud, and the breaking of Eminem as a major talent, not some white boy wannabe. And that's Hinds's point: the music isn't about money; it is about creative artists expressing themselves.

Who is he describing?
- Grew up in Compton
- Hang out at a club in Compton called the Penthouse
- Hang out at a park called Kelly Park; that's where you meet up with Eric Wright
- You get kicked out of your house, end up living next door to O'Shea Jackson
- With those two guys and two others, you form a group that makes rap history

Here's the story of Dr. Dre. That just one story: there's a lot more in these bits and bites from a hip-hip life. From the crowded noisy streets of Brooklyn to the noisier more crowded streets of Haiti, this book looks at the good, the bad, and the ugly of hip-hop.

Holt, David. Spiders in the Hairdo

Have you heard the one about the lady that bought a little dog in Mexico and brought it back as a pet? She was pretty disturbed later when she found out she adopted a Mexican sewer rat!

Or what about the lady that discovered a deep-fried rat in her Kentucky Fried Chicken? I heard that's why they changed the name to KFC—because it really wasn't chicken anymore.

And then, have you guys seen pictures of women from the 1960s, when they had huge tall beehive hairdos—like Marge Simpson? One time a lady found a huge nest of black widow spiders living in her hair!

And I know you've heard this one. A teenage couple goes out to a deserted road in their car. They're sitting quietly in the car when they hear a warning on the radio: "Attention, attention. This is an alert from the Minneapolis police. An insane killer has escaped from prison; he has only one hand—and a hook on the other. Make sure you lock your doors and stay inside until this menace is captured."

"Oh no, we should leave right away," says the girl.

"Nah," says the guy, "We're cool—he's nowhere near us."

"No, really, I'm getting scared," says the girl. "I want to leave. Now."

"Fine," says the boy, quickly slamming on the gas pedal and peeling down the street.

And when they get home, the boy gets out to go around the side of the car and open the passenger door. And do you know what he finds there? A bloody hook that had been ripped from an arm when he stepped on the gas.

Do you guys believe these stories? Have you heard them before?

They're called urban legends. Urban legends are stories that aren't really true, but people have been telling them as true for years and years. Did anybody ever say to you, "This didn't happen to me, but it did to my friend . . ."? That's an urban legend. And if you want to read about more urban legends, try this one: *Spiders in the Hairdo,* by David Holt.

Jackson, Phil. More Than a Game

What happened to the USA 2004 Olympic basketball team? Great one-on-one players, great stars, but somehow they couldn't work together as a team. What happened to the Los Angeles Lakers? They should have won it all. They should have been a dynasty like the Celtics in the 1960s, the Knicks in the 1970s, or the Bulls in the 1990s. Great players, but did they ever really come together as a team?

How could this happen? Perhaps because the players forgot that basketball is more than a game. Maybe because they thought they were bigger than the game, or at least bigger than the coach. One of the great NBA coaches of all time, and a former NBA all-star himself, is Phil Jackson.

Few coaches won as many championship rings as Jackson, and few have coached as many talented players. And few have every taken the time to write a book to tell the stories of those teams, those players, and how basketball is more than a game.

What's it like to coach Michael Jordan or Kobie or Shaq? What's it like to prepare a defense against Reggie Miller or Patrick Ewing? What's it like to be under the spotlight and on the hot seat during the long NBA season? What's it like to be the best in the world? Jackson tells his story, the story of his players, and the story of the 1999–2000 Lakers—the first of the three titles Jackson would win with the Lakers. Now Jackson is gone, Shaq is gone, and a shell remains of a team that could have been the best ever but wasn't, perhaps because they forgot that basketball, even in the NBA, is more than a game.

King, Stephen. "The Moving Finger" from Nightmares and Dreamscapes

To me, the most frightening thing about Stephen King is this: the size of his books. I mean, come on: *The Stand* is like 2,000 pages. That's why I prefer his short stories: quick in, quick out, and he can scare the hell out of you with just a few words, ten pages, and one moving finger.

Howard Milta was sitting alone in his apartment when he heard a scratching sound coming from the bathroom. His wife was out, getting ice cream, and he was watching *Jeopardy* on TV when he heard the sound. Figuring it was a rat in the bathtub, he arms himself with a broom and then enters. Looking in the bathtub, he sees nothing, but he hears the sound. Looking in the sink he sees it: a finger poking its way out of the drain hole in the basin: the nail scratching the surface, looking for a way out.

I didn't see that, Howard says, returning to his chair to watch more *Jeopardy*.

His wife returns, the sound goes away, and life is back to normal.

Howard needs to pee. He goes into the bathroom, looks at the sink, nothing there. He puts a drain stop in the hole, just in case, and goes to the toilet. Then he hears it: the sound of the drain stop popping out of the drain. He zips up, looks over, and the finger has returned.

That night he pees in the kitchen sink as he listens to the scratching sound from the bathroom.

The next morning, he decides to stay home from work and figure it out. He walks into the bathroom—the sound is louder now, and the finger seems longer, stretching out of the hole. He retreats again, leaving the house, and heads for the local store, where he purchases a large bottle of liquid drain cleaner, but just as he is about to leave the store he sees something else: hedge trimmers, on sale.

"Take this! Lunch is served, you bastard!" The finger smokes as the flesh burns when Howard pours the entire bottle of drain cleaner, but the fumes are too much: he vomits just before he passes out.

When he awakes, he hears the sound of flesh sizzling, but it is his own flesh, as the finger, or what is left of it, has reached out of the sink, and has wrapped itself around Howard's ankle. He manages to struggle free, running out into the living room when he has a thought: the electric hedge trimmers.

"I'm coming to kick ass and chew bubble gum, and I'm all out of gum!" Howard screams as he slams the batteries into the trimmer, and reenters the bathroom, only to find that the moving finger has—

Korman, Gordon. Son of the Mob

Vince Luca has some problems. He finally got a date with Angela O'Bannon—and it really seems like she likes him. That is, until she sees the body in the trunk of his Mazda Protégé.

And then there's Kendra—now she really *does* like him. Except there's that small matter of her father being the FBI agent that's trying to put Vince's father in jail.

And the small matter of his brother running an illegal gambling site on Vince's Web site.

And his mom burning a mobster's hand in a chicken pot pie.

And of course his Dad, "Honest Abe" Luca, a mobster who makes Tony Soprano look like a real wimp.

But other than that, Vince is having a swell time in high school. If only he wasn't trying to run a loan-sharking business on the side.

LeBlanc, Adrian. Random Family

Unlike *The Coldest Winter Ever,* which is fiction, this is the real deal. Jessica lived on Tremont Avenue, on one of the poorer blocks in a very poor section of the Bronx. She dressed even to go to the store. Chance was opportunity in the ghetto, and you had to be prepared for anything. She didn't have much of a wardrobe, but she was resourceful with what she had—her sister's Lee jeans, her best friend's earrings, her mother's T-shirts and perfume. Her appearance on the streets in her neighborhood usually caused a stir. Guys in cars offered rides. Grown men got stupid. Women pursed their lips. Boys made promises they could not keep.

Jessica was good at attracting boys, but less good at holding on to them. She fell in love hard and fast. She desperately wanted to be somebody's real girlfriend, but she always ended up the other girl, the mistress, the one they saw on the down-low, the girl nobody claimed. Boys called up to her window after they'd dropped off their main girls, the steady ones they referred to as wives. Jessica still had her fun, but her fun was somebody else's trouble, and for a wild girl at a dangerous age, the trouble could get big—especially when she meets Boy George.

Random Family is the story of young people trying to outrun their destinies. Jessica and Boy George ride the wild adventure between riches and ruin, while Coco and Cesar stick closer to the street, all four caught in a dance between survival and death. Friends get murdered; the DEA and FBI investigate Boy George; Cesar becomes a fugitive; Jessica and Coco endure homelessness, betrayal, the heartbreaking separation of prison, and, throughout it all, the damage of poverty. Together, then apart, these four young people make family wherever and however they can find it.

Mirriam-Goldberg, Carol. Write Where You Are

Whether you write in your journal to express your emotions, fears, and goals, or whether you branch out into poems, stories, or essays, writing can help you learn about yourself. It can be your place of refuge and illumination, your comfort from the stresses and confusions of your life. You can learn who you are and what you want to do with your life through writing. As the author says of herself, "Most of all, writing brought me home. As I filled up journals, I felt my life had meaning. I felt I belonged and was welcome on the page. No one could ever take this away from me." This may well be the greatest value of writing.

Writing is one of the most portable occupations—all you really need is paper and something with which to write. You can freewrite your way into ideas, brainstorm your freewriting into new ideas, cluster your brainstorming, and sort your clustering, each time going deeper into your thinking until you've developed and organized an idea. While she explains how to write stories, poems, and essays, she includes definitions of all those terms you learn in English class, like the difference between tone and voice. Not only are her explanations easy to understand, but she also pumps you up to dive into her exercises and start writing yourself.

Here's a story start: imagine yourself at age twenty-five. What will you look like? What will your job be? Move in your imagination to when you're fifty! How will your thinking and attitudes be different? What will you know then that you wish you knew now?

An inviting format, lots of writing examples from teens, and tons of quotes and "Did You Know?" notes in the margins make this an interesting read. And writing really is better than just thinking about a problem, because thinking keeps everything in your head, but writing it down empties it out of you and onto the page, so you're free from it. You also won't forget anything because you can reread what you've written. When you see the patterns of your thinking, you might be surprised to see some solutions to your problems as well.

Moore, Alan. League of Extraordinary Gentlemen (graphic novel)

Before the Justice League, before the Fantastic Four, and even before the X-Men, there was another group of superheroes who came together to save the world from an evil madman who would destroy it.

Each brings a talent to the table, and each wants something else: a shot at redemption. Once heroes, they have all fallen out of favor with the public.

The place is London, England. The time is 1898.

The evil is simple: a madman who is firebombing London, taking lives, and causing terror. Can no one stop it?

Enter Mr. Allan Quartermain, an adventurer known for his deadly shot, who has hit hard times and is now a hopeless opium addict.

Enter Hawley Griffen, a scientist who discovered the ability to turn himself into nothing—into an Invisible Man.

Enter one Dr. Henry Jekyll and his alter-ego, Mr. Hyde.

Enter Captain Nemo, who commands the submarine the *Nautilus* but can barely control his violent tendencies.

These adventurers will risk their lives to save the world as it prepares to enter the twentieth century. Although they are all good men, when faced with evil, they will resort to any means necessary. In vivid color, Alan Moore tells the story of good versus evil. Blood will be spilled, bones will be broken, and lives will be lost, but fear not, for behold this *League of Extraordinary Gentlemen*.

Myers, Walter Dean. Fallen Angels

Richie Perry doesn't have a lot of options: he's just graduated from high school in Harlem. The year is 1967. He wants to get away from home, away from his alcoholic mother. He'd like to go to college, but there's no money, so instead he's going to Vietnam.

With graphic language and more graphic scenes of the horror of war, Myers tells the story of Richie and the other members of his platoon. They're all in Vietnam for a different reason, but they want the same thing: to get out alive, since death is all around them. From the mines hidden under the ground they walk on, from the snipers in the jungle, from the enemy that seems to strike only at night, and from the chaos that was the Vietnam War.

But don't take my word for it. On Amazon.com, I looked up customer reviews of *Fallen Angels,* and almost all of them said the same thing: This is the best book I've ever read. This is typical: "*Fallen Angels* is one of the few books I've ever read, and I was really into it. Richie sounded like a lost teenager that didn't know what he was going to do and decided to join the Army. Walter Dean Myer really went into some graphic description; that's what made the book as excellent as it is. It really gave me a good understanding about what the soldiers went through in Vietnam. Now I realize why my friend's dad doesn't talk about it. I thought that it was really sad that a woman would actually plant a mine on her child and blow them all up."

If war is hell, then welcome to the jungle.

Myers, Walter Dean. **Shooter**

The question is always why.

After every school shooting, you turn on the TV and you get the talking heads, the outraged members of the community, and the families of the victims asking that question: Why did this happen in our school, in our city, and to our children?

Walter Dean Myers, the author of the book *Monster,* asks the same question, and you'll be surprised—and maybe angry—at the answers he provides. As with *Monster,* Myers isn't going to lay it out sweet and neat on the table. He wants to make you think and make you feel what it is to experience one of these "incidents." That's what they call it: an incident.

But the fictional shooting in this book is different in one small way: One of the kids, Cameron Porter, who is involved—and how involved he is, is up for you, the reader, to decide—is an African American at a school with few other black students. He's an outsider looking in, and he's not always welcome. He's quiet, does well in school—so then we're back to the question of why.

Why did he fall under the "spell" of Leonard Gray? Why did he go with him to the shooting range? Why did he join the secret society? The question is always why. The book is full of questions, as Cameron is interviewed by the FBI, by a psychologist, and by the police. What happened that day at Madison High School?

The question is always why?

Was it the fascination with guns? The taunting of bullies? Problems at home? Those are excuses, but Myers isn't interested in those; he's looking for an explanation, he's looking for the answer to the question of why, he's looking to get into the mind of the shooter.

Naylor, Phyllis Reynolds. **Jade Green**

When Judith Sparrow went to live with her uncle—in his big creepy house—he told her not to bring anything green.

> Don't bring your green shoes.
> Don't bring your green hat.
> Don't bring your green cloak.
> Don't bring your green dress.

And, most importantly, whatever you do, don't bring that picture of your mother—the one you have in the green frame.

But Judith does bring something green. And scary things begin to happen in her uncle's house. Scary things that *nobody* wants to talk about. Creepy sounds are just the beginning, and Judith begins to wish she'd listened to her uncle in *Jade Green,* by Phyllis Reynolds Naylor.

Northcutt, Wendy. Darwin Awards II

Could you imagine a more boring job than working at a toll booth? All day every day standing there taking money hour after hour. Two toll takers, one snowy day, decide to liven up the day by having a snowball fight. Since no snow fell around their covered booths, they scraped snow off vehicles as they paid their toll. So, one of the toll takers reaches out of his booth, grabs a big hunk of snow from a tractor trailer truck. As the truck pulls away, the toll taker notices, a little bit too late, that his sleeve got caught on a piece of metal. He was dragged out of the booth, down the highway, and later became the first snowball fight fatality of the year.

But some people don't want to work at boring jobs to earn money; instead, they try to steal it. Like the guy in upstate New York who decided to rob an insurance company. Unable to open the safe, he decided to steal the entire six hundred pound safe. He was doing pretty good until he got to the stairs, where he decided to back it down. Here's a lesson: if you understand the laws of gravity, putting yourself under a six hundred pound safe at the top of a flight of stairs is not a good way to live. In fact, it is a lousy way to die.

Both of these people may have lost their lives, but they won something: a Darwin Award. Scientist Charles Darwin's theory is that only the strongest survive. Well, it appears the smartest, too. This book is filled with stories like these of people who removed themselves from the gene pool through an act of outrageous stupidity. And don't even ask about the man killed by the vacuum cleaner.

Paulsen, Gary. Canyons

In some cultures, there is a test a boy must face before he can be considered a man. Native Americans have long had such a tradition, and this is the story of one young Indian boy's test to become a man. His name is Coyote Runs. The test is to join other Apaches on a raid to steal horses from Mexico and bring them back to his tribe. Despite the gunfire and the men chasing them, Coyote Runs passes his test. He is a man, but not for long.

For on his way back home, soldiers attack. Coyote Runs and others take off for safety into a canyon, but he is shot in the leg. He falls from his horse and crawls to a safe hiding place. As he hides, he believes he is safe. But then he sees it. The trail of blood running from his leg; the trail of blood leading soldiers directly to him. One of the soldiers leans over, puts his gun next to Coyote Run's face. Coyote Run whispers to himself: "Take me, spirit." He knows he is to die, but he wants to be buried back in his homeland with his ancestors in an ancient sacred place. He tries to will himself there: "Take me, spirit," but before he can work magic, the soldier puts the gun up next to Coyote Run's forehead and then pulls the trigger.

One hundred years later, a young man named Brennen is camping in the Arizona wilderness. He's glad to be away from home. He lives with his mother, but they don't talk much. He's not really interested in anything except running and camping. One hundred years later, Brennen is camping by a canyon in Arizona and having strange dreams, or is it really happening? He thinks he hears a voice, a voice whispering to him, "Take me, spirit." He leaves his sleeping bag and walks around the canyon, the voice seemingly louder now, "take me spirit." He is walking when he sees it: a skull; a human skull with a bullet hole right in the middle of the forehead. A human skull that seems to be calling him, that seems to be saying "Take me, spirit." Two young men, separated by one hundred years of history, are joined together. Brennen must take the skull to an ancient sacred place. That is his test, as he runs in the canyons and changes from a boy into a man.

Piven, Joshua. **As Luck Would Have It**

Steve Roberts is driving home after a long day, and he's not feeling too good—no doubt thanks to that greasy Big K Party Store Hot Dog he had for lunch. He's listening to the radio, and on the news they're reading off the winning lottery numbers for the Big Game, where the jackpot is up over three hundred million dollars. He's not the kind of guy to play the lottery, never has, but earlier that day when he went in to the Big K to get something to eat, he found he only had a $100 bill. He got the food, and got his change in tickets. Since he's never played before, he doesn't have any lucky numbers, so he has the kid working at the Big K Party Store generate random numbers. He's driving home, but he can't drive, listen, and read the numbers from the tickets, so he tunes it out. He gets home, has a beer, has something else to eat, and goes to bed.

The next morning, he's having his coffee while getting ready for a long work day. His wife has *Good Morning America* on, like always, and Steve's barely paying attention, when he notices something. The person being interviewed on the show looks familiar. It is the person from the Big K store who sold him the lottery tickets. He races to find the tickets, checks the numbers, and finds a match. Time stands still when Steve realizes he's just lucked into 363 million dollars. After a moment of joy, the terror kicks in: How will his life change? What if someone steals the ticket? What if someone kidnaps his kids or wife and holds them for ransom? What if? What if?

Luck is the impossible answer to the question what if? In this book, *As Luck Would Have It,* you'll read stories like those of Steve Roberts who lucked into money, or people who were in the right place at the right time. But also here are stories of people who were in the wrong place at the wrong time—lost at sea or stranded in the mountains—and other tales of survival where luck triumphed over reason. They say you have a better chance of getting struck by lightning than winning the lottery; well, that story is in here to: about a man who is struck by lightning and lives.

Preston, Richard. **The Hot Zone**

Charles Monet isn't feeling well when he climbs aboard the Kenya Airways flight. His head is throbbing, the kind of headache where even your eyeballs ache. By the time he climbs on the plane, he is worse. Waves of nausea hit him as the plane is in midair. He grabs the airsick back, and then it happens.

Vomit. Black vomit. Piles of black vomit pour into the bag, the stench fills up the airplane, and others become sick. The vomiting stops when the strokes begin, as blood begins clotting in his veins. He isn't dying; he is death.

The plane lands, and he is rushed to the hospital. Before the doctors can see him, Charles Monet explodes like a human bomb. He has crashed and is bleeding out. With his head between his knees, the vomiting starts again, but there is no black vomit. Only blood rushing up his throat and out his mouth. Then comes a sound like a paper being torn in half as his bowels open up and a deluge of blood emerges from his anus. But not just blood, actual pieces of intestines are flaking off and rushing out with the blood. He is crashing and bleeding out.

Everyone in the hospital is shocked by these happenings, but little did they know that in the pool of blood, there is a virus—the Ebola virus—and it is just waiting to find a new home, another victim to crash and bleed out.

Soon the virus finds a new home: a laboratory in Reston, Virginia, an area near Washington, D.C. If it spreads, it will be the end of the world as we know it. It falls to a team of specialists to risk their lives to kill the virus by stepping into the Hot Zone. And, in case you're wondering, yes, this *is* a true story.

Rapp, Adam. **Buffalo Tree**

Feel up to learning another language? Not of another country but of another place. This is life in Hamstock, a juvenile correctional facility. Let's start easy:

- What is a juvy? (a resident in Hamstock)
- Where is your patch? (cell)
- What's a square? (cigarette)

- What's a click? (time)
- Cribbed? (steal)
- Clipping hoodies? (stealing hood ornaments)
- Ribstick? (baton or nightstick)
- Chuck? (fight)

A young man named Sura is the main character in this book. He's got some serious clicks for clipping hoodies. He's trying to stay out of trouble and trying to stay strong. He wants to make it out alive. His patch mate, ColyJo, might not be so lucky. He's raw meat in Hamstock for the correctional officers and for the other juvies.

Then there's the buffalo tree. What's a buffalo tree? The buffalo tree is a test. It's a real tree, an old dead tree, in front of one of the buildings at Hamstock. If you want to prove you are tough, you climb the buffalo tree.

There's some other words in here you probably know, most of them four letters long. This isn't *Holes;* there isn't much funny here. No one is digging in the dirt; they are just trying to survive. Sura wants to make it out alive. He's not so sure if ColyJo will. Could you do it? Could you deal with chucks, live in a patch, and trade for squares as you watch the clicks go by? Could you stand the pain of the ribstick? Could you pass the test of the buffalo tree?

Rees, Douglas. Vampire High

Poor Cody Elliot. His parents moved him to a new town—new house, new school, and new friends. It would be bad enough if the school and the friends were normal, but they're not quite like those of Cody's old school. You see, Cody's new school is Vlad Dracul High, and the school's team is the Impalers. Here are some weird things about Cody's new school: the principal is seven feet tall and has a pet wolf. The students are all tall, pale, and wear sunglasses—even in the winter. Some of them have pointy teeth. And *none* of them seem to like Cody at all. Or maybe they like him too much . . .

Shales, Tom. Live from New York!

Other than being funny, what do these four movies have in common?

1. *Beverly Hills Cop*
2. *The Waterboy*
3. *Austin Powers*
4. *Animal House*

Other than selling tons of CDs, what do these four musical acts have in common?

1. Usher
2. The Rolling Stones
3. 50 Cent
4. Nelly

Other than being famous, what do these four people have in common?

1. Snoop Dogg
2. Halle Berry
3. The Rock
4. Al Gore

What is the common thing between these and Chris Rock, Eddie Murphy, Mike Myers, David Spade, Bill Murray, Will Ferrell, and Billy Crystal? Simple: "Live from New York, it's Saturday Night!" For almost thirty years, at 11:30 in New York, the lights came up in Studio 8H for ninety minutes of comedy, music, and controversy. Here is the story of the show told by the people who lived it, and like the show, it is uncut, unedited, and often uncensored.

Shan, Darren. **Cirque Du Freak**

When Darren Shan was younger—say, about your age—he found a flyer for a freak show. Cirque Du Freak, it said—come see snake boy, the wolf-man, and Larten Crepsley and his giant spider Madame Octa.

Nobody under eighteen is allowed, but Darren and his friend Steve do what you'd do if you *really* wanted to see something that wasn't allowed: they sneak in. And what they see there I can't even begin to describe to you. A werewolf bites off an audience member's hand, and Steve—who's obsessed with vampires—recognizes Mr. Crepsley as a famous vampire! And if you know anything about vampires, you know they're pretty dangerous and not to be messed-around with. So when Darren decides he wants to "borrow" Madame Octa—that's the giant spider—things go from bad to worse. If you need a scary book for a cold night, try *Cirque du Freak* by Darren Shan. There are now ten books in this series.

Sleator, William. **Rewind**

Three wishes. You've all heard stories about people who get three wishes and almost always end up worse off than when they started.

Peter, the main character in this book, starts off pretty bad—dead. He has a fight with his adoptive parents, gets angry, and runs out the door and is struck by a car. When he wakes up, he finds himself hovering over his own funeral, listening to his parents talk about him. He hears his mother say: "Peter always acted without thinking." But now he has to think because he hears a voice, a strange disembodied voice, offering him a chance to "rewind" his life and change the past. He doesn't have to stay dead if he gets it right. It seems easy enough.

The first time he rewinds his life, he puts sugar in the gas tank of the car that hit him. That means the car won't start, so when he runs out into the street, he won't be hit. It means he will live. Instead, he is hit by a taxi.

Second chance. He rewinds his life back a month, but again, the results are the same, and he remains dead. The clock is ticking.

Third chance, last chance to rewind. For this third chance, there is only one thing left for Peter to do to avoid the final accident. Only one thing to do to live again. And that is . . .

Soto, Gary. Afterlife

So Chuy is about ready to make his move on the girl of his dreams. He's standing in the bathroom checking his hair, checking his look. The guy next to him, he notices out of the corner of his eye, is wearing these really cool shoes. Normally, Chuy doesn't talk to people he doesn't know, but he's in a good mood; he's got the adrenaline pumping through his veins. So he says something, and the guy responds by jabbing a knife deep into Chuy's body, and soon the red blood is pumping through his veins out onto the white bathroom floor (show cover).

This is the story about a teenage boy's coming of age—after death. Soto kills off his main character Chuy by page four, yet that is just the beginning, as the rest of the book follows Chuy in the afterlife as he observes his friends, his family, strangers, and even his murderer while in a ghostlike state. But it's not the big stuff that makes *Afterlife* a page-turning read; it is the small scenes: Chuy worrying that his mother will find his pack of never-to-be-used condoms, his ghost-to-grave apology to his grandfather, and the moment of silence held for him before a school basketball game. The message is that Chuy was just an average kid that no one paid much attention to, which is the opposite of Crystal, a teen ghost girl that Chuy falls in love with halfway through the book. It's all here: love, violence, lies, and life. Well, afterlife.

Strasser, Todd. Can't Get There from Here

Have you ever spent the night on the streets? In a shelter? In a cardboard box? That's the life Maybe—that's her street name; she left her real name and family behind a long time ago—and her friends are living on the streets of New York City. *Can't Get There from Here* tells what Maybe and her friends do in order to survive, although sometimes they don't. They have this one person who hangs with them: Country Club. His story is typical. His name was Alex; they called him Country Club because he came from money, but that was a long time ago. Like the rest of them, money is hard to come by, and more meals are eaten from the garbage than from a restaurant. Alex was ADD, and the doctors could never seem to get his meds right, so he was either too wired or too tired. So he started doing badly in school, especially when he hit his teen years. Then the depression started, and he started missing more school. The more school he missed, the further he got behind. The further he got behind, the worse he did. The worse he did, the more discouraged and depressed he became. By sixteen, he'd given up on school and on the meds prescribed by doctors, taking care of his own medications—drugs and alcohol. By seventeen, he was out of his house and on the streets—that is, when he wasn't spending the night in jail for petty larceny or loitering or public intoxication. He got himself to New York City and soon took to the streets, running with Maybe and the rest of her friends—at least for a little while.

It was a few days after the new year that Maybe and her friends saw Country Club again. It was in an alley. There was a used Christmas tree lying on its side; Country Club was lying on his back. Both of them were green; both of them were dead. Country Club was the first of this group of homeless teens to die on the streets: his death won't be the last or the worst. The saddest thing is that for many of them, life on the streets is better than life at home. So when they talk about a better place to live, they realize the sad truth: they can't get there from here.

Stratton, Allan. **Chanda's Secrets**

Chanda, sixteen, remembers the good times, when she lived with both parents on a cattle post in sub-Saharan Africa and even later on when her family moved to Bonang. Her family's troubles began after her father was killed in the diamond mines. Her first stepfather abused her; the second died of a stroke; the third is a drunken philanderer. Although Chanda lives in a world in which illness and death have become commonplace, it is not one in which AIDS can be mentioned.

The horror and desperation of families facing this disease is brought home when her latest stepfather's sister dumps the dying man in front of their shantytown house. Before Chanda can get help from the hospital caseworker, he disappears and the wagon that brought him is burned. Her mother leaves to visit her family on the cattle post, and Chanda is forced to give up her dream of further education to care for her younger sister and brother. Her grandparents tell Chanda that her mother is fine, just tired. And thin. They never tell her what she already knows: that her mother is dying of AIDS. But what if? What if her mother contracted the disease from her first stepfather? What if? And what about her best friend Esther. Esther always has money. Esther poses for pictures for the tourists, but is that all? What if? All around Chanda she smells it and senses it and asks the question: What if?

Stubbs, David. Cleaning Out My Closet

His life sucked.

He's getting nowhere and nowhere fast. He's drinking too much, fighting too much with his wife, not working enough or making enough to support her and his daughter, and his music career is going nowhere.

His life sucked.

His wife left but then moves back home, and he moves into a house with some friends who forget to pay the rent, so he's evicted, but that doesn't stop him. He squats in the house—no heat, no electricity. He's working dead-end jobs, at country clubs and pizza joints. He's trying to make a name for himself at open-mike nights, but a name won't pay the bills.

His life sucked.

He finally gets some money together with his friends, all of them borrowing it from their mothers to record his first record. It comes out, and it disappears. No one is playing it; no one is talking about it; and his hometown paper didn't even review it. No one is listening.

His life sucked.

He's hooked up with some guys. Their idea is to lose their old names and take on new ones. Given how well he's done with his old name, new one can't hurt.

He's sitting on the toilet, and given where his life, his career, and his future seem to be going, its only right that he's on the toilet. And then the name hits him and a legend is born.

Slim Shady. Marshall Mathers. Eminem.

Trueman, Terry. Inside Out

Dirtbag and Rat are their names; they are always yelling at Zach, putting him down, telling him what to do—like kill himself. Dirtbag and Rat don't exist in the real world; they only exist inside the mind of Zach, a sixteen-year-old schizophrenic.

Schizophrenia is a chronic and severe brain disorder that affects approximately two million people in the United States. Symptoms include delusions, hallucinations, disorganized thinking, and markedly disorganized behavior. While it can not be cured, it can be treated with antipsychotic medications.

Zach sits in the coffee shop waiting for his mother to bring his medication so the voices won't start, telling him what to do. Like kill himself.

But there are other voices, not in his head, but loud voices in the coffee shop. Loud voices of two young men about Zach's age, who walk into the coffee shop, pistols drawn, and announce "this is a robbery." But as the cashier opens up the register, Zach and the gunmen hear the sound of sirens and screeching tires.

The robbers force everyone into a back storeroom as they try to figure out what to do. Zach can barely hear their voices because he's starting to hear other voices, that of Rat and Dirtbag shouting inside of his head and the sound of the SWAT team moving into position outside. Inside and outside the tension grows by the minute as the robbers and the police are at a stand-off. Inside and outside the noise grows in Zach's head. In this game of chicken between the cops and robbers, someone needs to make a move. As the minutes pass, the tension builds, like in a card game, and Zach is very much the wild card turning the story inside out.

Williams, Terrie. Stay Strong: Simple Life Lessons for Teens

What do actor Eddie Murphy, rapper P. Diddy, singer Janet Jackson, author Stephen King, and comedian Chris Rock all have in common? Well, they are rich. What else? They are all represented by Terrie Williams. Terrie Williams is the queen of promotion. She gives these people advice on how to run their careers, and now she's written a book to give young people advice on how to make decisions in their life.

While the book kicks off with an introduction by Queen Latifah and then contains lots of quotes from other celebrities, the message here isn't about being famous; it is about finding yourself and learning, to quote Spike Lee, to do the right thing. The book is filled with quotes and stories from young people who are facing the same roadblocks. There's a lot of stuff here, but a lot of it boils down to the basics: Life ain't fair, but what you do still matters. Make a difference, stay strong, and learn these life lessons.

Williams-Garcia, Rita. Like Sisters on the Homefront

Gayle doesn't like going to school. She doesn't like doing her homework. She doesn't like listening to her mother. The only thing she likes doing is hanging with her homegirls—the southside homegirls: Lynda, Terri, and Joycie. The four had been friends since day care—ditching Bible studies, study hall, and ballet classes; protecting each others' secrets and lies; always there for each other. And of course besides her homegirls, there's Gayle's man Troy. And before Troy, there was her baby's father.

But now Gayle's mom has had enough of Gayle sitting around doing nothing—just hanging out with her friends. When Gayle gets pregnant—again—her mother puts her foot down. Gayle's getting out of the city—away from her mama, away from Troy, away from her homegirls—and going to live down south with her mama's family, a family full of religion and into everybody's business. And at her uncle's house, Gayle can't sit around—she has to work. There's no TV, no music, no hanging out, and no boys. It's a serious prison, and Gayle just knows it will be the worst summer ever . . . until she meets Great, her mother's grandmother, who's just like Gayle.

Wittlinger, Ellen. **The Long Night of Leo and Bree**

Bree: Her boyfriend Jesse is driving her nuts—he's getting so clingy—and her mom is insane. Bree doesn't usually go to the bad part of town, but she just needs to be somewhere different, where nobody knows her. So she goes out—looking for something different.

Leo: It's the anniversary of his sister's murder—something he's never really gotten over. His mom deals with it by drinking all the time, his Gramma yells at him, and he just can't stand to be in the house one more minute; so he goes out—looking for trouble.

Bree finds something different and Leo finds trouble. And pretty soon it's a matter of life and death—and a very long night for both of them.

Wright, Richard. **Native Son**

Before Sister Souljah, Terri Woods, or even Walter Mosley, there was Richard Wright. He was the first major African American novelist, and in his novel *Native Son,* he paints a sad, desperate portrait of black life in the big city. Some things change, and some don't.

Bigger Thomas lives in a squalid one-room apartment in a Chicago South Side black ghetto. He shares the apartment with his mother, his younger brother and sister—Buddy and Vera—and with rats. Rats are everywhere. At first Bigger is afraid of one of the rats, but the fear allows him to kill the rat—to corner it, to torture it, then to kill it. That first chapter tells you about the story of the book: Bigger Thomas *is* that rat: he will act out of fear, he will kill, and he will be cornered.

At his mother's insistence, Bigger follows a job lead from a relief agency and becomes a chauffeur for the Daltons—a wealthy, liberal white family. Mrs. Dalton is blind, while her husband is blind in another way: while he is a liberal and talks about "helping the negroes," he makes his money as a slumlord. On his first evening working, Bigger secretly escorts the Daltons' twenty-three-year-old daughter, Mary, to a meeting of the Labor Defenders—a Communist-front organization to which she belongs, despite the objections of her parents.

Afterward, he spends an uncomfortable interval driving around and drinking with Mary and her boyfriend, Jan Erlone. Mary gets drunk, and Bigger is forced to carry her to her bedroom. When Mrs. Dalton, who is blind, enters the room, he fears detection and, to prevent Mary from crying out and revealing his presence, places a pillow over her face. After Mrs. Dalton leaves, Bigger discovers that Mary has suffocated. He needs to dispose of the body. Then he remembers the furnace downstairs.

While the book is over sixty years old, it has lost none of its power. Part hard-core suspense fiction and part social commentary, Richard Wright presents Bigger Thomas as a symbol of black men in the United States. America, meet Bigger Thomas, your native son.

Reading Survey

1. How would you describe your view of reading?
❑ Love reading—I enjoy reading for pleasure and for school
❑ Really enjoy reading—I enjoy reading for pleasure when I have the time
❑ Tolerate reading—I will read for school, but not for pleasure
❑ Hate reading—I will read only if I had to

2. How would you rate your own reading skills?
❑ Advanced—I like to read books meant for people in higher grade levels
❑ Above Average—I read some at my grade level and some above it
❑ Average—I am comfortable reading books for people at my grade level
❑ Below Average—I can read books at my grade level, but sometimes have trouble
❑ Poor—I have trouble reading most books at my grade level

3. Outside of school, how many books did you read a month?
[ ]zero   [ ]1–2   [ ]3–5   [ ]6–10   [ ]11–15   [ ]16–20   [ ]More than 20

4. When you do read, what do you read most? PLEASE CHECK ONE
[ ]books   [ ]magazines   [ ]comic books   [ ]newspapers   [ ]Web sites

5. If you read books, what type of books? PLEASE CHECK ONE
[ ]fiction/stories   [ ]nonfiction/true stories   [ ] graphic novels

6. In fiction, what THREE types of books do you like best?
[ ]Adventure   [ ]Historical   [ ]Fantasy   [ ]Science Fiction   [ ]Romance
[ ]Urban   [ ]Humor   [ ]Mystery/   [ ]Realistic   [ ]Horror
[ ]Other: Suspense

7. **In nonfiction, what THREE types of books do you like best?**

   [ ]Biography   [ ]History   [ ]Health   [ ]True crime   [ ]Science

   [ ]Sports   [ ]Humor   [ ]Music/TV/   [ ]Self-help   [ ]Poetry

   [ ]Other: Movies

8. **In magazines, what type of magazine do you like best? Choose only ONE**

   [ ]Music   [ ]Sports   [ ]Fashion   [ ]Video game   [ ] TV/Movies

   [ ]Other:

9. **If you said you tolerated or hated reading, why? Check all that apply**

   ❑ I like reading, just not reading books

   ❑ In books, I just can't get into the stories or relate to the characters

   ❑ Reading is boring compared to other things I could be doing with my time

   ❑ Reading makes me tired/causes headaches

   ❑ I'm not good at it

   ❑ Books take too much time

   ❑ Friends make fun of me

   ❑ Other

10. **If you said you tolerated or hated reading now, when you were younger did you:**

    [ ]love to read   [ ]enjoy reading   [ ]tolerate reading   [ ] hate reading

11. **What grade are you in?** [   ]

12. **Are you?** [ ]Male or [ ] Female

Bibliography

"A Core Collection of Graphic Novels." *School Library Journal* 48 (August 2002): 44–46.

Abrahamson, Richard F. "Collected Wisdom: The Best Articles Ever Written on Young Adult Literature and Teen Reading." *English Journal* 86 (March 1997): 363–70.

Abramson, Marla. "Why Boys Don't Read." *Book*, January 2001, 86.

"Adolescent Literacy: A Position Statement." *Journal of Adolescent and Adult Literacy*, September 1999, 97–110.

"Adolescent Literacy Research." *Education Daily* 35 (December 24, 2002): 4.

Agnew, Mary. "DRAW: A Motivational Reading Comprehension Strategy for Disaffected Readers." *Journal of Adolescent and Adult Literacy* 43 (March 2000): 574.

Alessio, Amy, and Kevin Scanlon. *Teen Read Week: A Manual for Participation.* Chicago: Young Adult Library Services Association, 2002.

Alford, Jennifer. "Learning Language and Critical Literacy: Adolescent ESL Students." *Journal of Adolescent and Adult Literacy*, November 2001, 238.

Allen, Janet. *It's Never Too Late: Leading Adolescents to Lifelong Literacy.* Portsmouth, NH: Heinemann, 1995.

———. *Reimagining Reading: A Literacy Institute.* Portland, ME: Stenhouse, 2002.

———. *Yellow Brick Roads: Shared and Guided Paths to Independent Reading 4–12.* Portland, ME: Stenhouse, 2000.

Allen, Janet, and Kyle Gonzalez. *There's Room for Me Here: Literacy Workshop in the Middle School.* Portland, ME: Stenhouse, 1998.

Allen, Susan M., and Deborah Regan Howe. "A Novel Approach: A Teacher-Librarian Collaboration Brings Young Adult Literature into the Classroom." *Voice of Youth Advocates* 22 (December 1999): 314–17.

Allington, Richard L. *What Really Matters for Struggling Readers.* New York: Longman, 2001.

———. "You Can't Learn Much from Books You Can't Read." *Educational Leadership* 60, no. 3 (2002): 16–19.

Altmann, Anna E., and Gail DeVos. *Tales, Then and Now: More Folktales as Literary Fictions for Young Adults.* Englewood, CO: Libraries Unlimited, 2001.

Alvermann, Donna. "Adolescents and Literacies in a Digital World." *Reading Online*, June 2003, 35–38.

Alvermann, Donna, et al. *Reconceptualizing the Literacies in Adolescents' Lives.* Mahwah, NJ: Lawrence Erlbaum, 1998.

Alvermann, Donna, and Stephen F. Phelps. *Content Reading and Literacy: Succeeding in Today's Diverse Classrooms.* Boston: Allyn and Bacon, 2005.

Ammon, Bette D., and Gale W. Sherman. *More Rip-Roaring Reads for Reluctant Young Adult Readers.* Englewood, CO: Libraries Unlimited, 1998.

———. *Worth a Thousand Words: Picture Books for Older Readers.* Englewood, CO: Libraries Unlimited, 1996.

Anderson, Sheila B. *Extreme Teens: Library Services to Nontraditional Young Adults.* Englewood, CO: Libraries Unlimited, 2005.

———. *Serving Older Teens.* Englewood, CO: Libraries Unlimited, 2004.

Angelis, Janet. "What about Older Readers?" *Education Week*, November 7, 2001, 48.

Applegate, Anthony J. "The Peter Effect: Reading Habits and Attitudes of Preservice Teachers." *Reading Teacher* 57, no. 6 (2004): 554+.

Asselin, Marlene. "Bridging the Gap between Learning to Be Male and Learning to Read." *Teacher Librarian* 30 (February 2003): 53–54.

Ayers, Rick, and Amy Crawford. *Great Books for High School Kids: A Teacher's Guide to Books That Can Change Teens' Lives.* Boston: Beacon Press, 2004.

Backes, Laura. *Best Books for Kids Who (Think They) Hate to Read: 125 Books That Will Turn Any Kid into a Lifelong Reader.* Roseville, CA: Prima, 2001.

Baird, Susan G. *Audiobook Collections and Services.* Fort Atkinson, WI: Highsmith, 2000.

Baker, Linda. "The Role of Parents in Motivating Struggling Readers." *Reading and Writing Quarterly* 19 (January–March 2003): 87–107.

Ballard, Susan D. *Count on Reading: Tips for Planning Reading Motivation Programs.* Chicago: American Association of School Librarians, 1997.

Bartel, Julie. "The Good, The Bad, and the Edgy." *School Library Journal* 51 (July 2005): 34–38.

Baxter, Kathleen A., and Marcia Agness Kochel. *Gotcha Again! More Nonfiction Booktalks to Get Kids Excited about Reading.* Englewood, CO: Libraries Unlimited/Teacher Ideas Press, 2002.

———. *Gotcha! Nonfiction Booktalks to Get Kids Excited about Reading.* Englewood, CO: Libraries Unlimited, 1999.

Bean, Thomas W. "Making Reading Relevant for Adolescents." *Educational Leadership* 60 (November 2002): 34–37.

Bean, Thomas W., and John E. Readence. "Adolescent Literacy: Charting a Course for Successful Futures as Lifelong Learners." *Reading Research and Instruction* 41 (Spring 2002): 203–9.

Bean, Thomas W., and Karen Moni. "Developing Students' Critical Literacy: Exploring Identity Construction in Young Adult Fiction." *Journal of Adolescent and Adult Literacy* 46 (May 2003): 638–48.

Beers, G. Kylene. "Literacy: What Matters Now?" *Voices from the Middle* 10 (March 2003): 4–6.

———. "No Time, No Interest, No Way! The Three Voices of Aliteracy." *School Library Journal* 42 (February 1996): 30–33.

———. "No Time, No Interest, No Way! Part 2." *School Library Journal* 42 (March 1996): 110–13.

———. *Reading Strategies Handbook for High School*. Austin: Holt, 2000.

———. *When Kids Can't Read, What Teachers Can Do: A Guide for Teachers, 6–12*. Portsmouth, NH: Heinemann, 2003.

Beers, G. Kylene, and Barbara Samuels. *Into Focus: Understanding and Creating Middle School Readers*. Needham, MA: Christopher-Gordon, 1998.

Bell, Sherri. "Transforming Seniors Who Don't Read into Graduates Who Do." *English Journal* 93 (May 2004): 36–41.

Biancarosa, Gina, and Catherine E. Snow. *Reading Next: A Vision for Action and Research in Middle and High School Literacy*. Washington, DC: Alliance for Excellent Education, 2004.

Bilz, Rachelle Lasky. *Life Is Tough: Guys, Growing Up, and Young Adult Literature*. Metuchen, NJ: Scarecrow Press, 2004.

Black, Susan. "Reaching the Older Reader." *American School Board Journal* 192 (April 2005): 50–53.

Blackburn, Mollie V. "Boys and Literacies: What Difference Does Gender Make?" *Reading Research Quarterly* 38 (April/May/June 2003): 276–87.

Bloestein, Fay. *Invitations, Celebrations: Ideas and Techniques for Promoting Reading in Junior and Senior High School*. New York: Neal-Schuman, 1993.

Bodart, Joni Richards. *World's Best Thin Books: Or What to Read When Your Book Report Is Due Tomorrow*. Metuchen, NJ: Scarecrow Press, 2000.

Booth, David. *Even Hockey Players Read: Boys, Literacy and Learning*. Portland, ME: Stenhouse, 2002.

Braxton, Barbara. "Bait the Boys and Hook Them into Reading." *Teacher Librarian* 30 (February 2003): 43–44.

Bromann, Jennifer. *Booktalking That Works*. New York: Neal-Schuman, 2001.

———. *More Booktalking That Works*. New York: Neal-Schuman, 2005.

Brooks, Bruce, Katie O'Dell, and Patrick Jones. "Will Boys Be Boys? Are You Sure?" *Voice of Youth Advocates* 23 (June 2000): 88–92.

Brown, Margie K. "Silverstein and Seuss to Shakespeare: What Is in Between?" *English Journal* 90 (May 2001): 150–52.

Brozo, William G. "Taking Seriously the Idea of Reform: One High School's Efforts to Make Reading More Responsive to All Students." *Journal of Adolescent and Adult Literacy* 47 (September 2003): 14–23.

———. *To Be a Boy, to Be a Reader: Engaging Teen and Preteen Boys in Active Literacy*. New York: International Reading Association, 2002.

Brozo, William G., and Michele L. Simpson. *Readers, Teachers, Learners: Expanding Literacy across the Content Areas*. Upper Saddle River, NJ: Merrill/Prentice Hall, 2003.

Brozo, William G., et al. "I Know the Difference between a Real Man and a TV Man: A Critical Exploration of Violence and Masculinity through Literature in a Junior High School in the 'Hood'." *Journal of Adolescent and Adult Literacy* 45 (March 2002): 530–38.

Bruce, Bertram C. *Literacy in the Information Age: Inquiries into Meaning Making with New Technologies.* New York: International Reading Association, 2003.

Bruggerman, Lora. "Zap! Whoosh! Kerplow! Build High-Quality Graphic Novel Collections with Impact." *School Library Journal* 43 (January 1997): 22–27.

Bryan, Laura. "Y-Rap (Young Readers Art Project): A Pragmatic Solution for Reluctant Readers." *Reading Improvement* 41 (Winter 2004): 235–42.

Burgin, Robert. *Nonfiction Reader's Advisory.* Englewood, CO: Libraries Unlimited, 2004.

Burke, Jim. *Reading Reminders: Tools, Tips and Techniques.* Portsmouth, NH: Boynton/Cook, 2000.

Carlsen, Robert, and Anne Sherrill. *Voice of Readers: How We Come to Love Books.* Urbana, IL: National Council of Teachers of English, 1988.

Carter, Betty. "Formula for Failure: Reading Levels and Readability Formulas May Not Inspire Kids to Read." *School Library Journal* 46 (July 2000): 34–37.

Carter, Linda Purdy. "Addressing the Needs of Reluctant Readers through Sports Literature." *Clearing House* 71 (May/June 1998): 309–12.

Closter, Kathryn, Karen L. Sipes, and Vickie Thomas. *Fiction, Food, and Fun: The Original Recipe for the Read 'n Feed Program.* Englewood, CO: Libraries Unlimited, 1998.

Cole, Jill. "What motivates students to read? Four literacy personalities." *Reading Teacher* 56 (December 2002/Jan 2003): 326–33.

Coleman, Jennifer. "Ready, Set, Motivate!" *Library Media Connection* 23 (March 2005): 30.

Cook, Sybilla, Frances Corcoran, and Beverly Fonnesbec. *Battle of the Books and More: Reading Activities for Middle School Students.* Fort Atkinson, WI: Highsmith, 2001.

Cooper-Mullin, Alison. *Once Upon a Heroine: 400 Books for Girls to Love.* Chicago: NTC/Contemporary, 1998.

Cox, Robin Overby. "Lost Boys." *Voice of Youth Advocates* 25 (August 2002): 172–73.

Cox, Ruth E. "From Boy's Life to Thrasher: Boys and Magazines." *Teacher Librarian* 30 (February 2003): 25.

———. *Tantalizing Tidbits for Teens: Quick Booktalks for the Busy High School Library Media Specialist.* Worthington, OH: Linworth, 2002.

Cox Clark, Ruth E. *Tantalizing Tidbits for Middle Schoolers: Quick Booktalks for the Busy Middle School and Jr. High Library Media Specialist.* Worthington, OH: Linworth, 2005.

Crawford, Philip. "Graphic Novels: Selecting Materials That Will Appeal to Girls." *Knowledge Quest* 31 (November/December 2002): 43–45.

———. "A Novel Approach: Using Graphic Novels to Attract Reluctant Readers and Promote Literacy." *Library Media Connection* 22 (February 2004): 26.

Credaro, Amanda. "Teen Reads: It's All in the Packaging." *Library Media Connection* 21 (January 2003): 30.

Crowe, Chris. "Young Adult Literature: An Antidote for Testosterone Poisoning: YA

Books 'Girls—and Boys—Should Read.' " *English Journal* 91 (January 2002): 135.

Curtis, Mary. *When Adolescents Can't Read: Methods and Materials That Work.* Cambridge, MA: Brookline Books, 1999.

Daniels, Harvey. *Literature Circles: Voice and Choice in Book Clubs and Reading Groups.* 2nd ed. Portland, ME: Stenhouse, 2001.

Darby, Mary Ann, and Miki Pryne. *Hearing All the Voices: Multicultural Books for Adolescents.* Metuchen, NJ: Scarecrow Press, 2001.

Darwin, Marlene, and Steve Fleischman. "Fostering Adolescent Literacy." *Educational Leadership* 62 (April 2005): 85–87.

Davis, Mary. "Improving Reading by . . . Reading." *Voices from the Middle* 8 (May 2001): 51.

DeVos, Gail. *Storytelling for Young Adults: A Guide to Tales for Teens.* Englewood, CO: Libraries Unlimited, 2003.

Dickerson, Constance B. *Teen Book Discussion Groups @ the Library.* New York: Neal-Schuman, 2004.

Doyle, Miranda. "Sex, Drug Deals, and Drama." *Voice of Youth Advocates,* August 2005.

Dreher, Stephen. "A Novel Idea: Reading Aloud in a High School English Classroom." *English Journal* 93 (September 2003): 50–53.

Dresang, Elizabeth T. *Radical Change: Books for Youth in a Digital Age.* Bronx, NY: H. W. Wilson, 1999.

Dugan, JoAnn R. *Advancing the World of Literacy: Moving into the 21st Century.* Carrollton, GA: College Reading Association, 1999.

Early, Maureen, et al. "What Activity Has Been Most Effective in Assisting High School Students to Read Successfully?" *English Journal* 93 (May 2004): 20–23.

Ediger, Marlow. "Struggling Readers in High School." *Reading Improvement* 42, no. 1 (2005): 34–39.

Edwards, Kirsten. *Teen Library Events: A Month-by-Month Guide.* Westport, CT: Greenwood Press, 2002.

Elliott, Joan B., and Mary Dupuis. *Young Adult Literature in the Classroom: Reading It, Teaching It, Loving It.* Newark, DE: International Reading Association, 2002.

Ericson, Bonnie O. *Teaching Reading in High School English Classes.* Urbana, IL: National Council of Teachers of English, 2001.

Fader, Daniel. *The New Hooked on Books.* New York: Berkley, 1976.

Fisher, Douglas. *Improving Adolescent Literacy: Strategies at Work.* Upper Saddle River, NJ: Pearson/Merrill/Prentice Hall, 2004.

———. "Setting the 'Opportunity to Read' Standard: Resuscitating the SSR Program in an Urban High School." *Journal of Adolescent and Adult Literacy* 48 (October 2004): 138–50.

Flagg, Gordon. "Not Your Father's Superheroes." *Booklist,* February 1, 2003, 988.

Flood, James. *Literacy Development of Students in Urban Schools: Research and Policy.* Carrollton, GA: International Reading Association, 2005.

Flowers, Tiffany. "Exploring the Influence of Reading for Pleasure on African American High School Students' Reading Achievement." *High School Journal* 87 (October/November 2003): 58–62.

Furi-Perry, Ursula. "Dude, That Book Was Cool: The Reading Habits of Young Adults." *Reading Today* 20 (April–May 2003): 24.

Gallagher, Kelly. *Reading Reasons: Motivational Mini-Lessons for Middle and High School.* Portland, ME: Stenhouse, 2003.

Gallo, Donald R. "How Classics Create an Alliterate Society." *English Journal* 90 (January 2001): 33.

Gambrell, Linda B. "Creating Classroom Cultures That Foster Reading Motivation." *Reading Teacher* 50 (September 1996): 14.

Gambrell, Linda B., et al. "Assessing Motivation to Read." *Reading Teacher* 49 (April 1996): 518.

Ganske, Kathy. "Questions Teachers Ask about Struggling Readers and Writers." *Reading Teacher* 57, no. 2 (2003): 118–28.

Garrett, Jeffrey. "Info-Kids: How to Use Nonfiction to Turn Reluctant Readers into Enthusiastic Learners." *Bookbird* 41 (May 2003): 59.

Gentile, Lance M., Merna M. McMillan. "Why Won't Teenagers Read?" *Journal of Reading* 20 (May 1977): 649–54.

George, Marshall A. "What's the Big Idea? Integrating Young Adult Literature in the Middle School." *English Journal* 90 (January 2001): 74.

Gillespie, John Thomas, and Catherine Barr. *Best Books for High School Readers: Grades 9–12.* Englewood, CO: Libraries Unlimited, 2004.

———. *Best Books for Middle School and Junior High Readers.* Englewood, CO: Libraries Unlimited, 2004.

Gillespie, John Thomas, and Corinne Naden. *Teenplots: A Booktalk Guide to Use with Readers Ages 12–18.* Englewood, CO: Libraries Unlimited, 2003.

Goetze, Sandra. "At-Risk Readers Can Construct Complex Meaning: Technology Can Help." *Reading Teacher* 57 (May 2004): 778–80.

Goldfinch, Ellen. "Reading Aloud to High School Students—What a Pleasure!" *Book Report* 21 (November/December 2002): 16–17.

Goldsmith, Francisca. "Earphone English." *School Library Journal* 48 (May 2002): 50–53.

———. "The Emergence of Spoken Word Recordings for YA Audiences." *Young Adult Library Services* 1 (Winter 2003): 23–26.

———. "Graphic Novels as Literature." *Booklist,* February 1, 2003, 986.

———. *Graphic Novels Now: Building, Managing, and Marketing a Dynamic Collection.* Chicago: American Library Association, 2005.

Gorman, Michele. *Getting Graphic: Using Graphic Novels to Promote Literacy with Preteens and Teens.* Worthington, OH: Linworth, 2004.

———. "Graphic Novels and the Curriculum Connection." *Library Media Connection* 22 (November 2003): 20–22.

———. "What Teens Want: Thirty Graphic Novels You Can't Live Without." *School Library Journal* 48 (August 2002): 18–22.

Greenlee, Adele A. "The Lure of Series Books: Does It Affect Appreciation for Recommended Literature?" *Reading Teacher,* November 1996, 216–25.

Guild, Sandy, and Sandra Hughes-Hassell. "The Urban Minority Young Adult as Audience: Does Young Adult Literature Pass the Reality Test?" *New Advocate* 14 (Fall 2001): 361.

Gutchewsky, Kimberly. "An Attitude Adjustment: How I Reached My Reluctant Readers." *English Journal* 91 (November 2001): 79.

Guth, Nancy. "Adolescent Literacy: Seven Principles." *Reading Today* 19 (August 2001): 23.

Guthrie, John T., et al. *Reading Engagement: Motivating Readers through Integrated Instruction.* Carrollton, GA: International Reading Association, 1997.

Harmon, Janis, et al. "Tutoring Struggling Adolescent Readers: A Program Investigation." *Reading Research and Instruction* 44 (Winter 2004): 46.

Hebb, Judith L. "Reluctant Readers Reading." *English Journal* 89 (March 2000): 22–26.

Henderson, Darwin L., and Jill P. May. *Exploring Culturally Diverse Literature for Children and Adolescents: Learning to Listen in New Ways.* Boston: Pearson Allyn and Bacon, 2005.

Herald, Diana Tixier. *Teen Genreflecting: A Guide to Reading Interests.* 2nd ed. Englewood, CO: Libraries Unlimited, 2003.

Herz, Sarah K., and Donald R. Gallo. *From Hinton to Hamlet: Building Bridges between Young Adult Literature and the Classics.* Westport, CT: Greenwood, 1996.

Hibbing Anne, Nielsen. "A Picture Is Worth a Thousand Words: Using Visual Images to Improve Comprehension for Middle School Struggling Readers." *Reading Teacher* 56, no. 8 (2003): 758+.

Hobgood, Jane. "Finders Keepers: Owning the Reading They Do." *Voices from the Middle* (April 1998): 26–33.

Holmes, Kerry P., et al. *Engaging Reluctant Readers through Foreign Films.* Metuchen, NJ: Scarecrow Press, 2005.

Honnold, RoseMary. *More Teen Programs That Work.* New York: Neal-Schuman, 2005.

———. *101+ Teen Programs That Work.* New York: Neal-Schuman, 2003.

Howerton, Duana. "Help for High School Students Who Still Can't Read." *English Journal* 934, no. 5 (2004): 77–81.

Hubert, Jennifer, and Patrick Jones. "Overlooked Books of the 1990s." *Booklist* 97 (July 2001): 1998–99.

Inglis, Jane. "Gentle Persuasion: Some Strategies with Reluctant Readers: Successful Experiences at a School for Students Aged 13 to 18." *School Librarian* 44 (February 1996): 7–8.

Ingram, Patricia. "Hooks for Reluctant Readers." *Education Week* 23, no. 13 (2003): 26.

International Reading Association. "IRA Literacy Study Groups Module Focuses on Adolescent Literacy." *Reading Today* 20 (December 2002): 34.

Irvin, Judith L., Douglas R. Buehl, and Ronald M. Klemp. *Reading and the High School Student: Strategies to Enhance Literacy*. Boston: Allyn and Bacon, 2003.

Isaac, Megan Lynn. *Heirs to Shakespeare: Reinventing the Bard in Young Adult Literature*. Portsmouth, NH: Heinemann, 2000.

Ivey, Gay, and Karen Broaddus. "Just Plain Reading: A Survey of What Makes Students Want to Read in Middle School Classrooms." *Reading Research Quarterly* 36, no. 4 (2001): 350+.

Jay, M. Ellen, and Hilda L. Jay. *Ready-to-Go Reading Incentive Programs for Schools and Libraries*. New York: Neal-Schuman, 1998.

Jetton, Tamara L., and Janice A. Dole. *Adolescent Literacy Research and Practice*. New York: Guilford Press, 2004.

Jobe, Ron, and May Dayton-Sakari. *Info-Kids: How to Use Nonfiction to Turn Reluctant Readers into Enthusiastic Learners*. Portland, ME: Stenhouse Publishers, 2002.

———. *Reluctant Readers: Connecting Students for Successful Reading Experiences*. Portland, ME: Stenhouse Publishers, 1999.

Johnson, Keith. "Children's Books in a High School Library?" *Book Report* 19 (March/April 2001): 6–8.

Jones, Jami. "Priority Male." *School Library Journal* 51 (March 2005): 33.

Jones, Patrick. "Nonfiction: The Real Stuff." *School Library Journal* 47 (April 2001): 44–45.

———. *What's So Scary about R. L. Stine?* Metuchen, NJ: Scarecrow Press, 1998.

Jones, Patrick, and Dawn Cartwright Fiorelli. "Overcoming the Obstacle Course: Teenage Boys and Reading." *Teacher Librarian* 30 (February 2003): 9–13.

Jones, Patrick, Patricia Taylor, and Kirsten Edwards. *A Core Collection for Young Adults*. New York: Neal-Schuman, 2003.

Kan, Katherine L. *Sizzling Summer Reading Programs for Young Adults*. Chicago: American Library Association, 1998.

Kaplan, Elaine Bell. " 'I Want to Read Stuff on Boys': White, Latina, and Black Girls Reading *Seventeen* Magazine and Encountering Adolescence." *Adolescence* 38 (Spring 2003): 141.

King-Shaver, Barbara. *When Text Meets Text: Helping High School Readers Make Connections in Literature*. Portsmouth, NH: Heinemann, 2005.

Klock, Geoff. *How to Read Superhero Comics and Why*. New York: Continuum, 2002.

Knickerbocker, Joan L., and James Rycik. Growing into Literature: Adolescents Literary Interpretation and Appreciation." *Journal of Adolescent and Adult Literacy* 46 (November 2002): 196–208.

Knowles, Elizabeth, and Martha Smith. *Boys and Literacy: Practical Strategies for Librarians, Teachers, and Parents*. Englewood, CO: Libraries Unlimited, 2005.

———. *Reading Rules: Motivating Teens to Read*. Englewood, CO: Libraries Unlimited, 2001.

Koelling, Holly. *Classic Connections: Turning Teens on to Great Literature*. Englewood, CO: Libraries Unlimited, 2004.

Krashen, Stephen. *The Power of Reading: Insights for the Research*. Englewood, CO: Libraries Unlimited, 1993.

Krogness, Mary Mercer. *Just Teach Me, Mrs. K: Talking, Reading and Writing with Resistant Adolescent Learners*. Portsmouth, NH: Heinemann, 1995.

Kropp, Paul. *Raising a Reader: Make Your Child a Reader for Life*. New York: Doubleday, 1996.

Kuta, Katherine Wiesolek. *What a Novel Idea! Projects and Activities for Young Adult Literature*. Portsmouth, NH: Teacher Ideas Press, 1997.

Langemack, Chapple. *The Booktalker's Bible: How to Talk about the Books You Love to Any Audience*. Englewood, CO: Libraries Unlimited, 2003.

Lause, Julie. "Using Reading Workshop to Inspire Lifelong Readers." *English Journal* 93 (May 2004): 24–30.

Leone, Peter E., et al. "Organizing and Delivering Empirically Based Literacy Instruction to Incarcerated Youth." *Exceptionality* 13, no. 2 (2005): 89–102.

Leonhardt, Mary. *Keeping Kids Reading: How to Raise Avid Readers in the Video Age*. New York: Crown, 1996.

———. *99 Ways to Get Kids to Love Reading, and 100 Books They'll Love*. New York: Three Rivers Press, 1997.

———. *Parents Who Love Reading, Kids Who Don't, How It Happens and What You Can Do about It*. New York: Crown, 1993.

Lesesne, Teri S. "Developing Lifetime Readers: Suggestions from Fifty Years of Research." *English Journal*, October 1991, 61–64.

———. *Making the Match: The Right Book for the Right Reader at the Right Time, Grades 4–12*. Portland, ME: Stenhouse Publishers, 2003.

———. "One Hundred of Our Best Ideas: Young Adult Literature with Staying Power." *Voices from the Middle* 10 (May 2003): 54.

Leslie, Roger, and Patricia J. Wilson. *Igniting the Spark: Library Programs That Inspire High School Patrons*. Englewood, CO: Libraries Unlimited, 2001.

Libretto, Ellen V., and Catherine Barr. *High/Low Handbook: Best Books and Websites for Reluctant Teen Readers*. 4th ed. Englewood, CO: Libraries Unlimited, 2002.

Littlejohn, Carol. *Keep Talking That Book! Booktalks to Promote Reading*. Worthington, OH: Linworth, 2001.

———. *Promote Reading through Booktalks: More Than 125 Exciting Booktalks for Middle School Students*. Worthington, OH: Linworth, 2002.

———. *Talk That Book: Booktalks to Promote Reading*. Worthington, OH: Linworth, 1999.

Livingston, Nancy. "Nonfiction as Literature: An Untapped Goldmine." *Reading Teacher* 57 (March 2004): 582–85.

Lyga, Allyson A. W., and Lyga Barry. *Graphic Novels in Your Media Center: A Definitive Guide*. Englewood, CO: Libraries Unlimited, 2004.

Mahiri, Jabari. *What They Don't Learn in School: Literacy in the Lives of Urban Youth*. New York: P. Lang, 2004.

Makowski, Silk. *Serious about Series: Evaluations and Annotations of Teen Fiction in Paperback Series*. Metuchen, NJ: Scarecrow Press, 1998.

Manning, Maryann. "Coaxing Kids to Read." *Teaching Pre K–8* 35 (March 2005): 80–82.

Manz, Kathleen Kennedy. "Reading Researchers Outline Elements Needed to Achieve Adolescent Literacy." *Education Week* 24, no. 8 (2004): 10.

McCabe, James. *The Wasted Years: American Youth, Race, and the Literacy Gap.* Metuchen, NJ: Scarecrow Press, 2003.

McCardle, Peggy, and Vinita Chhabra (eds.) *The Voice of Evidence in Reading Research.* Baltimore, MD: P.H. Brookes Pub., 2004.

McCardle, Peggy D., and Vinita Chhabra. *The Voice of Evidence in Reading Research.* Baltimore: P.H. Brookes, 2004.

McEwen, E. K. *Raising Reading Achievement in Middle and High Schools.* Thousand Oaks, CA: Corwin Press, 2001.

McFann, Jane. "Boys and Books." *Reading Today* 22 (August/September 2004): 20–22.

McGrath, Anne. "A New Read on Teen Literacy." *U.S. News & World Report*, February 28, 2005, 68–71.

Miller, Steve. *Developing and Promoting Graphic Novel Collections.* New York: Neal-Schuman, 2005.

Milliot, Jim. "NEA Finds Rapid Decline in Reading: 'Reading at Risk' Study Says Leisure Reading Is a Dying Activity; Calls for National Debate." *Publishers Weekly*, July 12, 2004, 5–6.

Moen, Christine Boardman. *Read-Alouds and Performance Reading: A Handbook of Activities for the Middle School Classroom.* Needham, MA: Christopher-Gordon, 2004.

Moje, Elizabeth Birr, et al. "Reinventing Adolescent Literacy for New Times: Perennial and Millennial Issues." *Journal of Adolescent and Adult Literacy* 43 (February 2000): 400.

Mondowney, JoAnn G. *Hold Them in Your Heart: Successful Strategies for Library Services to At-Risk Teens.* New York: Neal-Schuman, 2001.

Monseau, Virginia R., and Gary Salvner. *Reading Their World: The Young Adult Novel in the Classroom.* Portsmouth, NH: Boynton/Cook Publishers, 2000.

Mooney, Maureen. "Graphic Novels: How They Can Work in Libraries." *Book Report* 21 (November/December 2002): 18–19.

Moore, David W., and Kathleen A. Hinchman. *Starting Out: A Guide to Teaching Adolescents Who Struggle with Reading.* Boston: Allyn and Bacon, 2003.

Moore, David W., et al. *Struggling Adolescent Readers: A Collection of Teaching Strategies.* Carrollton, GA: International Reading Association, 2000.

Morton, Kay. "The Big Easy: Working with Reluctant Readers." *School Library Journal* 45 (February 1999): 47.

Moss, Barbara. "Exploring Sixth Graders' Selection of Nonfiction Books." *Reading Teacher* 56 (September 2002): 6–16.

Mueller, Pamela. *Lifers: Learning from At-Risk Adolescent Readers.* Portsmouth, NH: Heinemann, 1998.

Newkirk, Thomas. *Misreading Masculinity: Boys, Literacy, and Popular Culture.* Portsmouth, NH: Heinemann, 2002.

Nichols, C. Allen. *Thinking Outside the Book: Alternatives for Today's Teen Library Collections.* Englewood, CO: Libraries Unlimited, 2004.

Nichols, Mary Anne. *Merchandising Library Materials to Young Adults.* Englewood, CO: Libraries Unlimited, 2002.

Nilsen, Alleen Pace. "The Future of Reading." *School Library Journal* 51 (January 2005): 38–39.

Norton, Bonny. "The Motivating Power of Comic Books: Insights from Archie Comic Readers." *Reading Teacher* 57, no. 2 (2003): 140+.

———. "When Is a Teen Magazine Not a Teen Magazine?" *Journal of Adolescent and Adult Literacy* 45 (December 2001/January 2002): 296–99.

Odean, Kathleen. *Great Books about Things Kids Love: More than 750 Recommended Books for Children 3 to 14.* New York: Ballantine, 2001.

———. *Great Books for Boys: More than 600 Books for Boys 2 to 14.* New York: Ballantine, 1998.

———. *Great Books for Girls: More than 600 Recommended Books for Girls Ages 3–14.* New York: Ballantine, 2002.

O'Dell, Katie. *Library Materials and Services for Teen Girls.* Englewood, CO: Libraries Unlimited, 2002.

O'Donnell-Allen, Cindy, and Bud Hunt. "Reading Adolescents: Book Clubs for YA Readers." *English Journal* 90 (January 2001): 82.

Osborn, Sunya. "Picture Books for Young Adult Readers." *ALAN Review* 28, no. 3 (2001): 24.

Pavonetti, Linda M., et al. "Accelerated Reader: What Are the Lasting Effects on the Reading Habits of Middle School Students Exposed to Accelerated Reader in Elementary Grades?" *Journal of Adolescent and Adult Literacy* 46 (December 2002): 34.

Pawuk, Michael. "Creating a Graphic Novel Collection at Your Library." *Young Adult Library Services* 1 (Fall 2002): 30.

Ray, Virginia Lawrence. *School Wide Book Events: How to Make Them Happen.* Englewood, CO: Libraries Unlimited, 2003.

Reeves, Anne R. *Adolescents Talk about Reading: Exploring Resistance to and Engagement with Text.* Carrollton, GA: International Reading Association, 2004.

Reid, Rob. *Something Funny Happened at the Library: How to Create Humorous Programs for Children and Young Adults.* Chicago: American Library Association, 2003.

Reid, Suzanne. *Book Bridges for ESL Students: Using Young Adults and Children's Literature to Teach ESL.* Metuchen, NJ: Scarecrow Press, 2002.

Rex, Lesley A. "The Remaking of a High School Reader." *Reading Research Quarterly* 36, no. 3 (2001): 288, 299–314.

Reynolds, Marilyn. *I Won't Read and You Can't Make Me: Reaching Reluctant Teen Readers.* Portsmouth, NH: Heinemann, 2004.

Reynolds, Tom K. *Teen Reading Connections.* New York: Neal-Schuman, 2005.

Robb, Laura. "Helping Reluctant Readers Discover Books." *Book Links* 7 (March 1998): 51.

Rosen, Roger. "The Inside Story." *School Library Journal* 46 (June 2000): 39.

Ross, Catherine Sheldrick. "If They Read Nancy Drew, So What? Series Book Readers Talk Back." *Library and Information Science Research*, Summer 1995, 201–36.

Rycik, James A., and Judith L. Irvin. *What Adolescents Deserve: A Commitment to Students' Literacy Learning*. Newark, DE: International Reading Association, 2001

Schall, Lucy. *Booktalks and More: Motivating Teens to Read*. Englewood, CO: Libraries Unlimited, 2003.

———. *Booktalks Plus: Motivating Teens to Read*. Englewood, CO: Libraries Unlimited, 2001.

———. *Teen Genre Connections: From Booktalking To Booklearning*. Englewood, CO: Libraries Unlimited, 2005.

Schoenbach, Ruth. *Reading for Understanding: A Guide to Improving Reading in Middle and High School Classrooms*. San Francisco: Jossey-Bass, 1999.

Schwartz, Gretchen E. "Graphic Novels for Multiple Literacies." *Journal of Adolescent and Adult Literacy* 46 (November 2002): 262–65.

Schwartz, Linda, and Kathy Parks. *Raising Ravenous Readers: Activities to Create a Lifelong Appetite for Reading*. Santa Barbara, CA: Learning Works, 1998.

Scieszka, Jon. "Guys and Reading." *Teacher Librarian* 30 (February 2003): 17–18.

———. *Guys Write for Guys Read*. New York: Viking, 2005.

Smith, Karen Patricia. *African-American Voices in Young Adult Literature: Tradition, Transition, Transformation*. Metuchen, NJ: Scarecrow Press, 2002.

Smith, Michael, and Jeffrey Wilhelm. *Reading Don't Fix No Chevy's: Literacy in the Lives of Young Men*. Portsmouth, NH: Heinemann, 2002.

Snow, Catherine E., and Gina Biancarosa. *Adolescent Literacy and the Achievement Gap: What Do We Know and Where Do We Go from Here?* New York: Carnegie Corporation, 2003.

Stephens, Claire Gatrell. *Coretta Scott King Award: Using Great Literature with Children and Young Adults*. Englewood, CO: Libraries Unlimited, 2000.

Stevenson, Sara. "When Bad Libraries Go Good." *School Library Journal* 51 (May 2005): 46–48.

St. Lifer, Evan. "Tending to Johnny: Does the Gender Gap Affect What Boys Read?" *School Library Journal* 50 (August 2004): 11.

Stoke, Barrington. "New Help for Older Reluctant Readers." *Bookseller*, January 18, 2002, 43.

Strickland, Dorothy, and Donna Alverman. *Bridging the Literacy Achievement Gap, Grades 4–12*. New York: Teachers College Press, 2004.

Stringer, Sharon, and Bill Mollineaux. "Removing the Word 'Reluctant' from 'Reluctant Reader'." *English Journal* 92 (March 2003): 71–77.

Strong, Richard W. *Reading for Academic Success: Powerful Strategies for Struggling, Average, and Advanced Readers, Grades 7–12*. Thousand Oaks, CA: Corwin Press, 2002.

Sullivan, Edward T. "Race Matters." *School Library Journal* 48 (June 2002): 40–41.

———. *Reaching Reluctant Young Adult Readers: A Handbook for Librarian and Teachers*. Metuchen, NJ: Scarecrow Press, 2002.

Sullivan, Michael. *Connecting Boys with Books: What Libraries Can Do*. Chicago: American Library Association, 2003.

Tatum, Alfred. "Breaking Down Barriers That Disenfranchise African American

Adolescent Readers in Low-Level Tracks." *Journal of Adolescent and Adult Literacy* 44, no. 1 (2000): 52+.

———. *Teaching Reading to Black Adolescent Males: Closing the Achievement Gap.* Portland, ME: Stenhouse, 2005.

Taylor, Donna. "Not Just Boring Stories: Reconsidering the Gender Gap for Boys." *Journal of Adolescent and Adult Literacy* 48, no. 4 (2004): 290+.

Taylor, Rosemarye. "Creating a System That Gets Results for Older, Reluctant Readers." *Phi Delta Kappan* 84 (September 2002): 85.

Taylor, Rosemarye, and Richard McAtee. "Turning a New Page to Life and Literacy." *Journal of Adolescent and Adult Literacy* 48 (March 2003): 476–80.

Thimmesch, Nick. *Aliteracy: People Who Can Read But Won't.* Washington, DC: American Enterprise Institute for Public Policy Research, 1984.

Thomas, Rebecca L., and Catherine Barr. *Popular Series Fiction for Middle School and Teen Readers: A Reading and Selection Guide.* Englewood, CO: Libraries Unlimited, 2005.

Tovani, Cris. *I Read It, but I Don't Get It: Comprehension Strategies for Adolescent Readers.* Portland, ME: Stenhouse, 2000.

Trelease, Jim. *Read-Aloud Handbook.* New York: Penguin, 2001.

Turner, Gwendolyn Y. "Motivating Reluctant Readers: What Can Educators Do?" *Reading Improvement,* Spring 1992, 50–55.

Umstatter, Jack. *Readers at Risk: Activities to Develop Language Arts Skills in the Inclusive Classroom.* San Francisco: Jossey-Bass, 2005.

Valencia, Shelia. "Behind Test Scores: What Struggling Readers Really Need." *Reading Teacher* 57 (March 2004): 521–30.

Versaci, Rocco. "How Comic Books Can Change the Way Our Students See Literature: One Teacher's Perspective." *English Journal* 91 (November 2001): 61.

Walter, Virginia A., and Elaine E. Meyers. *Teens and Libraries: Getting It Right.* Chicago: American Library Association, 2003.

Weiner, Stephen. *Faster than A Speeding Bullet: The Rise of the Graphic Novel.* New York: NBM, 2003.

Welch, Rollie. "What Do Teens Read in One Day? A Teen Read Week Log." *Voice of Youth Advocates* 24 (October 2001): 257, 316.

Welldon, Christine. "Addressing the Gender Gap in Boys' Reading." *Teacher Librarian* 32 (April 2005): 44.

Whelan, Debra Lau. "Librarians Respond to Decline in Reading." *School Library Journal* 50 (September 2004): 17.

Wilhelm, Jeffrey D. "Getting Boys to Read: It's the Context!" *Instructor* 112 (October 2002): 16.

———. "It's a Guy Thing." *Voices from the Middle* 9 (December 2001): 60–63.

———. *You Gotta BE the Book: Teaching Engaged and Reflective Reading with Adolescents.* New York: Teachers College Press, 1997.

Wilhelm, Jeffrey D., Tanya N. Baker, and Julie Dube. *Strategic Reading: Guiding Students to Lifelong Literacy, 6–12.* Portsmouth, NH: Boynton/Cook Publishers-Heinemann, 2001.

Williams, Bronwyn. "Are We Having Fun Yet? Students, Social Class, and the Pleasures of Literacy." *Journal of Adolescent and Adult Literacy* 48 (December 2004/January 2005): 338–42.

Worthy, Jo. "A Matter of Interest: Literature That Hooks Reluctant Readers and Keeps Them Reading." *Reading Teacher* 50 (November 1996): 204–12.

———. "'On Every Page Someone Gets Killed!' Book Conversations You Don't Hear in School." *Journal of Adolescent and Adult Literacy* 41 (April 1998): 508–17.

———. "Removing Barriers to Voluntary Reading for Reluctant Readers." *Language Arts* 73 (November 1996): 483–92.

———. "What Johnny Likes to Read Is Hard to Find in School." *Reading Research Quarterly* 34 (1999): 12–27.

York, Sherry. *Children's and Young Adult Literature by Latino Writers: A Guide for Librarians, Teachers, Parents, and Students.* Worthington, OH: Linworth, 2002.

Zadora, Amanda. "Wrestling with Reading." *Teaching K–8*, April 2002, 58–59.

Afterword by Alex Flinn

Alex Flinn is the author of *Breathing Underwater, Breaking Point, Nothing to Lose,* and *Fade to Black.* All of her books have appeared on the Young Adult Library Services Association (YALSA) "Quick Picks" for Reluctant Young Adult Readers list or the Best Books list, most of them scoring both honors. Portions of these remarks were first delivered at the American Library Association 2005 Annual Conference during a session sponsored by YALSA's Quick Picks Committee entitled "Reaching the Reluctant Reader."

I think I'm particularly qualified to speak on the subject of motivating reluctant readers, not only because I attempt to write "literary" fiction that reluctant readers will read (I'm very proud to have published books that made both BBYA *and* Quick Picks) but also because I *was* a reluctant reader in high school—and to some degree, I think I still am.

I know that Gail Giles, being a former teacher, probably has a really good perspective on this from an educator's standpoint. So I'm here to offer the bored teenager viewpoint (even though I'm in my thirties, those scars run deep). To this day, whenever I pick up a book and realize that it's going to be a tender, southern coming-of-age story, in which the main character is going to learn lots of "relevant" things from wise older mentors with names like Velma Lee Hornswaggle, my eyes glaze over in my head. I want a book with a *plot,* baby, not just a theme. I have a painfully short attention span, and I want to read books that grab me by the eyeballs and force me to keep reading. So that's what I try to write.

I wasn't always a reluctant reader. I read a lot of books until the seventh grade—the year they made us read *Shane.* I just couldn't. I just wasn't into cowboys, and even though my mom, who was born in the 1940s, would probably have thought it was a pretty cool book, it didn't mean much to me. So I didn't read it. And that was the first time in my life I realized that it was possible to just *not* read a book that was assigned for English class. So from seventh grade until twelfth, I became a reluctant reader, a CliffsNotes reader. I read maybe half of the books that were assigned for school. If they sounded interesting, I read them; if they didn't, I read the CliffsNotes. I've often told teachers that one of the big selling points for reading my books in schools is that there are no CliffsNotes for any of my books.

I did, however, read in my spare time. I was raised to read, so it didn't occur to me not to—only that I hated the books we had to read for school. What I mostly read were Agatha Christie mysteries, books like *Flowers in the Attic, The Godfather,* the occasional Danielle Steel, and an up-and-coming author named Mary Higgins Clark. No one was giving me YA, though it did exist. I think I always knew I should have been reading good literature, but most of what was given to me as "good literature" was just painfully boring and not relevant to my life. So I read junk. I think, for the most part, that books written for young-adult reluctant readers are of higher quality than most of the stuff I read as a teenager. Because they are specifically written for young adults, they're not just sensational books; they deal with themes that are relevant to teens.

What I liked—which has become my guiding principle in writing books for teens (and I never thought of myself as writing for reluctant readers specifically, as I think most teenagers who read YA are reluctant readers to some degree)—were books where stuff happened. My life as a teenager was tremendously dull—only child; two doting parents; bored at school; no sex, drugs, or hope of rock and roll. So since nothing interesting ever happened to me in my entire life, I liked to read books where something happened, something *big.* Murder attempts. The Mafia. Kids getting locked in an attic. My favorite Danielle Steel was the one about a girl losing her face in a car accident and having reconstructive surgery.

As a reader, and as a writer for YA, aka reluctant readers, this has translated into a few basic principles. First, I want a book that can be summarized in a single sentence in a way that sounds interesting. My new book, *Fade to Black,* for example, is about a hate crime against an HIV-positive student, told in three viewpoints. Interested?

Second, I want to know what the book is about by reading the first chapter because my time is valuable and my attention span is short, and I'm not going to read beyond the first chapter if it doesn't sound interesting, so don't describe the scenery. In *Breathing Underwater,* a book that could be summarized in a single sentence as "This is a book about a teenage boy whose girlfriend takes out a restraining order against him after he hits her," it was pretty easy to let my readers in on what was happening in the first chapter. I started out in the courthouse. I used the phrase "restraining order" on the second page and clarified that as "girlfriend trouble" in case my readers didn't know what a restraining order was. Nick was in the courthouse with his dad—smoldering tension between them—looking at Caitlin, his ex-girlfriend—smoldering tension between them—while she testified that he had hit her.

Oh, and I let the readers know that the characters had sex—right there in the first chapter, too—just in case they were interested.

My next book, *Breaking Point,* also had a good one-sentence premise: Two boys plant a bomb at their prep school. But it was harder to write the first chapter in that book because I couldn't start with the bomb. I started with the main character, Paul, going to prep school and pretty much being a geek. But there are a lot of books about people not fitting in, and they're not all ragingly interesting to reluctant readers. I wanted my readers to know that this was a book about a crime, so I added a prologue in which Paul is getting out of jail on his eighteenth birthday, and he thinks that this would never have happened if he hadn't gone to school with Charlie Good. So then that first chapter, in which Paul's acting geeky and then meets Charlie Good, seems suddenly . . . interesting. What happened to make this geek into a criminal? And that's what keeps kids reading the book. I get a lot of mail about this book, and usually it says stuff like, "This is the only book I've ever finished."

A hugely important element is a great first sentence. I once took a workshop with Richard Peck, where he said, "A good first sentence is one that makes the reader ask why." I took this to mean that a first sentence should provide the reader with just enough information that the reader *cares* but should also leave the reader with unanswered questions to keep him reading.

I'm especially proud of the first sentence of my novel *Nothing to Lose,* which is about a guy who is on the lam with a traveling carnival while his mother is on trial for murdering his stepfather.

The first sentence is, "I shouldn't have come back to Miami." This sentence gives you a bit of information: The main character is in Miami. He's left Miami, but now he's back—and he's regretting it. But it raises more questions than it answers. Who is the main character? Why did he leave Miami? Why did he come back? Did someone make him leave or come back? Who? Why shouldn't he have come back? I think these are enough questions that the reader will definitely read a few more pages. Then, I hook the reader in by showing Michael, lying to police about his identity, making up an assumed name, and coolly lying about his age. *Nothing to Lose* was featured in Chapter-a-Day last year when it came out, and the kids who posted about it on their message board were all atwitter about the fact that Michael lied to the cops. The average reader would immediately know that *something was happening* within those first few pages, and by the end of the chapter, it was clear that Michael's mother was on trial for murder and he was hiding out, operating the Whack-a-Mole game at the carnival.

Maybe the most important element of a reluctant-reader book is plot. The plot is the something that is happening in the book. My books revolve around issues that appear in the news—bad stuff. But I think that anything that is interesting will do. For example, the premise of The Princess Diaries books probably makes them good reluctant-reader fare.

I think the plots of my books appeal to reluctant readers because they're about kids who are involved in the legal system (I write from my own experiences as a former lawyer). This is a neglected segment of the reading population because you never hear about teens wanting crime fiction. But considering that I can turn on the TV and watch *CSI Miami, CSI New York, CSI Las Vegas, NCIS, Boston Legal, Law and Order, Law and Order: Special Victims' Unit*—not to mention *America's Most Wanted* and *COPS*—I think there's definitely an interest there. I talk to a lot of teens who want to be lawyers or police officers.

In a well-written book, some plot element will occur at roughly quarter points, meaning that a quarter of the way through the book, something big happens; halfway through, something bigger happens; three-quarters through, something happens that really ups the stakes in a big way; and then the climax and ending. My writing mentor, Joyce Sweeney—who has also written a lot of Quick Pick books, including the recent *Head Lock*—once said, "You know you're in trouble, plot-wise, if when you are summarizing your plot, you're using a lot of words like *realize* or *understand*." In a good book that reluctant readers will appreciate, you use action words to describe your plot. For example, the plot points in *Nothing to Lose* include words like "kiss" or "bludgeon."

In *Nothing to Lose,* there are actually two plots because the book takes place in two two-week periods; last March, when Michael decided to run away with the carnival, and this March, when Michael came back. The present-tense plot basically deals with Michael being on the lam from police and deciding whether he should come out of hiding to testify on his mother's behalf. At the same time, he is searching for the girl he lost, a carny named Kirstie. So there's danger, crime, romance, loss—all the things I'd have liked as a teenager.

But it's the past-tense plot that drives the book and probably keeps reluctant readers reading even though this is the longest of my books. In the first scene of the past-tense plot, Michael comes home from a party and inspects the house to see if anything is amiss or out of order in an attempt to figure out if his mother is okay. Finally he goes to bed, but his mother comes into his room and lets him know that her husband has threatened to kill both her and Michael if she ever leaves him. In the first quarter of the book, we hear about Michael's troubles at home and school, culminating in the first plot point: a friend of Michael's talks him into going to the carnival with him. There, he meets Kirstie, a beautiful carny who kisses him on the mouth in the first five minutes. He is hooked. Troubles at home continue, but Michael is drawn into the carny life, and in the second plot point, Michael confronts his abusive stepfather, who tells him that he will have him arrested if he tries to do anything to protect his mother. Michael has nowhere to turn. In the third quarter of the book, Michael is falling in love with Kirstie, and she is trying to talk him into running away with the carnival. He's more interested in having sex, but when he finally gets her into bed, the beeper in his jeans pocket goes off. (I planted the beeper there several chapters earlier so the reader is waiting for it to go off. Playwright Anton Chekhov said, "If you have a gun on the mantel in Act 1, it must go off in the third act.") Michael answers it and finds that his mother has been badly beaten and hospitalized. He realizes that her husband will someday kill her. In the last quarter of the book, the carnival is leaving town. Kirstie almost talks Michael into going away with her, but Michael realizes that even though there's nothing he can do to help his mother, he has to stay with her. But then, in the climactic moments—Oh, I can't tell you what happens. Sorry. But it's interesting enough to keep even the most reluctant readers going once they start.

The final important element in reaching reluctant readers is characters who are interesting. Note that word: "interesting." I've heard a lot about how characters have to be likable or someone teens can relate to or someone they'd want to have as a best friend. But I'm not sure that is really it. In fact, I've read a lot of YA books in which the author has attempted to create a really "typical" teen, and I have to say they are usually boring. When I was reading YA books to learn more about the genre, I realized that I really didn't need to like the character. I realized this solely because of the sections of *The Chocolate War* that are narrated by the character of Archie Costello. Archie is, of course, brilliant and diabolical, and . . . fascinating, and I loved him because he was so little like myself or people I knew. There are a lot of books narrated by typical teens, but there are still reluctant readers, so I try to make my characters something a little more interesting.

My most recent book, *Fade to Black,* is—I think—my most reluctant-reader-friendly book. Although it has literary elements, including a narrative in free verse (which reluctant readers like, by the way; Sonya Sones's books are huge with reluctant readers), it also has a lot of good reluctant-reader elements. It's short—under 200 pages. It has a great premise—a hate crime against an HIV-positive student and a plot that is about something they've been hearing about all their lives, HIV. Moreover, because it shifts between three viewpoints—*and the viewpoint shifts are really the point of the book,* to show how different people look at the same situation, like *Rashomon*—there is always something happening, always something to keep the readers' interest. I tried to create utterly fascinating characters: a boy with HIV, who is the victim of a crime; a girl with Down's syndrome, who witnesses it; and a character named Clinton, who is accused of the crime. In fact, we find out early on that Clinton has done something else. My favorite character is Clinton because I enjoy the circularity of his logic. I really like trying to get into the minds of people who do things that most people wouldn't view as acceptable. I think reluctant readers do, too.

Because of my experiences, both as a reluctant reader and as an author whose books are appreciated by reluctant readers, I believe that there is a book out there to hook every reader. One of the most exciting things for me as an author is when a kid writes to me and says, "I never read a whole book before," or "I hate to read, but I was up all night reading your book." I hope that they'll just keep reading from then on.

Title Index

Subject Index

Author Index

50 Cent, 227

About the Authors

Patrick Jones is the coauthor of *Connecting Young Adults and Libraries,* 3rd edition, with Michele Gorman and Tricia Suellentrop (Neal-Schuman, 2004). His previous books for Neal-Schuman include *A Core Collection for Young Adults* with Patricia Taylor and Kirsten Edwards (2003) and *Do It Right: Customer Service for Young Adults in School and Public Libraries* with Joel Shoemaker (2001). In spring 2006, Walker & Company published his second young adult novel entitled *Nailed.* The Young Adult Library Services Association selected his first young adult novel *Things Change* for the 2005 Quick Picks list. He served on the Quick Picks committee for three years in the early 1990s. He is a longtime reviewer for *Voice of Youth Advocates* magazines and has a regular "What We're Reading" column on NoveList.

Patricia Taylor has been an editor, writer, and teacher most of her life. She is the author of the novel *Last Night and the Night Before* (Infinity, 2006) and coauthor of *A Core Collection for Young Adults* with Patrick Jones and Kirsten Edwards (Neal-Schuman, 2003). Twenty years in a high school classroom have given way to her present incarnation as full-time writer and educational consultant. In 1990, she was selected as a Top Ten Teacher in the State of Texas by the University of Texas and in 1995 was named Humanities Teacher of the Year by the Texas Endowment for the Humanities. She conducted training seminars for the Bureau of Educational Research on reaching reluctant teen readers, and is a contributing writer to NoveList.

Maureen L. Hartman was the driving force behind the Minneapolis Public Library's Teen Central, which opened in the new Central Library in May 2006. She has worked for Minneapolis Public as a teen specialist, collection development librarian, and is currently the coordinator of youth and family initiatives. She served for three years and chaired the Young Adult Library Services Association Quick Picks committee, and conducts the seminar "The Best Books for Reluctant Teen Readers and How to Use Them in Your Program" for the Bureau of Educational Research.